TEACHING
YOUTH YOGA

A Yoga Mindfulness Curriculum for Kids

Darcie Peck

WIND RIVER
YOGA BOOKS

Disclaimer

This book does not offer medical advice to the reader and is not intended as a replacement for appropriate health care and treatment. For such advice, readers should consult a licensed physician.

ISBN number 979-8-9869592-0-7

Illustrations: Rachel Halbert and Elisa Reynard
Photos: Darcie Peck, Samantha Harnack, Brandi Burdine and Sublette County Chamber of Commerce
Cover Photo: Darcie Peck
Design & Layout: DannySkinz.com

"Teaching Youth Yoga" is a treasure of practices and in-depth background to bring the power of yoga, meditation, movement meditation, nature, creative reflection and embodying the flow for young people and educators in these soulful times. Thank you Darcie for passing the torch and wealth of your experience on behalf of all.

- Shiva Rea, Samudra Global School for Living Yoga

This book is dedicated to:

All the yogis that I have been so blessed to teach. To all the open-minded parents who have allowed me to do what I love. To my father who instilled positive thinking and shared his love of physical education and to my mother who inspired my culinary and artistic appreciation. This book is dedicated to you all. Thank you for being among my greatest teachers and supporters.

PREFACE

Aloha & Welcome

To all the beautiful people out there who have been touched by the teachings of yoga. Since you are reading this, I know you are interested in bringing yoga and mindfulness to the future leaders of tomorrow. Children need these teachings. The world needs you.

Let's take a deep breath together and honor this divine calling to share the gifts of yoga. Peace and love are powerful influences. The more you can live from that sincere, sacred space, the more you will impact the world. I am here to share what worked for me, to give you the tools that I use to teach, and to guide you through your own journey. I am so excited to share my passion with you and all I have learned along the way!

Teaching yoga is my purpose and has been since taking my first yoga class in 1996. Studying International Relations at the University of Colorado, my goal was to work for the United Nations to bring peace to developing nations. After my first yoga class, I realized that the only way to make a profound change was to first change yourself. For the first time in my life, I felt a deep-seated peace and connection to my higher self. I could feel my purpose for being alive: to share this incredible feeling of peace with others. I wanted to help everyone feel better in their own body and mind, to change the system from the inside out. I felt so naturally centered and inspired, and I wanted everyone to

responsible for one's decisions, and bringing presence into everyday awareness. It was important to me to help kids find gratitude and appreciation, even in the most mundane or difficult times. Above and beyond anything else, my mission was to remind my students of their greatness, uniqueness, and infinite potential. I did this by introducing yoga and meditation to my curriculum. Not only did I see a difference in my classroom and our daily routines, but the principal, staff, and caregivers wanted to learn more about how they could support children's physical and mental health through yoga and meditation techniques.

This experience of teaching yoga to young children in school led me to open my own yoga studio, Wind River Yoga, in a small rural community that had never had access or exposure to yoga. Here, I was able to implement my heartfelt yoga curriculum and create a comfortable and safe place for the young people of our community to learn, grow, thrive, and heal. My mission was to teach the tools to enable them to feel good, have clearer minds, and live healthier and be more empowered in their bodies. Ultimately, I wanted kids to witness their own essence and potential and feel comfortable, happy and relaxed in their own skin. In this relaxed state of being brought on by yoga and meditation, we can access feelings of joy and gratitude in everyday living. This is what I had wished for in my youth and had now found a way to give it to others.

> ## "The two most important days in your life are the day you are born, and the day you find out why." -Mark Twain[2]

feel this state of being, this heightened awareness. I wanted this peace to spread from one soul to the next. So, after I graduated college, I embarked on my first yoga teacher training course.

I have always been involved with children. In high school, I taught at an after-school activities program. In college, I tutored and worked with kids with additional support needs. After college, I taught pre-K at a private school. Inspired by my own life lessons and what I think is important to teach kids, my sessions with children were infused with teachings of being a good human, believing in oneself, being

Fast forward to 2020, when the world experienced major social, environmental, and political challenges and upheaval on all levels. I am still practicing, and I am teaching now more than ever. My passion for yoga still burns, and the quest to share all that I have learned along the way is of utmost importance right now. With this book, I am excited to inspire more teachers to discover their talents and their purpose and to share them with the world through yoga. My hope is for every child to have the gifts of yoga in their upbringing and to be able to navigate this world with confidence and ease. This is particularly important to me. I am here to share the knowledge and tools that have changed my life.

"Every single moment in life is yoga — every moment, the light and the shadow; every experience, the good and the weird; and every being, those you adore and those you don't. It's all yoga, and it's all purposeful for the evolution of your soul. We think we are separate, but that is the lie that we tell ourselves. We are connected to everything and everyone. Yoga opens our eyes so we can see clearly who we are and who we are to each other. This awakening gives us permission to be more joyous, connected, understanding, compassionate, and loving, right here, right now." -Seane Corn[1]

These sacred teachings have been passed down to me from my teachers and healers, and I am so humbly proud to offer them to you through my eyes, unique voice, and experience. I encourage you to interpret them in your own way and, if they have value to you, please share them with the children closest to you. If we can empower the hearts and voices of our youth, I believe this world can heal, and the next generations will be able to thrive. I believe yoga has the power to unite and make this planet a healthier, more loving place to live.

How to use this manual:

This manual begins with a background of what yoga and mindfulness mean to me through my personal experience and understanding. This is the wisdom inspired by my own journey. You will learn the fundamentals of how to construct your own in-person yoga, creative movement, breathing, art and meditation class. You will learn how to create a successful yoga room setting, explore how children learn and set yourself up for a soulful and meaningful yoga class.

The curriculum is designed as a year's exploration of the art of teaching youth yoga. It begins in August and ends in July (based on the State of Hawaii school calendar). Each month has a breakdown of yogic themes and philosophy, art exploration, meditations, movement therapy, breathing techniques, journaling, reflections, *seva* (volunteer work offered to the greater good) projects, and yoga sequences. The themes complement one another, and there are tools and reminders for all ages on how to move through life with grace, confidence, and ease. I have used these teachings in my yoga classroom for over twenty years. Now it's up to you.

You can use this manual however you like. For instance, you might begin reading to see which concepts are important for you and create lesson plans from that. You can also follow it month-to-month and pick and choose activities that feel empowering and appropriate for the age group and demographic you will be guiding. The guided meditations at the end of each chapter can be used for all ages. You can modify for kids or use them in your teen and adult yoga classes.

Ultimately, this manual will help you plan, encourage, create, uplift, and manifest beautiful, soulful sessions that hold wisdom from which everyone can benefit. The best thing about the process is that you can teach from your own experience. You get to share your truth and the life lessons most important to you. You will find that these practices are essential for creating strong, resilient children who are learning to be courageous, happy, relaxed, creative, and independent. These children need you. Our education system needs you. *Let's get started!*

CONTENTS

For more information or to purchase pure essential oils:

PART 1

INTRODUCTION

Teaching Youth Yoga

"Wake up lovers. It's time to start the journey. Let us kiss the ground and flow like a river toward the ocean. It's best to travel with companions on this perilous journey; only love can lead the way."

-Rumi[3]

What is Mindfullness?

There is a story I like to share with kids about a monk and his disciple that teaches the very essence of mindfulness. This story is from *40 Days to Personal Revolution*, a book by one of my yoga teachers, *Baron Baptiste*.

> There was a disciple who came to his master to receive his higher ranking as a monk. He entered the temple leaving his shoes and rice bowl outside and inside the master asked his student, "On which side of the rice bowl did you place your shoes?" The student got annoyed and impatient. "Why don't you ask me about all the enlightenment I am receiving in meditation, my *kundalini* rising, and my knowledge of God?" But the Master continued with his simple question about his rice bowl and shoes. The student could not answer. When the Master sent the student away to study for another nine years, the student protested such an outcome for such a small mistake. "This is not a small mistake," replied the Master. "You are not yet living from your center, because you have no awareness of what is right in front of you. You are not present in your everyday activities, and that is what it means to live meditatively. You must have your feet on the ground.[4]

To me, mindfulness is present-moment awareness. It's knowing what is right in front of you at all times, as described in Baptiste's story—being present at an elevated level means being acutely aware of our environment and what we are doing while also being capable of responding to life. Being mindful is also having the ability to decipher when we get lost in thoughts, whether we're dwelling on the past or anticipating the future, and then bringing attention back to the now. Repeating this over and over again strengthens the brain's awareness and ability to be present.

When we have control over our attention in this way, we can place that attention wherever we want it to go. Over time, we won't get so distracted by the "monkey mind," the mind that incessantly chatters and is all over the place. When the attention becomes steady and alert, so does our focus. With a less busy mind, we can experience deeper states of inner peace. In this heightened state of awareness, we can accept our thoughts and feelings better without being carried away by them. Teaching children yoga and aspects of meditation are great ways to help them gain mastery over their minds and become friends with their thoughts and feelings.

I always like to start with the basics of mindfulness. Firstly, being aware of ourselves and the world around ourselves. When you start to guide children on a yoga journey, you constantly remind them to breathe, feel, and be aware of their surroundings and their physical body in space. Bringing attention back into the moment and staying in a constant state of reflection is key to creating a heightened state of awareness.

This level of awareness can greatly impact the world. When we can learn how to think before we speak, for instance, then we are more aware of how our thoughts, words, and actions affect the greater good. We are simply more conscious and, therefore, more compassionate. Being more aware allows us to be in the moment within a busy day and also be centered. We all have a choice. We can either be taken down by the busyness of life or be able to respond skillfully. Mindfulness has a place in everyday moments of experience.

Someone asked the Buddha, "Are you a god?" and the Buddha said, "No." "Are
you a saint?" and the Buddha said, "No." "Then what are you?" they asked.
And the Buddha replied, "Awake." -Baron Baptiste[5]

Meditation

Mindfulness, when practiced for a duration of time with added technique, can develop into meditation. Meditation comes from eastern thought and philosophy. Modern meditation practices have roots in the traditional techniques of Tibetan Buddhism. One of my meditation teachers, Light Watkins, defines meditation very simply as "a comfortable, seated, and consistent, eyes closed practice of experiencing present-moment awareness and, when possible, quieting the mind."[6]

Mindfulness and meditation both strive to quiet the mind so that we can become still and awake to all that is but also relaxed and at ease. By choosing to sit or lie down, focusing on our breath, and stilling the thoughts, we essentially take a "time out" on life. This is crucial in how we absorb, assimilate, and process experience. If we don't take the time to unwind and let go of the thoughts in our heads, our minds and bodies become cluttered with too much outside information. This leads to stress and, eventually, the mind, body, and spirit become fragmented. Over time, this separation can lead to chronic ailments and dissociation. Taking time every day to awaken to the present moment, our thoughts, and our breath is one of the most important practices we can add to our lives. Over time, we become more observant, intuitive, centered, grounded, and healthy individuals. Our days will crave the time that we can carve out for ourselves to quiet the mind, release, and renew.

Yoga is Life

Originating in India, the practice and philosophy of yoga is over 5,000 years old. The father of classical *Ashtanga* (Eight Limbs of Yoga) is said to be Patanjali. Patanjali composed the Yoga Sutras, the art of righteous living, in 200 AD. This provided a framework for spiritual growth and mastery over the physical and mental body.

Yoga essentially means to yoke—or bring together—the mind, body, and spirit in present-moment awareness. It's an art and science (an organized system of knowledge that is repeatable, testable, and observable) dedicated to creating a union between the body, mind, and spirit, and/or with the individual soul and the higher realms.

Yoga is also a way to take care of the mind and body and has been used as an alternative medicine throughout history. Yoga practice is a blueprint for controlling restlessness in the mind and enjoying lasting peace through focusing our attention from the gross to the subtle and moving awareness through various levels of consciousness. As we practice, we become more present in our daily lives, responsive to the breath and

flexible in our bodies, so ultimately, our minds have a better chance to be still. Yoga liberates the body and prepares it physically for sitting safely and effortlessly in meditation for long lengths of time.

Yoga can help us establish or re-connect to faith. According to my yoga philosophy teacher, Dave Druz, yoga has a vastly different meaning than just being exercise. "Yoga means union of our individualized consciousness with Universal Consciousness or, in religious terminology, a union of the soul with God. A Self-realized person's consciousness (with a capital S) is one with Universal Consciousness. That person knows with the core of their being that they are one with the omniscience, omnipotence, and omnipresence of the divine."[8] When we realize this, we can realize our power and infinite potential, and perhaps some meaning behind life. Stepping into our power on and off the mat and being an active participant in our own evolution is one of the many benefits of our yoga practice.

Yoga can be observed differently and have different purposes. It doesn't have to be spiritual; it might just be a physical practice that helps keep the body and mind in shape. The best part is that you get to create your own meaning and make it a personal practice.

"Yoga takes you into the present moment, the only place where life exists."
- Patanjali[7]

Ultimately, yoga is a way to 'practice life' and participate wholeheartedly in a way that serves everyone at the highest. The way we eat, sleep, speak, and act is all influenced by our inner world's state. Yoga and mindfulness give us access to a safe and peaceful place inside ourselves when the outside world may seem chaotic. Our personal practice can be a path to love and devotion or simply to acknowledge the miracle of life and the phenomena behind the beating of the heart and the magic behind the breath. Yoga and mindfulness are incredible tools to keep us healthy, alleviate stress, and decompress inner tension and resistance. Yoga is a powerful resource to turn to in this life.

"We are spiritual beings
having a human experience."
-Pierre Teilhard de Chardin[9]

Yoga and Spirituality

Spirituality involves recognizing and accepting a higher power, beyond our own intelligence and will, with whom we can have a relationship. The higher power can provide us with an experience of inspiration, joy, security, peace of mind, and guidance that goes beyond what is possible in the absence of the conviction that such power exists. For the purposes of this manual, you can choose to refer to it in whatever way feels most appropriate. Your sense of power can be an abstract cosmic consciousness or as down-to-earth as the beauty of the ocean or mountains. It can be quite personal, in the case of Jesus or the Buddha. Hence, spirituality is about honoring our own journey and unique understanding of what that connection is.

Yoga can be defined as this divine connection to the source and a sacred relationship to a higher force. Dave Druz also says, "Yoga's inner practice deals with stilling our thoughts. This is what meditation is all about. Yoga's outer practices deal with eliminating the ego. The ego is the primary obstacle to Self-realization, realizing our oneness to God."[8] The ego creates separateness. When our consciousness is body-identified, it becomes that ego, the I-Me-Mine self-centered awareness. The more we detach from the whole, the more we are attached to these physical bodies (ego) and feel separate and alone.

"The meaning of life is to find our gifts, and the purpose of life is to give them away." -Pablo Picasso[10]

This all makes sense around the pre-teenage years when we become more identified with the body. This age group tends to identify more with the physical body. This leads to obsession and a desire to be and feel in control; control of our food intake, our exercise, control of how we look. It's a perpetual cycle that can spin out of control. It cuts us off from all spirituality and the knowledge that we are perfect just the way we are.

In yoga, we want to take care of the body and know that we are a part of something greater; we are unique and beautiful just the way we are. All of our souls are connected to something beyond this physical world. In this lifetime, we are truly spiritual beings having a human experience. Tools such as mindfulness, meditation, and yoga all have the ability to give us everlasting peace as we navigate through life. Teaching children these resources at an early age can be life-changing.

Traditional Forms of Yoga

Many different types of yoga have been in practice for centuries. Each has its own dynamic and purpose.

Jnana Yoga: Wisdom, true knowledge, including the study of ancient texts and teachings of the Great Masters as well as self-inquiry.

Bhakti Yoga: Devotion, love, and worship (to the Divine, guru, family, friends, nature or anything that creates strong emotional ties and reverence).

Karma Yoga: Action, service to others, acting without attachment.

Raja Yoga: The royal way. Meditation, and contemplation (self-disciplined practice like the Eight Limbs).

Hatha Yoga: Will and physical exercise. *HA* means Sun, and *THA* means Moon. It's about balancing opposites within the body.

Hatha yoga is one of the more traditional styles of yoga, and we'll be practicing this with the kids. In ancient Indian lore, there is a connection between the right side of the body and the energy of the Sun. The Sun is active and hot; it creates life and growth. The Sun's energy, in this context, is considered masculine, powerful, and has the ability to move energy. The left side symbolizes the Moon's energy. The Moon is passive and cool; it creates longer-lasting and sustainable energy, waxing and waning through a constant cycle. The Moon is associated with feminine energy; more introverted, steady, reflective and cool.

Hatha yoga is when opposing energies (Sun and Moon, masculine and feminine, right and left, warm and cold) are balanced or joined together. The theme of merging the opposites reveals itself in many ways of the yoga practice. There is a balance between strength and flexibility, right and left, support and surrender, effort and ease, knowledge of the known and unknown, and wisdom of the inner and outer bodies. From our direct experience, we can observe how the postures integrate a balance of right and left sides of the body while balancing many internal opposing forces. Teaching yoga to children at an early age helps develop their brains to connect the right and left sides. Yoga also stimulates the cerebellum, a gland in the back of the head that deals with coordination. The more that body awareness is developed at a young age, the more kids have trust and confidence when introduced to new activities and athletics. The more active the kids are, the better prepared they are to embrace relaxation techniques and meditation.

Methodology of Teaching

"As a teacher, I possess a tremendous power to make a child's life miserable or joyous. I can be a tool of torture or an instrument of inspiration. I can humiliate or heal. In all situations, it's my response that decides whether a crisis will be escalated or de-escalated, and a child humanized or dehumanized."
— Haim Ginnot[11]

How Do Children Learn?

As far back as the 19th century, researchers such as Lev Vygotsky, Jean Piaget, and Howard Gardner studied and shared with us an understanding of individual learning styles. Many educators and specialists have refined this research. I like to try these seven different learning styles in class and share examples from each of these categories.

Visual *(spatial)*

Individuals learn best through pictures and tangible items (dry erase board, books, show and tell).

Aural *(auditory)*

Individuals learn best through music, sound, and vibration (chanting, dancing, or sound healing with *mantras*).

Verbal *(linguistic)*

Individuals learn best through repetition of information, call and response and/or written work (journaling, dry erase boards, yoga packets).

Physical *(kinesthetic)*

Individuals learn best through experiences with the senses (stuffed animal yoga, yoga with props, chocolate meditation).

Logical *(mathematical)*

Individuals learn best through reasoning and logic (applied yoga philosophy, circle time talks).

Social *(interpersonal)*

Individuals learn best through group connection and interaction (partner yoga).

Solitary *(intrapersonal)*

Individuals learn best through self-study (reflection, journaling, intention setting).

Creating Space

When creating space for little yogis, all you need is the body, mind, and breath. It's important that the location is safe and comfortable, and the temperature is nice wherever you are, inside or out. Make sure all your students are dressed appropriately and have water. It's nice to have yoga mats or towels to sit and stretch on.

Nature is essential for an enhanced experience. Being able to go outside, sit in the grass, walk barefoot in the dirt, watch the clouds, listen to the sounds, smell the air, and feel the body and breath merge with present-moment awareness is especially important. Sometimes, it's just nice to take breaks to go outside and feel the Sun on the skin. Obviously, you want a safe outdoor environment.

Activities outdoors are vital for instilling gratitude and mindfulness into the things we sometimes take for granted; for instance, the Sun, a beautiful blue sky, or grass to relax on. We can feel more grounded and alive just savoring the elements on the skin. Bringing awareness to the beauty and miracles of nature will help children feel empowered to take care of this

special place and find a deep appreciation of themselves as part of it. We each have a duty and an obligation.

One of my teachers said that taking care of this Earth is our 'rent' here on the planet. We live in crucial times, and, more than ever, we need to be advocates for this planet. We need to love and respect her, but, most importantly, we need to feel her and have a deeper sense of heightened connection and adoration. Through yoga, breath, mindfulness, and nature, we can achieve this!

Enhancing the Learning Experience

My experience as a schoolteacher has taught me to have a couple of things on hand if you are adding elements of art, writing, and/or teaching yogic philosophy. These things are not necessary but can enhance the overall learning experience of your students.

For art: paper, scissors, markers, and glue.

For creative flow arts: jump ropes, hula hoops, poi balls, scarves.

For meditation or relaxation: music, sound instruments (bells, bowls, or chimes), various kids' yoga books, healthy food.

For circle time and teaching yoga philosophy: dry erase board or chalkboard.

For visual aids: when lessons are presented and accompanied by pictures, the learning process is enhanced.

For safety: emergency first-aid kit.

For liability: parental consent and your own individual liability insurance.

For cleanliness, breath work, and mood: I am a believer in pure essential oils, and I have experienced them affecting mood and emotions.

I always start class by putting on essential oil and begin with breath work to help center the kids and open their airways for energy and focus. Not only will the scent of the oils help shift awareness and attention, but they will also cleanse the air. If you diffuse the oils into the air, they will cut down on airborne germs, making the whole environment safer and cleaner. Also, the oils are helpful if a child hurts themselves or is distracted by their own boo-boos. You can use oils topically with kids to soothe and create trust. I like lavender for bumps and bruises and peppermint applied right to the belly button for kids with upset stomachs. ⚠ **If you are not trained or knowledgeable about pure essential oils and don't feel comfortable using them physically or topically in your class, you can always diffuse them in the air.** We explore the benefits of aromatherapy in the July chapter.

Class Control

In my experience working with children, it's imperative to honor their unique personalities and treat each child accordingly. Some kids have strong personalities, and some are shy and timid. I have found that, regarding the overall tone of the class, it's important to ignore unwanted behavior and attend to kids who are listening and paying attention with positive feedback. Children want to please, and this behaviorism model is favorable when you want the kids to follow you and your instructions. Once the child who was not listening starts to get involved, then you acknowledge the effort made. It's important to stay calm and collected and consistently model the behavior you would like to see in your class. If you are stressed or overwhelmed, children will pick up on that energy as well.

Important things to assess when you begin your class are the overall energy, kids with additional needs, and kids who have a tough time sitting near one another. Set your rules right at the beginning of class and plan accordingly. Strategically place the kids on their mats. Create an ideal environment by letting the kids know what you expect of them and what you will not tolerate.

Classes should be fun and inspirational. If a kid needs to rest or take some time to chill, it's good to be supportive of their ability to recognize their feelings. It's important to realize that every child has a different upbringing and to let go of any desired outcome or expectations. Yoga should be challenging, but also an enjoyable experience. When coaching the kids through postures, it's important to encourage and uplift. Every day is going to be different. Yoga is all about the path and not at all about getting to or reaching an end result. It's not about mastering the poses or comparing our bodies to our friends' bodies. It's all about the ability to show up, try our best, and listen to the body.

If you see kids becoming upset that they cannot do a pose or start to compare their bodies in any way to someone else, stop and switch up the class. Lovingly, talk about how we all are unique, and that yoga helps us see our strengths as well as what we can work on. Yoga brings us balance. Yoga is a self-discovery, and it's about what we all learn along the way: compassion, unconditional love, respect, boundaries, effort and ease, likes and dislikes. Yoga also helps us check in on what kind of day we have had and to take care of ourselves. It's always good to have the kids check-in with that. What foods have they been eating? How much sleep have they been getting? What is the stress load? What has their mind been thinking? All these questions are good to ask your students before you start your class.

Age-Appropriate Lessons

For children **ages 3—7**, storytelling is a vital part of the yoga process. Using children's books to teach lessons and incorporating yoga postures from animals and nature are wonderful teaching tools. Pictures also aid in cognitive development. Not only are pictures a useful source for labeling and classifying words, but they can lead to the ability to recognize objects in the mind and then use the body to perform the action, which is an essential skill for schoolwork. Since many of the *asanas* or physical postures done with children at this age have animal names, it's good to have pictures of these animals to see and talk about. A fun game is to go to the 'yoga zoo' or go on a 'yoga safari,' where you talk about different environments, animals, nature, and moving the body into different shapes and positions. This is a great teaching tool for little ones. Make-believe yoga is also a great teaching tool. Children can use their imaginations to make the postures exciting and informative.

As kids get older, from **ages 7—9**, they still love to become different animals, but now you can have deeper conversations about the importance of Mother Nature and how to care for nature and all her inhabitants. Using any type of animal spirit cards and creative yoga flows that honor and empower the animal kingdom are fun ways to teach. Adding art, music, chanting, and other fun meditational movements like *qigong* and yogic dance can help break up the class and move the energy in a different and profound way. Children are happy, curious, and naturally interested in life. This is a great age to explore all things yoga with fun games, art, and activities. I like to use the wall for *asanas* with this age group and work on stronger postures like downward dog and dolphin pose.

For my pre-teen/teens, **ages 9—15**, I instruct classes as if I were teaching "mini" adults. I use a lesson with a theme or a quote to inspire the class. I create time for discussion and sometimes journaling and a chance to check in with the kids and see what kind of day they have had. I use that feedback to influence the mood of the class. Sometimes, the sessions are about self-care with relaxing yoga and discussion. Sometimes, I use music to influence the mood. Music can help dictate the atmosphere you would like to create. Calming music is great for gentle, restorative yoga. An increased tempo can elevate the overall energy, and you can use that to your advantage to create a more dynamic, movement-inspired class.

Another great idea is to have kids connect with each other through art, food, games, and flow arts such as jump ropes, poi balls, and hula hoops. These classes can leave a lot of room for talking about current events, lifestyle, school, and all the demands and stresses the kids are facing. This is a perfect way to let the kids know they are not alone and that they can do this! Compassion and empathy are great ways to connect with your students and make these yoga sessions much more than just touching their toes. A nice relaxation at the end with affirmations and gratitude is also very important. There are so many other ways to bring yoga into your classroom, from telling a story to fun art projects and activities.

Mindful Sequencing

Most yoga classes have an intentional flow. There is a warm-up of breathing and gentle movement of the limbs such as the fingers, toes, ankles and wrists, arms, and legs. Perhaps add some neck stretches and cat/cow poses to warm up the spine. The middle section of the class starts to unify and heat the body and breath to greater gross movements and sequences like Sun salutations A and B. If you are working on a peak pose such as a back bend or an arm balance, then it's important to warm up the muscles and sections of the body that those poses use. The end portion of the class is the cooldown. This is a great time for slow, gentle stretching, breathing, inversions, restorative postures, and relaxation/meditation.

"Yoga is the space where the flower blossoms."
-Amit Ray[12]

Adjustments and Hands-On Assists

It's of utmost importance to ask before you provide hands-on assistance in postures. By giving the kids their own power, it helps them to create healthy and safe boundaries. If verbally cueing postures does not work, ask if you can come over and help. Most kids want help. For safety, it's important to spot the kids in yogic headstands, handstands, backbends, or any other postures where you feel they could potentially hurt themselves. Having the kids work with the wall is also a great way to empower and encourage without touching. Demonstrating poses and using props to help support the body in postures is also a powerful way to teach if you feel uncomfortable with hands-on assistance.

Importance of Relaxation

Taking time for rest and mindful meditation at the end of a yoga class has endless benefits. This is where yoga starts to do its work. The body relaxes, and all the energy, nutrients, and goodness flow throughout the entire body and happy chemicals to the brain. It's the gateway to deep concentration, meditation, and oneness. The practice of relaxation at the end of a movement session teaches the body to be still. Once the body maintains stillness, the mind can go inside and release. Try to carve five minutes for a wind-down at the end of each class, including relaxation, guided meditation, visualization, affirmation, and gratitude.

Closing Your Class

Once you have the kids mindfully arise from relaxation, have everyone sit like the Buddha, with their spines nice and long, and bring their hands into prayer position or onto their laps. It's nice to end class together with a collective breath. Guide the children to inhale a nice long, deep breath in and exhale with a big sigh out through the mouth. You can end class by saying the Sanskrit word, *Namaste. Namaste* translates to 'the light in me honors, salutes, and respects that light within you.'

Alternatively, you could simply have them say a prayer or intention internally, perhaps a dedication for Mother Earth. It's important to thank the children for practicing yoga with you. It's also important to let them know that all our thoughts, prayers, and wishes really do bless every living being and creature on the planet.

The Power of Affirmations

We are what we think. We reinforce that thinking when we believe in those stories in our minds. Negative thinking can be programmed into us in many ways in our critical years through family, friends, and schooling. Negative thinking causes self-criticism and self-loathing, which in turn are projected into the world, creating bullying, authoritarianism, and violence. Negative thinking can also compromise our immune systems and create disharmony in the body. Showing children how to recognize these emotions means we can set out to improve upon them. These emotions are a part of the human experience.

On the bright side, the more we can use positive affirmations to counter negative thinking, the better. During the class, use positive affirmations freely. For example, when you are in mountain pose, call out and have the children repeat: *I am strong. I am steady. I am powerful. I believe in myself.* In concentration and relaxation exercises, children can say to themselves: *I am calm. I am at peace. I am relaxed. I am OK.* The more positive we can be, the better. As the children get older, think of their positive affirmations internally and make this a steady practice. The more we can catch ourselves being lost in negative thinking and reach for a bank of positive thoughts or affirmations, the more we can talk our way through hard and challenging times.

Heartfelt Sharing

In teaching a yoga class, always start from where you're at. Try to teach from a place of genuine authenticity. A welcoming space is a safe place for kids to be able to share from their hearts. Nobody is perfect, and there are no pedestals. We are all equal, so share your own personal life experiences. For example, if you were bullied in class, take that lesson, and teach that it's not OK to treat each other badly. Make sure all students know their self-worth and that we are all equal. If you never felt like you belonged, make sure everyone in your class is recognized and that no one feels left out. Make sure all kids feel safe and confident.

Another example: Perhaps you did not have the best nutrition growing up, and your truth is to teach how to eat mindfully. Tap into the lessons you have learned so that you can share from that sacred and healing space. Allow the universal life force to flow through you, knowing that your intention to teach is powerful. Believe in that higher power to assist. Just know that everyone gets something extraordinary and real out of a class where you sincerely share from your own direct experiences. Encourage the children to share from their own experiences too.

Building a Practice of Gratitude and Appreciation

Just as the body is built from the foods we eat, our minds are built from the experiences we have. The flow of experience gradually sculpts the brain, thus shaping the mind. Oddly enough, our brains tend to hold onto negative experiences more than positive ones. This can lead to feeling negative and pessimistic, which can become a vicious cycle of suffering.

From an early age, it's important to savor the good or bring awareness to the good, especially when one is feeling down. It can be as simple as breathing in positive feelings and sensations. Savor the experience for ten to twenty seconds. Really take it in through all the five senses and feel it melt into the body. The longer the positive feeling is held in awareness, the more neurons that fire and thus wire together, creating a stronger, more positive memory. The brain starts to remember these positive feelings and sensations, which attracts more positive experiences.

Instilling a practice of gratitude and appreciation within your yoga classes helps keep children grounded in what is good and happy in their lives. In the end, it helps build positive emotions which benefit their physical and mental health. This will support children's motivation, presence, will, and wholeheartedness. These are small things we can add into our minds daily that will lead to big brain changes and the experience of living. This is why, at the end of *savasana*, it's a powerful place to breathe in the good and be aware of the simple, easy, and beautiful things in our lives.

De-Stress Our Children

We are living in a time of over stimulation. It can be difficult to focus with so many devices and distractions. In general, we spend more time inside on our computers than we do out in nature. When we do stop and take a breath, we tend to feel dissatisfied with the hustle and our accomplishments. Because of this dissatisfaction, we are constantly striving for more to fill the void. Once we have accomplished something, we are onto the next challenge or duty. We rarely stop and permit ourselves to just **be**. If we don't stop to enjoy and experience that which is right in front of us, we will miss the point of life. Our busy lives become a huge distraction, blocking us from finding out who we truly are. Once we stop to understand that this distraction creates real 'unrest' in body and mind, we can find ways toward creating wholeness. With steady practice, we can own up to our distractions and become responsible for our lives.

There are many ways to reduce the impacts of stress. The most powerful way to use the mind-body connection to improve physical and mental health in the classroom and with our children is through guiding the autonomic nervous system. Every time the parasympathetic nervous system is stimulated, the body, brain, and mind increasingly feel more peace and well-being. There are simple ways to turn on the 'rest and digest' part of our nervous system that can be introduced to kids early and can create incredible positive long-term impacts. Modalities such as *deep breathing, belly breaths, big exhalations, mindful body relaxation, guided imagery, sensory experiences, and intentional movements* are easy methods to enhance a peaceful and inspiring learning environment. We will be learning many forms of relaxation techniques throughout this curriculum.

As the child gets old enough to realize the stressors in life (whether that be school, home, relationships, or simply the demands of life), the ability to take refuge in quiet and stillness is very important. Calming the mind will not make sense to them if they don't have an awareness of the consequences of a busy, stressed-out mind. However, it's important to introduce meditation as a way to help tame those strong emotions we feel that we sometimes do not like, no matter our age.

For kids, introduce the *'tension-release breath'* and have them notice how they feel before and after. Guide them through the practice: inhaling, squeeze the arms, fists, biceps, and shrug the shoulders up to the ears and then exhale, letting it all go with a big sigh. Notice the before and after and take a minute in silence to soak in the peace generated by that breathing technique. Another helpful strategy is *breathing into the strong emotions*. Over time, these emotions lessen in severity by allowing the breath to dissolve the intensity.

Whatever age and technique you use, it's all about planting the seed, practice, and intention. Kids might not get it now, but they will when the time comes for them to pull from their resources. Sometimes grief, trauma, injury, and even sickness are triggers that wake us up to these practices.

"Mindfulness is a way of befriending ourselves and our experience." -Jon Kabat-Zinn[13]

Teaching Kids Meditation

Most people find it nearly impossible to clear their minds of thoughts when they start out on their meditation journey. It's a practice that, over time, gets easier. The benefits can also become more powerful over time.

There are many styles of meditation. At its core, meditation is about stillness and chaos, thinking and non-thinking, and deciphering the difference. It's about knowing when the mind gets lost in thought and then returning it to your one-pointed concentration. That could be on the breath, sounds in the room, the *mantra* 'OM', or simply resting awareness, either on aspects of the divine or your happy place. It's about catching yourself getting distracted and bringing yourself back to the moment. Whatever technique you use, with constant practice and awareness, the body and mind benefit tremendously. It's actually training the brain to become stronger and more resilient. Teaching the foundations of the practice itself is the first way to introduce meditation to kids.

You can use the term monkey mind to describe a mind that is full of energy, thoughts, and emotions. In meditation, we are trying to get the 'wiggles' and agitations out so it doesn't overload the system, and we can focus. When we become still and relaxed, our body grows and functions best. I like to emphasize that meditation techniques and quieting the mind are just as healthy as eating good food, exercising, and sleeping well. Meditation is equally important and is a valuable resource for the mind and stress.

Here are some ways to start practicing meditation with the kids.

Younger Kids: With kids **ages 3—5**, use a short and fun meditation either through visualizations, music, or instruments. For example, use crystal or singing bowls, chimes, or drums to create a mesmerizing and tranquil vibration in the mind that leads to further relaxation. A chant or a song is also very meditational for smaller kids to work on their focus and attention. If the kids come into class with a lot of energy or distractions, I like to get the "wiggles" out by some creative movement and perhaps some breath work like the tension-release breath, inhaling and squeezing fists, then exhaling and relaxing the body.

Middle-aged Kids: With kids **ages 6—8**, I like to use guided imagery like *yoga nidra* or adventure meditations across different lands. This age can be very receptive to restorative yoga and the use of props to get cozy and comfortable. I like to build up a portion of this meditation to not speaking and allowing the kids to be one with themselves. Music is nice to play for this part, so they do not feel uncomfortable or silly with the silence. I like to start with one minute of just being.

Older Kids: With kids **ages 9—15**, I like to use a shortened *yoga nidra* practice. I first guide the kids through a *sankalpa*, or intention setting, and then move from gross to subtle movement. I like to bring attention to the physical body and the breath to dive deeper into the more energetic layers like the mind, emotions, and the intuitive body. Here, I like to give them visualizations that are creative and impactful, like seeing themselves doing something that they love (hiking, surfing, playing, dancing) and from there allow them to discover that innate joy and fulfillment in rejoicing in things that bring joy in life. At the end of the meditation, I encourage the kids to be just a witness to their thoughts without having any judgments. Just notice the inner commentator. Notice the thoughts that distract us. Notice the thoughts that take us away from being present. Training the brain to do nothing is a huge reprogramming of the mind, and the more practice, the more inner peace is instilled.

If every eight-year-old in the world is taught meditation, we will eliminate violence from the world within one generation.
-Dalai Lama[14]

What is Yoga?

- Yoga is a way to become Self-realized (one with universal consciousness).

- Yoga is awareness of Self and self in the world.

- Yoga is a path to enlightenment, to see yourself clearly and practice mindfulness.

- Yoga is perspective. Each person gets something different out of the same teaching. There are many teachings.

- Yoga is to be practiced, not perfected—honor where you are today.

- Yoga is change, transformation, rebirth, gratitude, and service.

- Yoga is connection, union, and life-changing.

- Yoga is the action of regenerating love and remembrance of who you truly are (divine).

- Yoga is about being in a relationship with all aspects of ourselves.

- Yoga is about opening yourself up to the sanctuary of your practice.

- Yoga is about practice; every time you come onto your mat, you move into the ceremony, ritual, and sacred pace. Let's begin again!

- Yoga is a practice that meets you where you are right now.

- Yoga is an opportunity for intention setting. Dedicate all movement, change, and healing to that of the collective whole. Wish for peace for every living creature and being.

- Yoga is a way to become still.

Yoga Wisdom I Have Learned Along the Way...

Yoga is near and dear to my heart. These are some of the ways yoga has impacted my life and topics I like to share with my students of all ages.

Yoga is a way of life.
Bringing the mind into the present moment can help with change and transformation and can also illuminate truth and happiness. Celebrate the little things in life that feel balanced and beautiful. Be grateful for the changes that help us step out of our comfort zone and evolve.

Focus on the breath.
Just breathe, and everything shifts. Breath is a reflection of the mind, so when you slow down the breath, you slow down the mind and emotions. Energy is just vibration with information. Take time to slow down, name the feelings, breathe into them, and finish with soaking in positive thoughts or feelings. *Ujjayi* breathing is a great introduction to creating a connection to sound, texture, and temperature of the breath and the present moment. Breathe mindfully and intuitively. Soak in every oxygen molecule into every cell in the body. Love every aspect of your being as sacred and divine.

Listen to the body.
Take a body scan and see what the body is saying. Check-in with how you feel. Know your limits. Use the breath to move in and out of postures. Use the breath to remove negativity stuck inside the body by exhaling through the mouth. Get control of the breath and never let the breath get control of you. Relax your face, jaw, eyes, and mouth.

Trust the system.
Surrender to the greater good. Sometimes we don't get fast results; practice takes time to clearly see all the benefits. Don't give up. Give yourself a chance. Be open to the experience.

Mat as a mirror.
Every time we get on that yoga mat, we can say: Let's begin again. How we practice our yoga *asanas* on the mat reflects how we live our lives on the outside. Are we rigid, judgmental, hard on ourselves, and critical? Notice these aspects in our children. Can you practice self-love on the mat? Practicing the physical *asanas* can teach us so much about ourselves. World renowned yoga guru and activist Seane Corn states it perfectly: "We are all here to awaken to the infinite love within. All moments are holy. All beings are sacred."[2]

"We are all just walking each other home."
-Ram Dass[15]

Notes:

PART **2**

Patanjali's Eight Limbs of Yoga (1–4)

*"Your body is the child of the soul.
You must nourish and train that child."*
-B.K.S. Iyengar[1]

Patanjali's Eight Limbs of Yoga

According to the yogic sage Patanjali, the Eight Limbs of Yoga are a guide to living a righteous and truthful life. They are codes of conduct and rightful ways to live that can lead a yogi from suffering toward enlightenment. This yoga system creates a platform to teach from and is a great introduction to yoga. It gives the students a broader sense of what yoga is really about and how to be a good human and how to conduct ourselves in life. Yoga is not just a physical practice but entails many ways we can evolve as humans. Most importantly, we learn a whole lot about ourselves along the way.

Essentially, the first things children have to learn in life and in the classroom are to get along, be kind, and share. We also learn to wash our hands, be clean, and take care of our physical bodies. We are also learning what not to do, such as lie, steal, and cheat. These are simple rules that can be difficult to follow for anyone feeling any kind of lack or deprivation. The Eight Limbs offer a template for how to live consciously and experience consciousness. If there was a final goal in yoga, it would be to reach the last of the Eight Limbs, which is the ultimate state of enlightenment.

"The Eight Limbs work together. The first five steps—*yama, niyama, asana, pranayama,* and *pratyahara*—are the preliminaries of building the foundation for spiritual life. They are concerned with the body and the brain. The last three steps—*dharana, dhyana,* and *samadhi*—which would not be possible without the previous steps, are concerned with reconditioning the mind."[2] Together, this yoga system of being helps us move from our physical practice into our mental practice and ultimately into our spiritual practice. When we stop to quiet the mind, we seek to understand happiness and unhappiness at the deepest level, and can choose to change. This step of self-inquiry is important as we move through the layers of our being. We ultimately get to know ourselves better, can rest more comfortably in our own skin, and can choose to be less distracted by the outside world when we have a valued code of ethics to live by. We are truly stronger within ourselves when we have an awareness of this at an early age.

As we dive into the Eight Limbs of Yoga with the kids, each limb will have an explanation and ways to take action. Each limb will also have a sample practice (meditation, reflection, journaling, breathing technique, and yoga sequence) to share with the kids or whomever you teach. Starting off with the Eight Limbs of Yoga gives the children a platform for learning yoga basics and the paths to practice yoga in daily life. Yoga is about not only stretching the body but also stretching ourselves within our minds, our attitudes, our ways of living, and how we are in the world. It's important for kids to know that they can practice in many different ways so they can use their own unique capabilities and talents to be the best versions of themselves at every moment of the day. *So, here we go!*

First Limb –
Yama: *Proper Behavior*

The first limb, *yama*, deals with integrity, ethics, and principles. The *yamas* look at social behavior, including how you treat others and the world around you. They are a guide of moral 'do nots'. Do not harm, steal, lie, covet, or accept gifts bearing obligations. ***These are the five yamas.***[2]

1. Ahimsa: *Non-Violence*

Ahimsa means kindness to all things. It can also mean friendliness to yourself and others. It's about understanding how our actions and thoughts can either cause or alleviate suffering. For kids, it's simple: be nice, be kind, and share.

Generally speaking, *ahimsa* is more than just being non-violent. It's a way of life. The key to attaining *ahimsa* is through practicing yoga, mindfulness, and meditation. With the practices of being centered, present, and connected, and as you become increasingly Self-realized, you'll begin to feel a greater sense of connection with the world. This connection will naturally make you more compassionate, loving, and understanding, and less harmful. *Ahimsa* was Gandhi's entire strategy for liberating India from the British Empire. And, of course, Gandhi was an avid meditator.[3]

Gandhi said *ahimsa* is "a force which is more positive than electricity."[4] He also emphasized that *ahimsa* was not a negative state of harmlessness, but a positive state of love. It's about doing good, manifesting love, and having this love for all our enemies. We cannot be bystanders who ignore the evil in the world. We must actively participate in spreading love. This love is a primordial force that sustains, uplifts, and connects all souls together.

*We can express **ahimsa** in these ways:*

- Speaking and living from the heart.
- Treating others with respect and dignity.
- Expressing love, gratitude, and appreciation.
- Harm no living thing.
- Eat plant-based foods.
- Do not bully or demean.
- Be kind to yourself and others.
- Staying positive in words and actions.
- Non-judgment. Accepting others regardless of the situation.
- Loving oneself unconditionally.

Ahimsa *Practices*

Metta Meditation - *Loving Kindness Meditation*

Metta means love, friendliness, or kindness. It's something that you feel in your heart. *Bhavana* means to cultivate or to develop this mood or emotion. There are five stages for this meditation:

In the first stage, you feel *metta* toward yourself as you focus on feelings of peace, calm, and tranquility. You begin to extend these feelings into strength and confidence and, just as if a flicker of light turns into a bright flame, increase that light within your heart and extend to all parts of your body in feelings of joy and happiness. **Repeat to yourself**: *May I be well and happy.*

In the second stage, think of a good friend. Bring them to mind as vividly as you can, thinking of their good qualities. Feel that deep connection to your friend. Remember why you like them, and quietly **repeat to yourself**: *May they be well, may they be happy.*

In the third stage, think of a family member and repeat stage two.

In the fourth stage, think of Mother Earth and **repeat the mantra:** *May she be well and happy.*

In the fifth stage, think of someone that you have had a conflict with. Try not to get caught up in any negative feelings and just send them your *metta* of loving kindness and hopes for the relationship to resolve and feelings to neutralize.
In this stage, you can also send love and light to anything in the past that you might regret or have a hard time forgiving, whether it's a situation or an experience.

Chant - *Lokah Samastah Sukhino Bhavantu*

May all beings everywhere be happy and free, and may the thoughts, words, and actions of my own life contribute to that happiness and to that freedom for all. *Lokah Samastah Sukhino Bhavantu.*

As you chant or sing this, focus on positivity and love for all life and Mother Earth. May every prayer for yourself be a blessing to every living being and creature on this planet..

2. Satya: *Truth and Honesty*

Satya is associated with truthfulness; it literally means 'that which is.' This *yama* encourages us to speak the truth. We must see and discuss things as they actually are instead of how we wish they were. It's about being open to the truth, listening to the truth, and only telling the truth when you can speak it with honesty, kindness, and compassion.

*We can express **satya** in these ways:*

· Speaking up for yourself, your beliefs, and your rights.

· Practice clear, open and honest communication.

· Be truthful and do not lie.

· Use clarity in your intention.

· Be reliable.

· Keep promises, and don't make promises you can't keep.

· Do not say anything if you can't say something good. Try to be positive and help when you can.

· Let your practice be a way to observe and skillfully respond to how you feel fully.

· Be responsible for every thought, word, and action.

Satya *Practices*

Sat Nam Meditation and Reflection

Sat Nam translates to: '*I am truth and truth is my identity.*'

Inhale the word **Sat** internally
and exhale the word **Nam** internally.

Repeat ten times with ten breaths.

At the end of the meditation, reflect on what your truths are right now at this moment.
What do you believe in with all of your heart and soul?
Are you living your truth? Are you practicing what you preach?

3. Asteya: *Non-stealing*

Asteya can literally mean the non-stealing of others' possessions, but it can also mean the non-stealing of others' ideas, sentiment, love, and generosity. It's about being yourself and trusting in that relationship, and knowing that you have everything you need within yourself. Do not be someone you're not.

---

*We can practice **asteya** in these ways:*

· Be considerate of others' property, relationships, and time.

· Speak wisely. Choose words carefully and clearly.

· Don't steal other people's belongings.

· Time is precious, do not waste it or waste anyone else's time.

· Allow everyone's light to shine, be happy for others.

· Don't judge other people.

· Value and show gratitude and generosity.

· Have your own ideas, think for yourself.

· Do not be envious. Do not covet what others have.

· To not take credit for things you did not do, give credit where credit is due.

Asteya *Practices*

Presence Meditation - *Being Aware of Thoughts*

Being unaware of yourself and where you are cuts you off from the experience of being in the moment. The more that happens, the more of your life you miss. We rethink and reconsider events, and our minds wander. That's natural, but if we let ourselves get too far off track, we lose ourselves. Slow down. Take a breath. Pause. Think and see things clearly. Yoga allows us to do this. Through yoga, you can train your mind to slow down and let yourself be aware of sensations, thoughts, and emotions as you experience them. One of the most important concepts of *asteya* is to remind yourself that you never get time back. Live in the moment and truly enjoy and appreciate what you have around you.

Practicing Abundance and the *Mantra*: *'I am enough.'*

Abundance means to have a great amount of something. With abundance, we have no need for other things. If we want to feel whole and happy with ourselves, we must practice understanding that we have enough, we are enough, and we will ultimately reduce our desires for more. Practice using the *mantra 'I am enough'* whenever you feel things like desire or that you lack enough or want things. Pay attention and observe how it affects your life.

"As you walk and eat and travel, be where you are. Otherwise, you will miss most of your life."
-Gautama Buddha[5]

4. Brahmacharya: *Going Within*

In a broad sense, *brahmacharya* means the preservation of one's energy. The literal translation is about sexual responsibility. In essence, this *yama* is about not giving all of your energy away or mindlessly allowing it to leak away. Find the moderate path. Be socially responsible. Learn from your mistakes. Avoid meaningless encounters and frivolous relationships. Control your urges; do not overeat, over-buy, over-want. Protect your energy and health by making conscious, smart choices. Ultimately, as we turn inward, we are no longer dependent on outside stimulation or pleasures to bring us joy. Inner peace is all we need.

Another way to look at it is to eliminate desire in general. We will discuss this idea later in the manual when we discuss the *Buddha and the Four Noble Truths*. But for now, the first truth is: Desire creates suffering. So, to eliminate desire is to control our urges to want. Ultimately, when we want things we cannot have or we have too much of something, it creates an undesired outcome. Try not to lust over things you think you need.

---

*We can teach and practice **brahmacharya** with young people in these ways:*

· **Everything in moderation.** If you eat something sugary or low in nutritional value, counteract it with something positive like exercise or healthy eating. Find balance.

· **Protect your energy.** If someone is mean to you, then know to protect your energy by perhaps not hanging out with them. You can respond with kindness or say a prayer that feels peaceful. If you're heading out into public or big gatherings, do some grounding energy visualizations to protect your energy. Check in with yourself and your intuition.

· **Try not to want frivolous things.** Resist advertisements. Control urges. Reflect on desires and simplify your life.

· **Harness your energy.** Take naps. Spend reflective time in nature. Quiet the mind with meditation. Read. Write. Journal. Make art, etc. Do peaceful things that regenerate your energy. Use this energy to connect to your spiritual self.

· **Be aware of desire.** Notice if you are always wanting things to make you happy. Notice if you are admiring other people's things and wishing that they were yours. Notice if you feel envious of other people's material items. Practice being grateful for what you have.

· **Be conscious with every step.** Have your higher purpose at hand with every choice, every action.

Brahmacharya *Practice*

Grounding Energy Meditation

Sit or lie down and imagine a bubble of light surrounding your body. Visualize that light wrapping around your body in a circle over and over. Envision the color surrounding you—gold, silver, red, purple, whatever comes to your mind. Now, shade in the bubble of light as if you were a painter and you were coloring the front, back, sides, top, and bottom of your bubble a beautiful iridescent, mother of pearl color. This bubble of light is a protection of your energy. No one can steal your peace. Now, relax into the space of not needing anything, not having to do, become, be or want anything. Feel yourself sink deeper into a tremendous state of peace.

Now, feel the sensation of not needing, wanting, or desiring anything, being totally fine with just you and what you already have. Notice how it feels to let your guard down and release all the things in life that we have to do, manage, accomplish, be and become. Notice how when that weight of the world lifts, you can just bask in that state of deep peace. You're not wanting, lusting over, desiring, or giving up your energy. Now, soak in the revitalization. As if you were a lamp and you were being plugged into an outlet. Feel every cell energized, restored, and renewed.

5. Aparigraha: *Non-Attachment*

Aparigraha means to neutralize the desire to want things. We generally suffer when we can't have the things that we want. When we want things, we can become obsessed and covet and hoard them. It's alright to have goals and possess things, but when desires control our lives or things bring us suffering when we don't have them, then we need to release those attachments. This *yama* is about consciously having things in our lives that we can take care of in a healthy way, supporting our highest values. It's about not identifying with our stuff and our belongings, but liberating ourselves into knowing that we are enough just as we are. It's about non-attachment, energetically releasing the ties to things.

> *We can practice **aparigraha** in these ways:*
>
> · Simplify your life by attaining and retaining only what you need.
>
> · Let go of past anxieties, negative thoughts that do not serve you in the highest. Free yourself from attachments.
>
> · Try not to over-collect and hoard. Be mindful of what you have and feel grateful for every item. Bring things into your life consciously.
>
> · Detach. Clear your space and release the things that no longer bring you joy and fulfillment.
>
> · Don't be possessive of things, thoughts, people, or places Give freely to others.

Aparigraha *Practices*

Energy Release Meditation
Imagine negative thoughts or experiences in a balloon and then cut the balloon and see it drift away.

Breathing into Big Emotions
Hold anything negative in the mind with tons of white light. Use your breath and breathe into it. Allow your breath to be bigger than that emotion. Really lean into it. Now inhale as deep as you can into that feeling and exhale out through the mouth and feel that emotion being freed from the body.

Peeling Back the Layers of Life Meditation
Imagine your life like an onion, and you are peeling back the layers of the world. As layer after layer falls away, release the weight of the world. All the duties, obligations, regrets, failures, hardships, challenges, tribulations are released from the mind and shed from the body. Release the ego, or any thoughts of the things that you think make up you: your hair, your clothes, your job, your talents. Let go of the untruths, shame, guilt, sorrow, and emotions. Release and let go of all of the superfluous ideas and things. Detach. That stuff doesn't define you. Let it go.

As the layers peel back, notice in the very middle of that onion is the pearlized center: iridescent, shiny, radiant, and beautiful, just like you are at the core of your existence. Radiant light. Bathe for a few moments in that bright, pure and luminous light. .

Second Limb –
Niyama: *Personal Observances*

The *yamas* are the foundation for the *niyamas*, for doing right. Together, the first two limbs show us how to take better care of ourselves and teach us to love ourselves and others so we can have a more meaningful life. They foster right-minded activities and allow positive energy to take hold in our lives by cleansing and purifying our body and mind. *Niyamas* relate to discipline and spiritual observations. They consider how we treat ourselves and allow us to cultivate our inner being and inner awareness. These are sometimes called observances or practices to attain a more spiritually rich life. These practices focus on purity of the mind and body, contentment in all situations, self-introspection, self-discipline, selfless service, and devotion to a higher power or to something greater than ourselves like the Divine, Mother Earth, the Sun, the Moon, and the Universe. The *niyamas* help us consciously connect back to ourselves and help us identify what is really important and true, lovingly and truthfully. **There are five niyamas[2].**

1. Sauca: *Purity*

Sauca translates to 'cleanliness' or 'purity.' *Sauca* reminds us of who we are fundamentally, when we let go of distractions and difficulties. We purify ourselves mentally and physically, internally, and externally. When we do it right, *sauca* can completely reinvent our well-being.

> *We can practice **sauca** in these ways:*
>
> · **Purity of environment.** Clear the things that create suffering: unhealthy foods, thoughts, clutter, and negative energies.
>
> · **Purity of space.** Keep your yoga space, house, business, and desk clean and clear.
>
> · **Purity of the body.** Take care of the cleanliness of your body by eating clean and whole foods.
>
> · **Purity of communication.** Notice thoughts, words, and distractions that do not serve you in the highest.
>
> · **Purity of thought.** Examine the intentions behind what you think, say, or do.
>
> · **Purity of the moment.** Practicing presence.
>
> · **Purity with relationships.** Make friends with your dark side. Find awareness of what blocks you from love and awakening.

Sauca *Practices*

Purity Meditation

Children are curious. They think about the world from a place of innocence, delight, and amusement. Use this 'beginner's mind' to think about the world around you from a child's perspective. As adults, we look at the world with skepticism, pessimism, or even thinking that we know what's going to happen. We forget to take in the wonder of the world. Do everything as if it's your first time. Wipe the slate clean and fresh. Encourage children to be their natural selves. Praise every moment and situation with fresh and new eyes.

Cleansing Meditation

Imagine yourself standing underneath a waterfall, and the water is cleansing all the negativity from the body. See that cleansing energy moving down into the Earth. See yourself as sparkling clean. Use your words to allow that energy to be rinsed. What are you cleansing in your life?

2. Santosa: *Contentment*

Santosa translates into 'contentment,' 'happiness,' or even 'delight.' *Santosa* can be thought of as present-moment graciousness, when everything around you feels whole and complete. It's loving yourself beyond all material possessions, wealth; without defining yourself by what you have. It's about being a fundamentally good person and believing that you are enough. *Santosa* sometimes means releasing the past or making peace with what is. It's about releasing guilt and regret, starting fresh each day with a positive outlook and open heart.

> *We can practice **santosa** in these ways:*
>
> · Appreciate what you have and who you are; be thankful.
>
> · Be grateful for the small things every day.
>
> · See the beauty in everything and everyone.
>
> · Find gratitude in nature.
>
> · Enjoy the simple things in life.
>
> · Find happiness, responsibility, and growth in every moment.
>
> · Live graciously and mindfully.
>
> · Be happy and live fully.
>
> · Slow down.
>
> · Be more like a happy and carefree child.

Santosa *Practices*

Gratitude Meditation

It is widely accepted that gratitude leads to happiness. The more gratitude you feel, the happier you are. Gratitude increases positivity as we hold on to good experiences and allows us to experience better health, overcome adversity, and build strong relationships. Gratitude manifests in many different ways, and there is no right or wrong way to show it. Gratitude is a skill and an awareness we need to keep passing down through the generations. Appreciation can go a long way in the world.

Think of all the things in your life that you are thankful for or make you feel balanced. Send the breath into the heart and just notice all the happiness and joy in your life. Remember the good and simple things. Hold on to the things in your life that make you feel supported and nurtured. Just pause in that state of gratitude and contentment and soak in the release of happy chemicals.

In your classes, ask the kids what they are grateful for. Allow them to share this with their friends and families. Gratitude journals that the children can write or draw in each week are also very powerful.

3. Tapas: *Self-Transformation or Heat*

Tapas can translate into 'heat,' 'disciplined practice,' or 'will power.' It can be a way to use and create energy in the body, mind, and voice. *Tapas* is a commitment to self-transformation. We burn up the old to make room for the new. *Tapas* is about developing practical habits that create long-lasting results. It's a practice to try to focus only on one or two things at a time. Use your will to get the results you want in life.

Tapas can be thought of as a spark of motivation inside your soul to help keep you on track and stay focused. *Tapas*—that inner fire you feel—motivates you to become who you are and to work through difficulties in life. Without *tapas*, we wouldn't have the courage to face problems and make progress on our spiritual journey. *Tapas* encourages self-love and self-awareness.

In Sanskrit, the word *tapas* means 'cleanse.' The modern-day yoga master TKV Desikachar explains that *tapas* is a "means by which we keep ourselves healthy and cleanse ourselves inwardly."[7] In yoga practice, *tapas* becomes our internal refinement.

"Action is movement with intelligence. The world is filled with movement. What the world needs is more conscious movement, more action."
-B.K.S. Iyengar[6]

We can practice *tapas* in these ways:

· Attention to body posture so that energy can flow.
· Attention to eating habits and what the body craves.
· Attention to the patterns of the breath. Create heat through *asana* or *pranayama* to purify the body and mind.
· Watch any heated temperament, control negative impulses and heated speech or language.
· Fasting or meditating for long hours.
· Commit to the practice.

Tapas *Practices*

Clearing Meditation

Sit or lie down and focus on your breath in the body. Notice your big toes starting to light on fire like candle flames. Focus on that feeling of fire ripping across the toes, into the whole foot, moving up the ankles. Follow those flames up both legs, hips, torso, chest, arms, fingers. Bring that heat and fire up through the throat, face, and head. Imagine the fire burning away all impurities. Stay with the flames for three to five minutes.

Candle Meditation

Candle meditation is known as *Trāṭaka*, and means 'gaze' in Sanskrit. It is one of the six techniques used for purification. Focusing the eyes is the basis of candle meditation. Candle meditation works by concentrating on a single focal point. This focus could be a candle or any small light source like a star, the Moon, it could also be an image of a flame in the mind's eye.

Candle meditation works because of how our brains process what we see. Our eyes send signals to the brain to process and decode. As we focus on the candlelight, our brains have a chance to slow down and ignore other distractions. Information is processed more easily, and we become more aware of the candle. Eventually, the flame absorbs our attention, and we become fully encompassed and relaxed. Once you achieve this, you can meditate effectively, looking at your past, present, and future with clarity.

Candle meditation works because it allows one to open their third eye, or *ajna chakra*, focusing on developing intuition and wisdom. Candle meditation makes psychic abilities stronger and is easy to do. It can help purify the mind from the constant chatter by giving the mind something to focus on. It also helps facilitate better reflection due to increased concentration. Feel the flame burn away the impurities. Now feel that same flame ignite the heart space with tremendous light.

Candle meditation with LED tea lights is a wonderful resource for children. They can use this meditation safely to help focus and clear their minds.

4. Svadhyaya : *Study of the Sacred Text and Oneself*

The literal translation of *svadhyaya* is "self-study," which invites us to examine our own nature, thoughts, and actions at the core. It's about nonjudgment and reflecting on those things that serve, and do not serve in our lives. It's about becoming aware of self-defeating thoughts and roadblocks that we put in our way. It's about honoring our own true nature, which is divine. Sometimes reading spiritual texts or so-called 'self-help' books can inspire you to look at yourself more intimately and spiritually. We can also start to feel more compassion and live more mindfully when we are inspired. *Svadhyaya* activates the wisdom mind and encourages us to connect more to the divine spirit inside.

We can practice **svadhyaya** *in these ways:*

· Self-study and self-inquiry.

· Spiritual quest. Get to know the Divine presence in your life. What are your beliefs in a higher power?

· Be accountable to actions, thoughts, words, and deeds. Learn from your mistakes and love yourself unconditionally without judgments.

· Contemplate and apply the scriptures or sacred texts. Ask yourself: how can I be better, love more, serve higher?

Svadhyaya *Practice*

Meditation: *So - Hum*, I Am That

Inhale *So* and exhale *Hum*, internally. Repeat for ten breaths. This breath meditation helps us release the chatter of the mind to align to the present moment, honoring the Divine aspects that we are. It also translates into *'I am that,'* which means I am of Divine energy. I am connected to that most magnificent power. I am one with the universe.

This is a simple yet effective meditation for children to help focus the mind through an internal *mantra*.

5. Isvara Pranidhana: *Surrendering to the Divine*

Isvara pranidhana is about surrendering, dedicating ourselves to the all-pervading consciousness or divinity. It means giving ourselves over to a higher purpose, allowing our souls to evolve to our own unique purpose. On the mat, it's about the practice; not being attached to the outcome, to focus on the journey and not be rattled by the 'bumps' along the way. There is no end result in yoga, but a continuous practice throughout every stage of life. It's about adapting to nature and the cycles of life. It's about releasing control of the things we have no control over and instead controlling how we think and feel about it all. We must take full accountability for all our actions and offer them to the goodness of all. Use our downfalls as lessons. Use our lessons as gifts.

We can practice **isvara pranidhana** *in these ways:*

· Acknowledge a higher power.

· Pray and worship according to your religious beliefs.

· Surrender yourself to the world beyond you.

· Bless your food and drink. Find gratitude in every moment.

· Devote yourself to something greater than yourself. Make everything an offering to a universal cause or truth, to that which is divine.

· Find your soul's purpose. Hold faith that the universe has something magnificent in store for you.

· Find peace and acceptance always.

Isvara Pranidhana *Practice*

Divine Meditation

Meditate on an aspect of the Divine. Imagine your heart energy reaching up out of your crown, connecting with that greater force, and then bringing that energy back down through the crown and into the heart.

Third Limb –
Asana: *Moving these Earth Suits*

The *yamas* and *niyamas* set the stage for *asanas*, for moving the energy in the body. *Asanas* are physical yoga postures or exercises which open and expand consciousness throughout the body. By focusing attention on different body parts with mindful movements and concentrated awareness, we open up the physical body, helping to release aches and pains. Yoga postures help us have more control over our bodies and our emotions, concentration, and intentions. When we deliberately move the body through various positions, these movements can help unlock pent-up emotions and feelings residing in the tissues. By creating a safe, intentional platform to move the energy within the body through *yoga asanas*, one can free themselves of blocked, negative energy and restore the body with fresh, oxygenated blood for renewal. Ultimately, this provides space for emotional healing.

Traditionally, *yoga asanas* were practiced in preparation to sit in stillness for meditation. Meditation can also help us gain control over our minds and emotions. Together, *yoga asanas* and meditation combat the stressors of life and aid in the aging process.

So, how does it work? Yoga practice reattaches us to the body from an external awareness. We move from outer experience to an inner experience, from gross to subtle. In allowing ourselves to reattach to our bodies, we realize our duty to live our lives guided by our body's ancient wisdom. A healthy life requires a healthy body. Yoga provides this connection between the physical and the spiritual. Once we are aware of and caring for our physical bodies, we can begin to dive inward. Once the body relaxes, the mind can find stillness. This is one of the many benefits of a steady practice.

Ultimately, *asanas* (postures) make way for *pranayama* (energy flow). Once we get the energy lines open in the body, the breath can literally take flight. The breath can work its way through the physical and unblock stuck emotion, old thoughts, and patterns. It can reinvigorate the mind and refresh our awareness of the present moment. When the body and breath start moving, we are working more harmoniously with our senses. We clear negative feelings out, and we can get rid of aches and pains, and more profoundly prepare the body and mind for stillness in meditation.

"My Body Is My Temple and Asanas Are My Prayers."
-B.K.S. Iyengar[6]

Yoga Asana: *Pointers and Practices*

Drishti

Drishti is a gaze point. It's a key factor in our yoga practice for balance and focus. When we fix our gaze at a single point, our mind relaxes, and we can enter a meditative state. When the gaze moves around the room, we can become scattered.

> When kids are having difficulty balancing in yoga class, have everyone find a focal point or *drishti* either on one spot in front of them or on a wall. I have discovered that when children lack confidence, especially young ones, they like to be silly, flop all around, and fall on their mats purposefully. In these cases, try attending to the good behavior, ignoring the unwanted behavior, and praising the ones who listen and follow the instructions. When the ones who were not following along do, praise their behavior too.

Breath

Breath is key. When the energy of the classroom is high and focus scattered, redirect attention to the breath. Allow the breath to be the most important component within each *asana*. Allow the breath to move everyone in and out of the postures with ease. Allow the breath to help with the inner alignment and form. Notice when the breath gets out of control. Slow down and send the breath into areas of resistance. Pause and reflect. Stay true. We never want the breath to get control of us. We always want to be in control of our breath.

> Teaching the kids to move with their breath will support their movements and the desired action and add a meditation component into the flow. Start by simply inhaling while raising the arms up and exhaling while lowering the arms down. Another exercise to try is to inhale while raising the arms up and exhale, leaning forward to fold the upper body down over the legs slowly and carefully (with bent knees if necessary). Inhale to come back up to standing. Try flowing with the breath through a Sun salutation.

Yoga Alchemy

Yoga is transformative. We can use yoga as a tool to shift perspective and give balance to our daily lives. Yoga meets us where we are today. For instance, if we are feeling lazy, unmotivated, and stuck in lack of movement or negative thinking, we might need a more stimulating practice to move out that dull energy like tapping, *kriyas*, and *surya namaskars*.

Conversely, if we are overstimulated and burnt out, we need replenishing practices like *yoga nidra*, *chandra namaskars*, *Yin* yoga and restorative yoga. These practices help us deeply reflect and support the inner state. These practices also slow down the body and allow one to connect to themselves, their breath, and nature. Checking in with how we feel daily can dictate movement therapy. Everyday our yoga practice can change. We will incorporate these practices throughout the curriculum.

Tapping

Tapping is an amazingly effective practice to get the energy to flow and transmute negativity into positivity while relaxing. There are many types of tapping. In Chinese medicine, tapping can be for both moving stagnant energy as well as instilling relaxation in the body. You can tap on areas that feel dull, such as the temples, forehead, or the back body. This is highly effective in creating energy. You can also tap on reflex points or meridians on the body, like the top of the shoulders, palms of the hands, inner ankles, or the bottoms of the feet. Kids love tapping. It is a fun way to wake up the energy in the body. Just by clapping the hands, the mind and body immediately come into the present moment. In January's curriculum, we will explore another style of tapping called the *Emotional Freedom Technique*, developed by Gary Craig.

Kriyas

Kriyas are breathing and movement exercises that stimulate the body and mind. They can alchemically shift negative feelings into positive sensations. The word *kriya* means action. *Kriyas* are a series of postures popular in *kundalini* yoga. The purpose is to use a sequence of postures, breath, and sound to affect physical and mental changes in the body, mind, and spirit. The idea is that an action leads to a manifestation. Different *kriyas* support the liver, balance the glandular system, stimulate hormones and the pituitary gland, increase flexibility, and so much more. Each *kriya* has a different outcome, and each works on your body on a deep level. Kids love moving and breathing. *Kriyas* are a great way to wake up the body's energy but also create tremendous focus to calm the kids and encourage concentration. *Kriyas* also help to get the 'wiggles' out.

> ### Flying Bird Kriya
> Sit comfortably and extend the arms to each side like bird wings. Vigorously start to move both arms up and down in micro movements like a bird flapping its wings. Inhale five short inhalations through the nose and exhale five short breaths out through the mouth. Keep repeating in this rhythmic style of breathing while simultaneously flapping your arms for one minute in unison.
>
> ### Twisted Root
> Sit comfortably and place your fingertips on each of the shoulders. Inhale through the nose and twist one way. Exhale through the mouth and twist the other way. Continue back and forth gently at your own pace for one minute.

Surya Namaskar

Surya namaskar is a yoga flow showing gratitude and appreciation for the life-giving energy that the Sun provides. The Sun represents power, energy, light and life. Your *surya nadi*, or Sun channel, runs along the right side of your body. Traditionally, *surya namaskar*—or Sun salutation—should be done in the morning around sunrise to honor the first light. There are many benefits to *surya namaskar*, including physical strength, balanced energies and coordination. The technique of *surya namaskar* makes you more mindful as you physically warm up all the joints through intentional flow.

Regularly practiced, *surya namaskar* increases awareness, guiding you to form a deeper connection between your body, breath, and consciousness. Kids love these dynamic movements. You can exhale on a forward fold, for example, and say *OM* aloud with the kids or 'howl' in upward dog. In a downward-facing dog, I like to bounce the legs and hips, hop into handstands, or simply take the dog 'for a walk.' There are many fun ways to make each posture exciting and new.

Chandra Namaskar

Chandra namaskar, or Moon Salutation, honors the energy of the Moon. You can do this series of gentle stretches to help relax and calm the mind at any time of day. *Chandra namaskar* cools and softens the body and is a wonderful way to wind down and get your body ready for a restful night's sleep at the end of the day. Traditionally, the Moon holds the divine feminine and connects it to nature.

This cool, receptive, inwardly focused divine feminine lunar energy can be found in each of us as well, opposing the more warm, active, and outwardly oriented solar energy. *Chandra namaskars* help channel the lunar energy and these cool, relaxing, and creative qualities. Kids love to move in a flowy, gentle, and nurturing way, especially if they have had a long

day at school. Be creative with a visual of that beautiful Moon shining upon your practice and energizing all the students with love and light. Incorporate the Moon into your classes by discussing Moon phases and the importance of new Moon and full Moon rituals.

Yoga Nidra

Yoga nidra is just the opposite of *kriya*. While *kriyas* are a faster-paced breathing and moving practice, *yoga nidra* is a more relaxed, subtle way to shift energy at will. *Yoga nidra* is a guided relaxation on the back that nourishes and revitalizes. *Yoga nidra* is both relaxing and mind-altering. Over time, by working with intention setting and moving consciousness throughout the body, one can feel more grounded, aware, less reactive, and more hopeful and loving. When the body is burnt out, we need practices to allow rest to happen. *Yoga nidra* supports the nourishing and cooling of the body and mind and deals with moving through the different brain waves to reach the optimum stage of theta brain waves to allow healing and restoration to happen. *Yoga nidra* is a practice that anyone can do. When guiding kids through *yoga nidra*, it's fun to be creative with a lot of description and visualizations. One of the most important aspects of *yoga nidra* is intention setting. We thoroughly go over how to conduct your very own *yoga nidra* in the March chapter.

Yin yoga and restorative yoga are also incredibly nourishing and important practices. *Yin* yoga will be explored in December's chapter and restorative yoga in July's chapter.

Forth Limb – **Pranayama**: *Breath Control*

Asanas set the stage for *pranayama*, for the breath to harmonize, circulate, and expand energy to all body parts. *Prana* (energy of life force) rides on the breath. When the physical body begins to open, *prana* can move and flow to help release blockages in the body and bring body and mind back into homeostasis. Mastery of the deep connection between breath, mind, and emotions is the goal of this breathing practice.

The great Indian poet Kabir was once asked by one of his students, "Kabir, where is God?" His reply was, "He is the breath within the breath."[10]

Pranayama is measuring, controlling, retaining, and directing the breath. The moment the in-flowing breath harmonizes with the out-flowing breath, the perfect relaxation and balance of the body occurs. All postures need breath to flow. When we are not mindful of our breath or are holding our breath, injury can happen in the body. The breath can be seen as a reflection of the mind. When we get hurt or feel threatened, our breath shortens. When we are calm and at ease, our breath softens and elongates. The more we can access control over the breath, the more peace and harmony we will experience. The more conscious we are of our breath, the more presence we have in our life.

The breath is a natural detoxifier. Working with the breath also creates an actual physical sensation of heat, or *tapas*, the inner fire of purification, as we talked about with the *niyamas*. This heat purifies the nerve channels in the body, also known as *nadis*.

The *nadis* (energetic lines or pathways) are like the meridians in Chinese medicine. The heat stimulated from breath helps the body remove excess waste along the *nadis* through exhalation. Inhalation helps expand, open the airways, and feed all the cells and tissues. The exhale helps to detox and dispel nervous tension. Each inhale creates energy, each exhale releases energy. Exhalations are so healing because they slow the body and mind down significantly. They have a grounding effect all over. Even breathing techniques where you elongate the exhale longer than the inhale have profound positive effects on the central nervous system, specifically the parasympathetic nervous system, helping to alleviate anxiety and depression. *Prana* can move along these energetic pathways, which is why it's important to focus on the breath always in yoga *asanas*.

"Breath is the King of the Mind."
-B.K.S. Iyengar[9]

It can take as few as six long, slow, deep belly breaths to switch the body; deactivating the sympathetic nervous system (fight or flight) and activating the parasympathetic nervous system (rest and digest). Breath is so powerful and can be a guide for us in our practice. The sound of breath can also help remind other students to breathe. Without breath, there is no life. Being aware of the breath can alchemically change the old to the new, negativity into positivity. It's a way we can shift our mood, minimize pain, support our nervous system, and connect to the now. It's also a way to give back to nature. The longer and slower you exhale, the more you are feeding the planet.

Prana translates into life-force energy. *Prana* is all of life. It is around us and within us. *Prana* flows through our breath. It is the energy of our voice and words; it's our health and vitality. We are all so very connected through breath. There is an old yoga belief that we are born with a certain number of breaths and the longer, slower, and deeper we breathe, the longer, and more vital life we will lead. When you are in control of your breath, your *prana*, no one can steal your peace. When you are more peaceful, it affects everyone in your force field. Our breath is powerful!

Breath is our lifeline, and teaching mindfulness and breathing to kids at an early age has endless benefits. When we slow our breathing down, we naturally slow our heart rate, and the brain waves come into a more receptive and relaxed internal atmosphere. As the parasympathetic nervous system turns on, all of our vital organs get oxygen, a natural release of happy chemicals (endorphins, serotonin, melatonin, dopamine) flood the body and the brain, and we can calm ourselves into an opportunity to be open and ready to learn. Having better breath control can help kids in many areas of their lives—test-taking, sports, homework, music, and arts. Being more conscious of their breath can also help kids be more in touch with feelings and emotions daily.

Ida and Pingala: *Two Channels that Circulate Prana*

Two channels circulate *prana*. *Ida* is the left channel associated with the left side of the body. *Ida's* characteristics include white, the Moon, reflective, feminine, cooling, and restorative. *Pingala* is the right channel associated with the right side of the body. *Pingala's* characteristics include red, the Sun, energy, masculinity, fire, and heat. The Sanskrit word *nadi* derives from *nad*, which means 'flow' or 'channel.' These energetic pathways allow *prana* to flow like water, finding the path of least resistance and nourishing all organs, nerves and tissues along the way. The *nadis* are like little rivers within the body that replicate energetic irrigation systems in the body.

The human body contains over seventy-two thousand *nadis* that channel *prana* to every cell in the body. The *sushumna* is the central *nadi* of the body. When this system flows freely, we are healthy and vital. When the *nadis* become weak, we get blocked and sluggish and can struggle with poor mental, emotional and physical health. The breathing technique *nadi shodhana* is beneficial nerve and energy cleansing as well as mind balancing.

Every ninety minutes or so, the channel switches from *ida* to *pingala* and vice versa. We are in a constant state of moving through two energies that literally support our every move. This is just one reason why our *asana* and *pranayama* practice is so important: to bring balance. We can tune into the subtle energies of our bodies and minds just by tuning into our breath and creating harmony in the moment. For example, if we are always on the go, we will burn out. If we lack movement, we can become sedentary, and our energy can diminish. With awareness of the two channels, we can literally restore life force to our entire being by being conscious of our breathing. We can also release a lot of pent-up emotion by properly channeling our breath.

Pranayama *Practice*

Balancing the Channels: *Ida and Pingala*

Close off your right nostril and take three breaths through the open nostril on the left side. Notice if it feels clear or blocked. Close off the left nostril and take three breaths in and out through the right nostril and notice how it feels. Now decipher. If the right nostril feels more 'open,' then your *pingala* channel is more open, and it's the best time to be active, get things done, strive for movement and accomplishment. If the left channel is more 'open,' then your *ida* channel is more energetically supporting slowing down, deep breathing, soothing meditations, restorative yoga flow, reading, writing, and replenishment. When we can identify these subtle energies in the body, we become more in tune with our biology and learn how to operate more efficiently in the world. Benefits of this breathing technique can include more energy, a stronger immune system, and less burnout. We can then learn how to flow and support our energy better..

Vayus: *The Five Winds*

Prana flows along energetic pathways in the body known as *vayus* or Sanskrit for wind. We all have five *vayus*; 'five winds.' The energetic qualities of the five winds of *prana* direct the energy flow to all areas of the body, thus aiding and supporting different functions of the body. This ancient wisdom was developed by yogis who found optimal health and well-being by consciously controlling their awareness and focus of the different *vayus*. If we work to cultivate a basic awareness of the *vayus*, we can deepen our body and breath awareness, bring consciousness and *prana* to that specific place, enrich our yoga practice and boost our health.

Awareness of the five *vayus* has many applications in yoga and is used to support the body within a *yoga asana*.

*The five **vayus** are:*

1. *Prana vayu* creates a focus to lift and open the upper body.
2. *Apana vayu* creates a focus to descend and ground the lower body.
3. *Vyana vayu* creates a focus of extending energy into the limbs and out to the edges of the skin.
4. *Samana vayu* creates a focus towards the core, consciously drawing energy from the periphery toward the midline.
5. *Udana vayu* creates a focus to engage the spinal muscles for correct and strong posture that draws energy in toward the midline, and supports a clear voice and intention and speaking the truth.

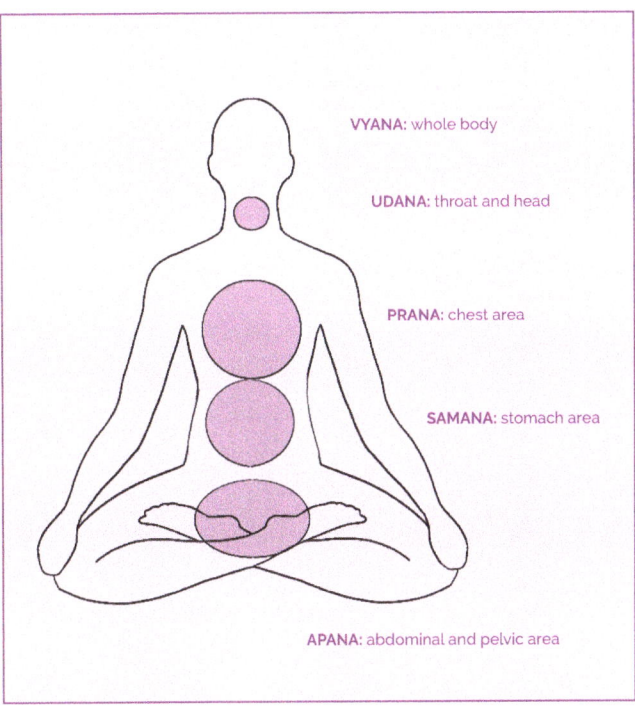

VYANA: whole body

UDANA: throat and head

PRANA: chest area

SAMANA: stomach area

APANA: abdominal and pelvic area

Experiencing the Vayus

Prana vayu is centered in the third eye. Its energy begins in the head and permeates the chest. The flow of *prana vayu* is inward and upward. It feeds the brain, eyes, ears, heart, lungs and chest and governs the reception of our senses. This *vayu* is very important because as you breathe in, *prana* moves into all of the other *vayus*. The slower, deeper and longer the breath, the more vital energy one can receive.

To experience prana vayu, inhale and feel the breath move from the lower belly up into the chest, heart and brain.

Apana vayu moves into the pelvic floor, sacrum and lower abdomen. The flow of *apana vayu* is down and out. Its nourishing energy aids the digestive, reproductive, and excretory systems. *Apana vayu* cleanses out toxins both physically and emotionally. Its grounding energy allows us to feel connected to the earth and our foundation.

To experience apana vayu, inhale and feel the *prana vayu* energy rise and, upon exhaling, feel this downward *apana vayu* energy move out through the feet. As the breath moves out, feel the release of anything that doesn't serve you on a physical, emotional and mental level.

Vyana vayu is located primarily in the heart and lungs and flows outward towards the limbs and the periphery of the body. It guides the circulation of blood, nutrition and energy to all edges of the skin.

To experience vyana vayu, inhale and feel your breath radiating outward from the heart and navel region to the arms, fingers, legs, and toes.

Samana vayu is centered in the abdomen and navel area. The flow of *samana vayu* moves inward from the periphery of the body toward the center. This *vayu* brings *prana* back toward the heart and guides the integration of all substances: food, air, experiences, emotions, and thoughts.

To experience samana vayu, inhale and feel *vyana vayu* move outward into the limbs and exhale, feel your breath and energy contract and gather towards your torso and navel region.

Udana vayu has a circular energy in the throat, neck and head region and aids in communication, and speaking with clarity and honesty.

To experience udana vayu, inhale and feel your breath engulfing the throat and upward into the head region and as you exhale, open the mouth with a nice *HAAA* sound.

"When you are breathing, you are feeling, and when you are feeling, you are dealing, and when you are dealing, you are healing."
-Baron Baptiste[11]

Vayu Movement Meditation *Practice*

This *vayu* movement meditation was taught to me by my teacher Shiva Rea. These are fun arm movements to do with the kids that warm up the body with the breath and aid in coordination and concentration.

Sitting comfortably on a block in *virasana* or standing with feet wider than hip-distance apart, bent and comfortable, rooting into the Earth through your feet. Turn your palms up in *hasta mudra*, to receive. Close your eyes and ask what you are feeding, nurturing, loving, or inviting into your life. By using an arm meditation, we will be expanding that intent throughout the entire body.

Prana vayu:
• Inhale. Arms float up toward the top of the head.
• Chant: **OM prana swaha** (I bow to the infinite energy of *prana*)

Apana vayu:
• Exhale. Palms down, arms float down.
• Chant: **OM apana swaha** (I bow to the infinite energy of *apana*)
• Repeat **prana vayu** and **apana vayu** for five to ten rounds.

Vyana vayu:
• Inhale from the heart, outward, until the arms stretch out to each side with openness. Feel the heart expand, bend the knees, and arch the back.
• Chant: **OM vyana swaha** (I bow to the infinite energy of *vyana*)

Samana vayu:
• Exhale and draw that energy back toward the heart/belly Bring the hands toward each other like you are cupping your heart with love or hugging a virtual tree, bend the knees, and curve the spine like a cat position.
• Chant: **OM samana swaha** (I bow to the infinite energy of *samana*)
• Repeat **vyana vayu** and **samana vayu** for five to ten rounds.

Udana vayu:
Place one foot in front of the other. On the inhale, allow the hands/arms to travel upwards from the throat region to the sky and outwards, away from the body, as you shift weight into your front foot. Exhaling, shift weight into the back foot, knees bent, bringing the arms/hands back down to root. Shift forward again, the arms simultaneously rising upward from the throat to the sky and forward and outward. Float the arms back down to the root in a circle as your weight shifts back. This is how the governing meridian in Chinese medicine flows; up the spine and down the front in a circle. Repeat in this circle for five rounds and then switch legs, back foot in front and the front foot in back.
• Chant: **OM udana swaha** (I bow to the infinite energy of *udana*)
• Repeat **udana vayu** for five to ten rounds on each side

PART **2**

CHAPTER **2** (September)

Patanjali's Eight Limbs of Yoga (5–8)

"It's through the alignment of the body that I discovered the alignment of my mind, self, and intelligence."
-B.K.S. Iyengar[1]

Fifth Limb –
Pratyahara: *Sensation and Stillness*

Pranayama prepares us for *pratyahara*. *Pratyahara* is a technique of drawing attention inward through sensory transcendence, a conscious effort to pull awareness away from external stimuli. By considering the senses without attachment, you can turn your attention inward and allow your body to relax. This provides a unique observance of our own attachments, cravings, or things that distract us from being present. When we are acutely aware of the senses, we see where our attention goes, what senses we are feeding into, and where we allow our energy to leak. As a result of this awareness, the senses no longer depend on constant stimulation, but become reprogrammed. The habits of a restless, scattered mind can be detrimental to our health, healing, and our ability to create and manifest. It could also inhibit growth in moving forward. *Pratyahara* allows us to shift our mindset to present moment awareness.

As we become deeply absorbed in our meditation, *pratyahara* occurs naturally. We are trying to still our thoughts and focus on nothingness. With our mind solidly focused, our senses follow. Mind first, senses after. Our senses sharpen as our meditation deepens, and we learn how to become aware of them, but not attached to them. We become empowered over our thoughts and our distractions through the beginning process of meditation. Through this process, we become friends with our minds and we are able to control our thoughts.

When you first begin to concentrate, it becomes a battle of the senses. As you master *pratyahara*, though, your mind can ignore the smaller senses like an itch or an annoying sound. You are no longer distracted. You are free from stimuli that could potentially 'steal the peace.'

Savasana is a great example of *pratyahara* practice. Corpse pose is a posture for relaxing and letting go. The purpose of this relaxation is to consciously withdraw from the external world, but still feel very much a part of it. Deep relaxation feels as if you are sinking down deep into the ocean floor. You are heavy and relaxed. You are still aware of the sounds around you, but they do not alter your relaxed state of being. This is a state of non-reaction. This phenomenon creates a space between a stimulus and how you respond to it. You are in the world, but not of the world. You simply peel back the layers of the world so you can rediscover your true self again. *Savasana* creates an opportunity to nurture a peaceful state of consciousness.

Kids' Yoga *and the Five Senses*:

Kids have an innate appreciation for the five senses. We learn about the world and ourselves through our senses. Using the five senses in education for children is great because of their increased awareness of external stimuli, and focusing on one particular sense can relax the mind and calm emotions. Kids' yoga is so amazing because we can essentially replicate nature and the world within our practice. By engaging kids' five senses, they figuratively embody the aspects of nature that correspond to the yoga postures, whether that is a flower, a cat, or a lightning bolt. Our senses give children something to concentrate on and learn from.

The five senses are a great way to begin a state of mindfulness by slowing down and tuning into our breath, noticing all that surrounds us. It allows our focus to bring us into the present moment. We can make it a listening meditation by concentrating on the sounds and noticing when the mind gets distracted with thoughts. We then bring it back to the sounds we hear on the outside. Engage the senses with the following meditations to help kids heighten their awareness and focus their minds.

Pratyahara *Practices*

Observation Meditation
Lie on your back and see if you can just observe. Observe the sounds, breath, temperature, the floor beneath you, the taste in your mouth, smells in the air without letting the mind go down the storyline. Be a witness to your thoughts, but not attached to them. Notice how your senses can pull you away from being present. Now see if you can just let go and be. Can you relax deeper and go within? Can you notice stillness and then thoughts? When thoughts come, Can you erase them and concentrate on nothingness?

From Gross to Subtle
Find a comfortable place to sit, lie down, or come into child's pose. Bring your awareness to the sounds in the room. Now bring your awareness to the borders of your mat. Now bring your awareness to the edges of your skin. Now bring your awareness to the sounds of your breath. Notice the texture, temperature, and sound of your breath. Now, can you feel the pulsation of your heart? Rest in this space inside the body.

Five Senses Relaxation Cues:

· Relax the eyes deeper into their sockets.

· Relax your tongue away from the roof of your mouth.

· Relax the jaw.

· Notice the air flowing in and out of the nostrils.

· Relax the inner ear.

· Relax your face.

· Relax your throat, heart, shoulders, arms.

· Relax your belly, spine, hips, legs, feet.

· Relax your fingers and toes.

· Relax your skin. Feel the edges of your skin soft and smooth like a warm, cuddly blanket surrounding all of your flesh and bones.

· Inhale, feel the body rise. Exhale, feel the body fall.

Five Senses *Meditation*

The sense of sight

Guide your group through a visual meditation. Be graphic in your description of wherever you are taking them: a dense, lush jungle; a dry, hot desert; swimming in blue, cool, crisp ocean water. Visually take yourself through a sight meditation and gaze onto something beautiful like a flower, sunset, tree, or colorful rainbow and stay with that focus.

The sense of hearing

Sing a song, read a poem, take your students through a sound meditation, maybe with live instruments or recorded music, or simply lay back and listen to your favorite song and be present with every word.

The sense of touch

Feel the earth under your feet. Notice the cool grass or the warm sand. Allow water to flow through your fingers. Feel the hot sun or cool raindrops on your skin. Cuddle with your pets. Hug someone you love. Take time to appreciate the feeling of the world around you. Find a restorative posture with props that support you. Notice each sensation.

The sense of taste

Imagine eating healthy and vibrant foods. Take the time to block out other senses and eat a meal in complete silence with your eyes closed. Allow chocolate to melt on your tongue. Take yourself through an *ayurvedic* tasting of different spices and herbs.

The sense of smell

Burn candles or incense, or diffuse essential oils and notice the relaxing scent. Bake a cake and sit with the aroma of chocolate. Smell the rain in the wind, the flowers in the air, sagebrush, plumeria, the ocean breeze or the forest floor.

Sixth Limb –
Dharana: *Intense Focus*

From *pratyahara*, we evolve to *dharana*, one-pointed concentration, letting go of any other thoughts that are related to the five senses.

As we move through the Eight Limbs, we become consciously aware, from the gross to the more subtle and from external to internal. As we become aware of things in the outside world, we become mindful of how we want to participate and conduct ourselves in this life. These are the lessons of the *yamas* and *niyamas* where we begin the practice of directing attention.

The *asanas* and *pranayama* further develop concentration through focused attention that helps clear bodily distractions. In *pratyahara*, our awareness of the five senses, and how deeply we attach to them, grows stronger. In *dharana*, we are giving the mind a tool to focus with. You slow the brain's thinking by concentrating on something very specific. When you lose track of the passage of time, you know you're concentrating deeply. This state of *dharana* is an opportunity to really see the fluctuations of the 'monkey mind' and observe the many endless thoughts the mind can easily attach itself to.

Our minds are easily distracted, but we can focus on our minds directly when we remove outside distractions from our bodies. *Dharana* is about using a modality to help keep the focus directed inward. We can slow our thinking as we concentrate on a single object. Think about a specific energy center, visualize a deity, or silently consider sound repetition. *Dharana* helps elongate the meditative experience and gives the practitioner something 'to do' rather than just still their thoughts.

"Yoga does not just change the way we see things; it transforms the person who sees."
-B.K.S. Iyengar[2]

Dharana *Practices*

Physical Concentration:
Focus the mind on a candle flame, a flower, third-eye *chakra*, internal heartbeat, the breath coming in through the nostrils, a picture of a *yantra*, *mandala*, or a deity.

Sound Meditation:
Focus the mind on sound using music, live instruments, or repetition of a *mantra*, like *OM* or *Sa Ta Na Ma*.

Energetic Meditation:
Focus inward on a *chakra* color or healing light inside the body.

Sa Ta Na Ma Meditation
We can clear and restructure our subconscious through *mantras*. Two of the basic ones taught by Yogi Bhajan are *Sat Nam* and its derivative *Sa Ta Na Ma*. They allow us to reorient the mind and open us up to the possibility of transformational change, or at least an attitude adjustment for the meantime. *Sat Nam* wakes up our divine identity and nurtures truth in our consciousness. It's a seed or *bija mantra* that literally means, *'I am that,' 'I am truth'* or *'truth is my identity.'* To practice, inhale internally the word, *SAT* and exhale internally the word, *NAM*.

Sa Ta Na Ma meditation is a powerful tool to focus the mind while creating profound change. It is a *mantra* for recognizing truth and honoring the cycle of life. For children, it is a wonderful way to start class because it creates focus and coordination with the hand movements synchronized with the sounds. It brings us into the now and creates an easy and peaceful resonance.

Sa is birth, the beginning of all that ever was and will be. (thumb and forefinger touch and press together).

Ta is life, the incarnation of infinite energy. (thumb and middle finger touch and press together).

Na is death, the return to the infinite consciousness. (thumb and ring finger touch and press together).

Ma is rebirth and a chance to begin again in joy of the infinite. (thumb and pinky finger touch and press together).

Chant: *Sa Ta Na Ma* three minutes aloud or singing; three minutes in an audible whisper; three minutes silently. Then sit in meditation for as long as it feels good. You can use the *Sa Ta Na Ma* hand meditation too by touching and pressing the thumb and fingers together (as I describe above) while you pronounce each syllable. *Sa . . . Ta . . . Na . . . Ma . . .*

Seventh Limb – Dhyana: *Meditation*

Once you've mastered *dharana*, you can strive for *dhyana* as you contemplate meditation. As you create devotion through a continuous flow of concentration, you focus not on one set point but on nothing at all. *Dhyana* is a state of being keenly aware without focus. It's a connection to pure consciousness rather than an effort that needs to be made. In fact, it's the absence of effort. Attention is drawn inward, and, in this quiet stillness, the brain produces few or no thoughts at all. It takes a lot of strength and stamina to reach this state of stillness. Sometimes this sensation feels timeless due to the calm you feel within the state of nothingness. It should feel light, airy, and very relaxed. In the state of *dhyana*, we fix the concentrated mind on an aspect of the Divine.

"Yoga is a light, which once lit, will never dim. The better your practice, the brighter the flame."
-B.K.S. Iyengar[3]

Dhyana *Practices*

Divine Meditation

Meditate on an aspect of the Divine: Love, light, wisdom, grace, beauty, compassion. Meditate on the feeling of an image of a great master (*for example:* Jesus, the Buddha, Krishna, Amma, Mother Nature).

Deity Meditation

Place a statue or picture of a deity you connect with in front of you as you meditate on their qualities. You can do an open-eye meditation or close your eyes and picture that deity. Gaze into their eyes and feel the healing energy. *Ganesh*, for example, is the remover of obstacles. Where in your life can *Ganesh* support you? Can he help you feel lighthearted and jovial? Or look at the face of the Buddha. Can you sit like him and relax into the moment? Can you emulate his serene and peaceful being? Now, can you move on with your day channeling every thought, word, and action in the spirit of that deity and their qualities?

Eighth Limb – Samadhi: *Enlightenment*

Dhyana, together with the other limbs, leads to *samadhi*, a feeling of ultimate bliss and oneness. There is a transcendence of the ego in this stage, a complete merging with universal consciousness and the interconnectedness of all living things. In this state, nothing else matters but this sublime union. This is the ultimate gift of yoga—the merging of the individual self with infinite consciousness: the soul with the Divine. It is a true feeling of connection and surrender.

Samadhi means 'harmony, to bring together, to merge or direct.' It's the state in which a yogi perceives the identity of his soul with spirit. Human consciousness becomes one with cosmic consciousness. Your mind and reason remain alert and awake as you go beyond consciousness, leaving behind the body and senses. *Samadhi* means union or true yoga, the end of the idea that we are separate from the world around us. Our mind ceases to distinguish between self and non-self. We realize an identity unified with the world around us and find liberation in awareness. The mind and thought become still, and we allow ourselves to experience truth and complete joy.

"Yoga allows you to find a new kind of freedom that you may not have known even existed."
-B.K.S. Iyengar[4]

Samadhi *Practices*

Meditation on the One Love Current

Lie down and allow your breath to deepen your relaxation. Feel yourself melt into that oneness. Feel completely immersed in the feeling of love. Allow that current of love to surround the inner landscape of your body and mind.

Infinite Ocean Meditation

Lie on your back, using pillows to provide support wherever you may need it (the knees, neck, arms, hips, back, etc.). Draw in breath and feel it enter through every pore of your body. As you exhale, allow the body to sink down deeper.

Imagine that you are lying on a bed of water in the vast ocean. You are floating on your back, feeling the waves gently support, massage, and palpitate the body. Feel safe and secure. Feel the wide beautiful ocean; the magnificence of its beauty and energy start to spark every cell in the body. Feel this infinite space inside. Feel connected to something greater, more powerful than yourself. Feel this connectivity to Mother Nature. Feel her feminine love as her gentle sway caresses every part of your being. Feel the coolness of the water spray over your skin and feel the heat of the Sun on your body. Feel weightless, but grounded. Relaxed and at ease. Feel effortless, floating as the water supports you. Feel this infinite and grand exchange. Feel the oneness and unity with all. Feel that divine essence as a part of you, supporting and guiding you.

The Eight Limbs of Yoga: *Summary and Reflection*

The Eight Limbs are the foundation of this curriculum of teaching youth yoga. The practical, physical, mental, spiritual, and philosophical teachings of the Eight Limbs provide the framework for all of the lessons in the following chapters. Turn back to the Eight Limbs often and absorb each one as you progress on your path.

Bringing yoga philosophy, like the Eight Limbs, into a physical yoga class is a fantastic way for kids to learn, have fun, express themselves, and communicate their feelings. Real yoga begins when we step off that mat and into the world, where we can practice some of these concepts and techniques. Self-inquiry is especially important in practice. Yoga is about learning from mistakes while striving to be the best version of ourselves possible.

Think about your life. Ask yourself if you are living truthfully, lovingly, and if you take full accountability for all of your actions. Do you have any regrets? What can you improve upon?

*These are great questions to **ask yourself** along the way:*

- Which of the Eight Limbs am I really good at practicing?
- Which of the Eight Limbs can I work on
- When I am in alignment with the 8 Limbs, how do I feel?
- When I am not in alignment with the 8 Limbs, where is my resistance?
- How is my body and my health? What does my self-care routine look like?
- Where am I strong & flexible? Where am I weak and tight?
- How is my mind, my breath and my mental health?
- Which yoga, meditation and or mindfulness practices are the most beneficial to me?
- What stimulates my curiosity? What do I like to study?
- What is the change I would like to see in the world?
- What is my passion, my dharma, my life's purpose?
- How and where can I be of service?

Class Discussion: *What is Yoga?*

After you have guided little yogis through the Eight Limbs, reflection is key. These are a few questions that can spark important discussion during circle time.

Discuss what yoga is all about. Allow the kids to give you their interpretation of the Eight Limbs. Have them explain the benefits of yoga and some of the practices.

PART **3**

CHAPTER **3** (October)

Overcoming Fear *and* Inviting the Light

"I wish I could show you when you are lonely and in the dark, the astonishing light of your own being."
-Hafiz[1]

October: *Overcoming Fear and Inviting the Light*

Fear is an inescapable part of being human. Taking the time to teach students how to manage their fears and develop strategies to control fear sets them up for confidence and independence as they grow. One way we can learn to move through fears in life is through self-regulation. Learning how to self-regulate allows children to discover how to process their emotions in a healthy and productive way. Learning how to talk ourselves through fears gives us the ability to manage them without acting out. As adults, many of us have learned to self-regulate without thinking about it. For instance, when we are feeling scared or overwhelmed, we might calm ourselves down through slow deep breaths or affirming in our minds that everything will be alright.

Yoga is a great tool for learning self-regulation techniques. A personal yoga practice can help us move our breath and our bodies, so our emotions do not get stuck or stagnant. We become more self-aware. We also have a chance to pause, reflect, and respond instead of reacting to the stressors of life thoughtlessly. Learning these tools early gives kids a chance to feel more confident and successful in the choices they make. It is essential to provide a safe space for kids to learn.

Fear can teach us a lot about ourselves. It represents the unknown and, if we can empower ourselves with breath, we have an ability to move through to the other side. Our breath's power can slow the emotional response so we can process and assess. Ultimately, fear can become an opportunity to succeed and grow, shedding light on our true inner strengths and values. Fear can give us that push to challenge us in the ways we need most. Embracing our fear will add to our self-esteem and resilience.

When we start to feel more confident, we emulate energy of super-powered strength and radiance. This strength becomes our ally in battling future fears. The 'excitement' comes from the challenge of stepping into our power and relying on our own selves. Having a steady yoga practice to fall back on, support from our families, teachers, friends, and faith in our higher self can all help us rise up to any occasion. It's all about doing the best we can in any situation. Wisdom is abundant in every experience. Life has a way of giving us what we need to grow and learn from.

This month, we will be highlighting resources and strategies for children to move through the most challenging fears. We will learn about customs and traditions that honor all the role-models, superheroes, teachers, mentors, deities, Goddesses, and energies in our life that uplift us and help us feel safe. We will get to be imaginative and creative and have fun reflecting on what we find scary and what we can do to channel that fear. Most importantly, we realize that we are not alone. Everyone experiences fear.

In Lesson One, we will learn some background on fear through yoga philosophy and teaching tools for kids like meditations, journaling, and breath work that can help children move through the hardest of times.

In Lesson Two, we learn about a traditional Indian custom called *Navaratri*, which celebrates *Shakti* Energy and Goddess (Divine Feminine) Energy. We will move through practices that ignite the feminine and the warrior qualities in ALL of us through art, affirmations, yoga flows, and meditations.

In Lesson Three, the powerful vibration of *AUM* (*OM*) is introduced, and by working with sound, breath, and art, we can learn how to bring that primordial vibration of peace offering to all parts of our being. We will also learn how to combat fear through chanting to send that peace out to all beings on the planet.

Finally, *in Lesson Four*, we will celebrate Halloween with fun art, journaling, and dance sessions to shake off any negativity. We will rejoice in the fun character strengths that we are emulating.

Lesson One – *Fearless Yoga*

Yoga Philosophy:
Samskaras, Maya, Samsara, and Moksha

If yoga can offer us anything, it's a stronger sense of self and determination. By believing in our breath and our bodies, we become more confident. By quieting the mind through meditation and relaxation, we are more peaceful and responsive. By using clear and powerful affirmations, we empower ourselves. These simple yoga tools can help us overcome our fears to be the best we can be and share our light with the world.

In yoga philosophy, there are certain ways to look at our fear, negative patterns, and imprints in the mind, and essentially, be freed from those cycles. One cycle is called *samskaras* (shadow tendencies), and the other is *maya* (illusion). *Samskaras* are impressions or negative beliefs that we have about ourselves. They are a direct result of a negative experience or imprint of a bad memory. As we age, they present themselves as habits, either from this lifetime or past lifetimes, that present a hindrance to our spiritual progress and to our day-to-day happiness. They become our shadow, our darkness. They are the things that we, perhaps, do not like so much about ourselves; traits or behaviors that do not serve us in the highest and might sneak up upon us in times of weakness. They could also be feelings generated from past regrets or events that were not forgiven and, therefore, have a lot of power over our lives. Sometimes these *samskaras* can be the result of *maya*.

> *"Fear is just excitement without the breath."*
> -Robert Heller[2]

Maya is often referred to as illusion or delusion. It's responsible for the false perception that things are separate from each other and from a higher power. When we feel separate, we feel alone, unworthy, not good enough. Unimportant. Our lives seem frivolous, and goals may seem unattainable. *Maya* is also the beliefs we hold about ourselves or the world around us that are really untrue; delusions. *Maya* was once explained to me as the 'dust on our lens of perception.' It's a state of being in which you feel clouded or cannot see clearly. We lose track of our soul's purpose when we forget or cannot see our unique, divine, and beautiful self. This can affect our *karma* (law of cause and effect) and *dharma* (righteous path).

The unceasing cycle of life, death, and reincarnation is known as *samsara*. There is an illusion that separateness exists, and believing that leads to a cycle of negative *karma*. This belief also perpetuates the cycle of action and rebirth. As we choose to know the realization that we are all connected, all part of oneness, we can break that illusion from *samsara* and reach *moksha*—liberation from *samsara*. In *moksha*, we are essentially free from the shadows and untruths that we think about ourselves because we are stepping into our divine light.

These yogic concepts can be skillfully interwoven into your kids' yoga classes. Having a *karma* talk is a great way to introduce the laws of cause and effect. When we are hopeful and helpful, we will start to attract that very nature. If we are negative and fearful, we will always be in that constant loop of emotion. The things that weigh us down are not permanent. We can choose not to let them weigh us down forever. We can choose to be freed. It is all perception. It's about trusting our good nature and goodwill, catching our negative self-talk, and being aware of the energies we are putting out there. Yoga empowers us to move through the delusion and to become one with our true selves.

Teaching children to be aware of their thoughts and their self-talk is the first way to change and move through hard situations. When we have a more positive outlook, fear and challenges will not seem so defeating. When we are confident, we have more power and energy to face the unknown.

Moving Through Fear

Yoga is about the journey. We all know how overwhelming and scary life can be at times. A consistent practice can help ground us and allow us to be a witness to our many thoughts and emotions. Moreover, yoga offers the tools to discharge the negativity so that it doesn't become dislodged, and find its way into the body and tissues. One of my teachers, Baron Baptiste, once said in class: "*Your issues are in your tissues, and what you resist will always persist.*"

If we do not address old, unwanted feelings, they will persist in some shape or form. It could be through patterning in our lives, a sickness, a disease, or situations in which you feel life is hitting you over the head with the same problem. Therefore, it's imperative to do the inner work to be truly free. If not, we can fall victim to limited beliefs and old pains that we have not chosen to forgive and forget. Through yoga and meditation, we can cultivate a relationship with ourselves that is not ruled by fear, one where we are willing to face the shadows and darkness.

> *"The only way to is through."*
> -Baron Baptiste[3]

Strategies for Kids

One of the most important things you can do at the beginning of a youth yoga class is to check in with your students. Talk about present-moment feelings. This empowers the student to check in with themselves consistently and have the compassion to breathe through heavier, more intense emotions. If a child can communicate their fear, it's important for us as teachers to validate their emotions and reassure them. Reassurance means coming up with a way to help them feel braver and more able to manage their fears by themselves.

Teaching breath-awareness is the key. When uncomfortable and fearful feelings arise, allow the breath to become slower and deeper. A wonderful way to think of it is to allow the breath to grow bigger than the emotion. Emotions are just energy in motion and, once conscious of emotion, we have the power to sit with it without reaction. This allows us to move through it and dissolve it. When you direct the breath into anxious feelings and sensations in the body, it has the power to neutralize and deactivate those strong emotions.

Breathing into Fear – *Breath Work Practices*

Ujjayi ~*Victorious Breath*

Ujjayi Pranayama is another practice that encourages us to focus our minds on the present. Be aware of what is happening right now and identify with the immediate experience. Doing this helps us master our conscious mind.

Ujjayi is the breath that is 'victorious' over denser, lower vibrations. It's a powerful tool in regulating our central nervous system. Our movement and breath are synchronized; we grow absorbed in this awareness. We settle our agitations, our mind slows and fluctuates less, and even if only for a moment, we feel a sense of balance.

Ujjayi is a warming breath that prepares the muscles for *yoga asana*. This technique slows the breath, calming the body and the mind. *Ujjayi* breathing stimulates the two channels in the body (*ida* and *pingala*) that help improve concentration, endurance, and energy levels, while releasing tension from the body. This allows more response time to deal with heavier emotions. Effective in soothing anxiety, fear, worry, and doubt, *ujjayi* can help us bring presence and mindfulness to our yoga practice.

Ujjayi *Practice:*

Inhale and exhale normal breaths. When you are ready for the *ujjayi* breath, inhale and feel the back of your throat contract as if you were sipping the breath. Feel the air tickle the back of your throat, making a slight snoring sound. Now imagine a mirror that is held in front of you and exhale with an open mouth *HAA* sound, so your breath may fog the mirror. Repeat, inhaling through the nose into the back of the throat and then exhaling, both from the mouth and the nose. Feel the air move through the back of the throat with an ocean sound. Now take that same sound in a breath through the nose and exhale through the nose. After you experience *ujjayi* breathing for a couple of rounds, relax your breath to its normal state.

Bhastrika ~ *Bellows Breath*

Bhastrika breathing or 'bellows breath' is a traditional breathing exercise in yoga that helps to increase *prana* or life force. *Bhastrika* energizes your body and clarifies your mind. If you feel low energy or you feel like you're moving in slow motion, *bhastrika* can clear the feeling of stagnation. Bellows breathing also increases your digestive power and boosts your metabolism. Because of this energy boost, you'll want to avoid bellows breathing in the evening close to bedtime. You may find yourself invigorated, and sleep becomes difficult.

When you find yourself in need of energy, try *bhastrika* breathing. It's known to help one be more assertive and confident as well as provide more energy. Listen to your body as you breathe this way. Sometimes bellows breathing makes you feel light-headed. Though the practice is safe, it's important to pause for a few minutes and regain your breath, breathing naturally until the discomfort passes. Then, you can resume bellows breathing more slowly and less intensely. Add sage or essential oils for a spiritual, purifying, and cleansing effect.

Bhastrika *Practice:*

Sit up tall, shoulders relaxed. Take a few deep breaths in and out from your nose. When you're ready to start, inhale through your nose and expand your belly fully out. As you exhale through the nose, draw that belly in with a little bit of force. Breathe from your diaphragm, keeping your head, neck, shoulders, and chest still as only your belly moves in and out with each breath.

Begin with ten *bhastrika* breaths, then breathe naturally for a few moments, allowing yourself to take in the sensations in your body and mind. Then, breathe again with twenty *bhastrika* breaths. Pause again to breathe normally. Finish with a round of thirty *bhastrika*. Think about how this cycle makes you feel.

Making Breath Bigger than Emotion

Sit in a comfortable position. Think of a strong emotion you are experiencing. Allow your breath to gradually become longer, until your breath is bigger than that feeling or sensation. Sit with the long, slow, deep breath until you feel the energy of the emotion lessen and dissolve.

Once you've returned to normal breathing, recall that emotion. If you feel there is still negative energy lingering, repeat this practice: deep, full, big breaths into the emotion. Then, rest and come back to normal breathing. End your session with a positive affirmation, for example, *I can do this; I am amazing; I am strong; I am powerful; I am healing; My body is healthy. It is going to be great.*

In the end, bathing yourself in the realities that *'I am Love, I am Whole, I am Balanced'* are great ways to seal off the healing of those deep emotions, to leave the mind and body feeling centered, grounded, connected, and reassured.

Moving Through Fear - *Meditation Practices*

Let the Energy of Fear Dissolve in Spaciousness

Tune into that feeling: The pure emotion of fear. Think about the fear and where it centers itself in your body. What thoughts does it evoke in you? Allow yourself to create a story surrounding this fear, focusing on how it feels. Where does it live in the body? What is the texture? Does it have a color? Fully consider the energy it brings to you.

How does this story expand? Is there more to the feeling than you first thought? Hold on to the fear, allowing it to grow and surround you. As it grows, so does your awareness of it. Hold that fear and its energy inside your consciousness. Don't try to make the fear go away, but think about how sharp it feels. Allow that sharpness to fade and the space around you to grow.

Work with the Opposite Feeling

When feelings of fear arise, embrace them. Instead of dwelling only on fear, think about the opposite. Perhaps the opposite of fear is faith. Think about a moment when you felt hopeful or courageous. Imagine that you're surrounded by loving and nurturing energy. Breathe in love. Let yourself feel this presence sending you love, courage, or faith. You can use affirmations like I am loved. I am brave. I have faith. The more you practice this transfer of fear to faith, hope, or love, the less effect the emotion of fear will have over you.

"Courage is only the accumulation of small steps."
-George Konrad[4]

Fear Becomes Strength - *Journaling Session*

We can add yoga philosophy into our kids' classes by first guiding the kids into recognizing the emotion.

Is it a fear, a doubt, a worry, a regret? Usually, fear deals with the future, while anxiety and regret deal with the past. Doubt and worry deal with self-confidence. Validate that fear with the kids. Acknowledge that it's scary, uncomfortable, and sometimes stressful. We all experience some of the same emotions. We all can relate. We are not alone.

Is that feeling or emotion a truth, or is it made up because one is feeling lost, separate, and not whole? Do you believe something that is untrue? For instance, would everyone agree on your truth, or is it made up? Reassure the kids that they are brave and strong enough to move through whatever they are experiencing. Come up with a plan and a way to breathe through it.

Now, let's find a positive in this whole process. Offer encouragement. Did we learn anything because of these emotions? Can we find gratitude in the wisdom we discovered? Did we become stronger, more reliable, and more resilient because of the process? Who did we look upon or rely on for support? Acknowledge the resources used to move through the emotions and the life lessons that we learned.

"When you own your breath, nobody can steal your peace."
-Anonymous[5]

Lesson Two – *Shakti and the Goddesses*

Goddess Power

The Goddess, or divine feminine, embodies power and energy. This compassionate yet creative energy enlivens the world around us, our bodies, and our minds. Regardless of how we encounter the Goddess, whether intentional or spontaneous, this experience helps us find our source of empowerment within. The energy of the Goddess appears in many forms (nature and nurturer) and can benefit and inspire both men and women. The Goddess transcends gender, allowing men and women to tune into their vibrations and take part in their own unique power.

Each Goddess has unique qualities. They have separate talents and different rituals from one another. Over time, and still today, people have called on Goddesses when they need something in their lives. As you get to know what it is you seek in your life, you'll be able to determine which Goddess works in that area. Deity meditation and invoking the Goddess helps us get to know the different energies and personalities we mirror and can help our relationship with the inner source of sacred power. When we need insight or help, practicing with the Goddesses reminds us of unique aspects of ourselves that connect us to the cosmos, stimulating deep contemplation and opening up the layers of our soul, allowing us to receive the Goddesses' gifts of power to awaken and transform us. Goddess energy also helps us recognize and own the shadow aspects of ourselves, which may sometimes feel disruptive or uneasy but are necessary to embody our truth. Each Goddess is dedicated to guiding us into the deepest realms of our soul, opening us to the mystic within, and teaching us the skills to live empowered by the Sacred Feminine.[7] The Goddess not only gives us movement practices but *mantras* and affirmations to empower the mind. By feeling this external support through Goddess practices, we have the ability to move from untruth to truth, and from darkness to the light. In the next sections, we will be exploring three powerful Hindu Goddesses from India and learn about harnessing *shakti*. We will consider rituals to invoke positive qualities and processes to turn fear into faith and adapt those processes to youth yoga.

Invoking the Goddess

The beginning of October marks *Navaratri*, one of the biggest celebrations of the year in India. *Navaratri* symbolizes the spiritual victory of 'light over darkness, good over evil, and knowledge over ignorance.'[6] It's marked by nine nights of devotion and celebration of the Goddess, embodying the divine feminine, peaceful warrior qualities of these most powerful deities. The 'deity qualities' live in each and every one of us. The three Goddesses that are celebrated are *Durga* (Goddess of protection, one who eliminates suffering); *Lakshmi* (the Goddess of wealth and good fortune); *Saraswathi* (Goddess of flow, knowledge, music, art, wisdom, and learning).

The energy of the Goddess is truly transformational. It's she who embodies super-intelligence, the highest creative power. By cultivating a sincere connection with this profound energy, one can strive to be more loving, receptive, honoring, reflective, and, essentially, feel more connected to creation. Having inspiration is a powerful way to create change and transformation.

This feminine energy in Hinduism is called *shakti*. We all have *shakti* within us. *Shakti* is primordial, cosmic energy that represents the dynamic forces of ability, strength, effort, power, and capability that are thought to move through the entire universe. The divine feminine exists in male and female humans alike as part of the Goddess. The Goddess's power, *shakti*, manifests in the human body as beauty, luxury, joy, strength, and abundance.

In this next section, we will learn about three powerful Hindu Goddesses. There will be practices on incorporating their energies into our daily lives and instructing that within your own kids' yoga classes. Yoga flows, reflections, affirmations, and art projects will coincide with each Goddess. Through these practices, we will learn how to invoke the energies of the Goddess that we need in our lives. By learning about the Goddesses, we can be reminded of our true, powerful, and intelligent self that is always there.

In India, the celebration of *Navaratri* takes nine days to pay tribute to these Goddesses. With this curriculum, you can choose which Goddesses' unique qualities you would like to teach from or maybe just use the emulations they represent in your yoga flows, meditations, and affirmations.

Days 1–3: *DURGA*

Durga is the cosmic warrior. She battles ignorance and darkness within. *Durga* provides the power and strength for when we face challenging situations or find ourselves pushed backward. She allows for dramatic breakthroughs as she helps us slay our demons and negative forces around us. Her name means "hard to know" or "hard to conquer," and that is the power she brings into our lives when we call on her.[7] *Durga* is the Goddess of strength, courage, and protection. *Durga* represents the power to dispel the negativity of poverty, laziness, fear, evil, and criminal inclinations. She is a mountain Goddess, and her power is sacred strength over evil. She removes misery and protects from the evils of the world. *Durga's* ten hands are very symbolic. The weapons they hold are peaceful instruments of consciousness that are not used to harm. She has the conch that emanates the universal sound of *OM* (peace). The bow and arrow are symbols of energy. The lotus in half bloom symbolizes the human mind continuously evolving. The sword symbolizes knowledge. The discus spinning on her fingers represents that she controls the world. The trident is for peace and salvation. Her *mudra* is to let her devotees know they are protected from fear. The snake symbolizes moving from lower states of consciousness to higher states with an urge to experience bliss.

Days 4–6: *LAKSHMI*

Lakshmi is the Goddess of wealth, abundance, and prosperity. She carries the energies of luxury, wealth, and material power as she works, creating and nourishing worldly manifestations, and giving incredible wealth to those devotees. *Lakshmi* is the core of everything we desire. Her name means "good luck." *Lakshmi* is traditionally depicted as a beautiful woman of golden hue. She has four hands and sits or stands atop a full-bloomed lotus. She holds a lotus bud, which represents purity, beauty and abundance. The four corners of life align with her hands: *dharma* or purposeful action, *kama* or desires, *artha* or wealth, and *moksha* or liberation from the cycle of birth and death. Symbolizing her overflowing generosity, gold coins flow from her two hands. She represents abundance and money, making her welcome in shops and businesses in some parts of India. *Lakshmi* also gives spiritual gifts. When you feel bliss, for example, it means that *Lakshmi* is nearby. Her clothes are red, embroidered in gold, representing prosperity. She is truly beautiful, benevolent, and embodies the idea of harmony and balance.

Days 7–9: *SARASWATHI*

Saraswathi is the deity of language and intelligence. She is the deity of musicians, poets, writers, students, and orators. She is the power behind creative inspiration, the Goddess of wisdom, arts, music, literature, science, fine arts, technology, and creativity. She holds the spiritual light of renewal and vitality. *Saraswathi* represents a river and is all about flow, cosmic consciousness, creativity, education, and enlightenment. She is the energy of motivation and inspiration. *Saraswathi's* name means 'the flowing one.' Human learning is represented in her four hands: mind, intellect, alertness, and ego. She wears white as a symbol of purity and holds a gorgeously crafted stringed instrument called a *veena*; a book and a rosary for repeating *mantras*. The swan, her companion, is the bird whose beak separates the milk of wisdom from the water of material existence. *Saraswathi's* gift to the world allows us to find the divine in the world around us.[7] Spiritually, she represents releasing the old and making room for the new. She symbolizes a 'go with the flow' attitude. Sometimes we have to let go of control in order to let things unfold naturally. She symbolizes truth and speaking truth from the heart. *Saraswathi* stands for innocence and remembering that true light within ourselves. She believes that the universe has a unique plan for each and every one of us.

Yoga Flows, Reflections, and Affirmations

Durga Yoga

Ignite your personal strength and courage. Come into a horse stance or a wide squat where the knees are bent over the ankles and the toes are turned slightly out. As you inhale, take your arms overhead and imagine you have a sword. Exhale, taking that sword forward and down toward the Earth. Inhale, the arms moving sideways and up to grab the sword and exhale, the arms moving forward and down toward the Earth.

Durga yoga might involve imaginative sword cutting, riding a tiger or lion, shooting a bow and arrow, or a strong, dynamic warrior flow.
Reflections: What am I cutting through in my life? What am I letting go of? Which emotions, people, places, and/or things are not supportive of my evolution? What am I aiming for?
Affirmations: I can do this. I have the power to transform. I am strong and confident. I am a warrior.

Lakshmi Yoga

Embrace your life with love, abundance, and beauty. Come into Goddess pose (also known as reclined butterfly pose). Support the head and the knees if necessary. Inhale the beauty and abundance from nature that surrounds you. Exhale feelings of interconnectedness to Mother Earth and a deeper sense of relaxation and release.

Lakshmi yoga might involve side bends, spiral hands, prayer wheel, or soft, flowy, intelligently aligned yoga *vinyasa*
Reflections: How is my physical, mental, and spiritual wealth? Am I worried I won't have enough? How can I give back to the world?
Affirmations: I am bountiful, blissful, and beautiful. I am abundant. I have enough. I give to others unconditionally.

Saraswathi Yoga

Unleash your creativity, intuition, and wisdom. Use any of the *prana* flow arm meditations, either sitting or standing, to feel the breath in sync with creative movement and flow. Feel every breath like a whisper from the universe guiding you along your way. Now allow the breath and the body the freedom to move spontaneously.

Saraswathi yoga might include moving dogs, pulsations in plank and lunge positions, spontaneous cobra, wave motion within the *asanas*, and imagining gold spinning from the fingertips. Free form dance is also a beautiful expression of reflection. *Reflections:* What am I flowing through in my life? What am I creating, singing, playing, inspiring? What am I manifesting? What am I learning? What am I contributing to?

Affirmations: I trust what the universe has in store for me. I am enough. I am smart. I go with the flow. I am in tune with the natural rhythms of life. I am creating a positive influence in the world. I love what I do, and I am making a significant impact on the world.

Goddess Meditation

Close your eyes. Picture a Goddess before you. See her beauty, strength, wisdom, and power. Visualize a golden light pouring down through her crown into her heart, radiating love and compassion. Inhale that golden light from her heart into yours and feel the kind, gentle, pure, unconditional love and beauty fill your heart, your lungs, your blood, and every cell in your body. Radiate this love throughout your entire body. Know you are this *shakti*; the most creative, intelligent, beautiful, and powerful force in the universe.

Goddess Dance: *Spiral Meditations with Arms*

Start standing. Bring attention to your fingers. Begin to make waves with the fingers. Now move your whole hand as though you were wiping out a peanut butter jar, creating spirals with both hands. Start the motion from the wrists. Move the hands, floating them high or low. Bring the spiral movement into the elbows and then into the shoulders. Allow this free-form movement to take flight through the whole body as you feel this ethereal dance of cosmic energy. Spontaneously move the joints, limbs, hips, spine, neck, and head in a meditative dance. Feel and see the joints in the body moving fluidly. Feel the dance of the Goddess take flight.

Goddess Art Project

Print out coloring sheets of the images of Goddesses that you can find online. Kids can color the Goddesses or they can create their own. Discuss their specific meanings. What do the Goddesses represent? What are they here to do for planet Earth? Talk about the symbolization of what they hold in their arms. Talk about ways we might channel these attributes in life. We can always look to the Goddesses for knowledge and wisdom to help us get through the toughest of times. They emulate the qualities we already have, but sometimes forget we possess. Imagine you hold all the power of the Goddess. What would that feel like? What could you do? Have the kids journal their own powers on their Goddess page.

Lesson Three – *The Power of OM*

Invoking Peace

OM—sometimes spelled *'AUM'*—is a *mantra* or vibration often chanted at the beginning and end of a yoga class. *OM* represents the ever-changing sound of the universe. Yogis believe that everything that exists pulsates, generating a rhythmic vibration. As we chant *OM*, we become connected with the vibration of the universe. We experience life as a reflection of the movement of the entire universe; the rising and setting of the Sun and the Moon, the rise and fall of our breath, the ebb and flow of the tides, the beating of our hearts, the echo within a seashell, and the rustling of the wind through the leaves of a tree. *OM* is chanted in three parts. A - OU - MMM. Each syllable vibrates within our bodies. We can consciously recognize this by feeling the sound "A" pronounced "AHH" in the pelvis, the "U" pronounced "OOH" in the abdomen and heart, and the "M" sound in the head. The sounds open the energy in the *chakras* and emanate peace outward to all beings, all of creation.

I like to use the sound of *OM* in my yoga classes to help the kids further focus their energies inward. The sound of *OM* is so powerful that it can lessen any agitation or negative emotion by just breathing into it and chanting.

You can chant *OM* at the beginning and end of class and during different yoga flows where breath is exhaled. The sound helps raise the vibration of the internal body and clears the mind. If the kids come in with a lot of energy, *OM*-ing is a great way to channel that intense emotion within the yoga practice. It creates focus, concentration, and ease. It allows students to connect to the power of their voice.

The OM Symbol

The OM symbol represents different states of consciousness.

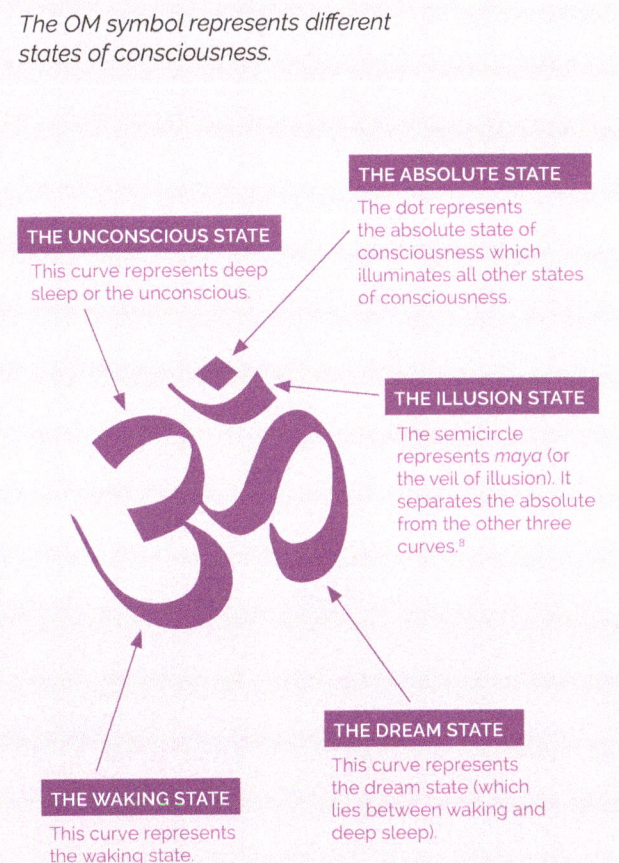

THE ABSOLUTE STATE
The dot represents the absolute state of consciousness which illuminates all other states of consciousness.

THE UNCONSCIOUS STATE
This curve represents deep sleep or the unconscious.

THE ILLUSION STATE
The semicircle represents *maya* (or the veil of illusion). It separates the absolute from the other three curves.[8]

THE DREAM STATE
This curve represents the dream state (which lies between waking and deep sleep).

THE WAKING STATE
This curve represents the waking state.

Experience the Power of OM

OM Breath Work
Inhale and breathe in *OM*. Allow the exhale to release slowly and softly to the inner sound of *OM*. Use the sound of a singing bowl to chant *OM* with. Do a sea of *OM*s with the kids where everyone takes three *OM*s at their own pace and breath. The sound is illuminating, powerful, and restorative. Know that the peace you are creating within is the peace you are creating without. Now send that peace out to bless all living beings on this planet.

OM Vibration Meditation
Sit down and place both hands on the belly. Inhale and exhale *AAHHHH*. Now, take your hands to your heart space and inhale and exhale *OOOOO*. Now, take your hands to the top of the head and inhale and exhale *MMMM*. Feel the inner vibrations. Know that with sound healing, you are bringing peace to all the vital organs, glands, muscles, tissues, all systems of the body, and the *chakras*. Sometimes it's fun to *OM* with the kids and ask them where they feel the vibration in the body. Let them tell you. Every answer is right.

OM Art
Take a piece of paper and draw an *OM* sign that is expanded and open on the inside, so there is room to doodle, color, or paint. When you are coloring on the inside, think of all the things in your life that bring you peace. Now wish them for everyone on this planet and beyond.

OM Bookmarks
Cut construction paper into the size of a bookmark. Show the kids how to draw the symbol *OM*. Have the kids decorate their bookmarks with the *OM* sign and explain to them the meaning of *OM*.

Lesson Four – Yoga at Halloween

Invoking the Inner Superhero *Movement Class*

In this class, we will approach overcoming fear by channeling our inner superhero! All the kids get to come dressed up in their favorite costume, and the discussion will focus on the different powers that we are invoking. Kids can talk about the powers they would like to have; invisibility, super strength, telepathy, levitation, the ability to walk on water . . . as far as their imagination takes them!

We'll begin with a strong, powerful yoga session and a fun and open dance circle where children take turns to dance in the middle of the circle so everyone else can copy their unique moves. Afterward, discuss the characters the kids are dressed as and think about the powers we emulate and embody in everyday life. Allow the kids to talk about the goodness they will be blessing the Earth with.

October Traditions: *Halloween*

In October, many traditions celebrate Halloween as a remembrance of people who have passed. Spiritually, it's about shedding our own identities and moving into the afterlife. Halloween is a custom of practicing becoming someone or something new.

The holiday begins the three-day observance of 'allhallowtide,' a time many cultures dedicate to remembering the dead, including saints, martyrs, and all who have passed on from this world. When we remember those who have gone, we remember their spirit and their positive vibrations. The darkest of nights is really a celebration.

Halloween is the perfect time to channel new energy. That could be by putting on a new face, becoming your hero, a role model, an actor, a villain and/or a favorite character. This is an opportunity to laugh, be someone different, and not take yourself so seriously. As we make-believe, we may feel we can embody those powers and strengths, maybe even feel like we are not from this planet just for one night. Halloween is a time of commemoration and imagination. For kids, it's a time to turn fear into excitement through being our own superhero, our own ally in life.

"You gain strength, courage, confidence by every experience in which you really stop to look fear in the face . . . . you must do the thing you think you cannot."
-Eleanor Roosevelt[9]

Superhero *Journaling Session*

The call for self-reflection and inner growth is continually unfolding for anyone on the path of self-discovery. Cate Stillman[10], a yoga teacher and *ayurvedic* practitioner, inspired this project. It's about acknowledging, unconditionally, the self in the now and thinking about who you would want to be, with superhuman powers guiding your way. It's a fun project to reflect upon with older kids who can theorize on being better versions of themselves.

1. Draw a picture of who you are now. What do you look like? Feel like? What do you dress like? What tools do you carry? Who are your friends? What are you reading, studying, thinking about? What are your habits? What do you eat? Where are your aches and pain? Your frustrations? Your challenges? Draw it all in. Use words, arrows, images, and uncover all of you at this very moment. If you're sad, draw a sad face. If you're strong, make sure you have lots of big muscles.

2. Draw another picture, but make it a picture of who you will be once you complete your hero's journey. Who will you become? What extraordinary life do you want to live? What do you look like? Feel like? Dress like? Turn yourself into a superhero with a cape, title, and nickname. The heroines have extra arms in the Vedic traditions, but you can create your image however you like. Give yourself as many limbs as you need to carry your special tools. What are those tools? What will be your mission? What will you be sharing with the world? How will you make planet Earth better? This picture represents the best version of yourself. Writing it down and talking about it helps make your superhero version of yourself a reality.

Invoke Your Inner Superhere - *Art Project*

Sarah Jayne Bleiweis, an artist and yoga teacher, inspired this project. Get butcher paper (a heavier paper, usually in a long roll) and trace the outline of the kids' bodies with chalk. Have them pose in a superhero action move when they lay on the paper. Kids then decorate their superhero. Once they're done, spray it down with hairspray to keep the chalk in place. Have the kids talk about their superpowers and what change they would like to see in the world.

· What important things will you be doing?

· What superpowers will you be blessing the Earth with?

· How will you make this world a better place?

Halloween Discussion and Dance

In this special class, we will be recreating Michael Jackson's *Thriller Dance*, calling it '*A Dance with our Shadows*.' We will explore fear and discuss the things in life that are scary. We will talk about how we can move with courage through our fears in life with the breath, a strong body and mind, and steady yoga practice.

Essentially, in this class, we will stand up to our fears and shadow tendencies and have a super-fun *Thriller* experience. Kids will be able to help choreograph this dance, and it won't be scary, but a fun chance to get some Halloween dance moves in. Creative dance is a way of dispelling and shaking off fear, discomfort, and shyness. Free movement creates confidence, spontaneity, courage, and self-awareness.

At the beginning of the class, go around the circle and ask the kids what is scary; the dark, spiders, snakes, ghosts, being alone, death, heights, etc. Relay to the kids that we all have things we are scared of. Give them confidence that it's normal to be scared, but we can create tools to breathe through these things in life that hold us back. Then, warm up with empowering yoga moves and open the body easily with some choreographed Thriller dance steps. In the end, everyone gets to make up their own dance moves to represent the things in life that they find scary.

Notes:

CHAPTER **4** (November)

Gratitude *and* The Buddha

"It's only through devotion and devotion alone,
that you will realize the absolute truth."
-Gautama Buddha[1]

November: Gratitude and The Buddha

November is a wonderful time for friends and family gatherings, to appreciate what you have, and to honor all the people in your life who love and support you. It's a time to be grateful and share that love with others. It's about recognizing that the light within yourself is the same light in others.

One of the greatest lessons we can teach our children is how to give without the expectation of anything in return. It's a practice of doing things when "love is the only commitment" to being in service of others and of the greater good. There are so many rewards to our random acts of kindness. Sharing our energy with people and the world is healthy for our body's inner chemistry. Our brain actually produces "happy chemicals" like dopamine, serotonin, and endorphins when we are giving for the sake of giving. Giving our energy to someone or something not only brightens someone's day, but has a ripple effect of giving people faith in humanity and inspiring someone else to give graciously. As we embark on the yoga path, we learn that being in service is one of the highest offerings. In yoga, this selfless service is called *seva*.

Selfless acts of kindness, praying for world peace, hoping for the best for a friend, and caring for an animal or the Earth are all great ways to extend love. The teachings of the Buddha are a wonderful way to open up the dialogue of love, compassion, unconditional love, sympathy, and empathy. The story of the Buddha inspires us to show love, be love, spread love, radiate love, live love, communicate love, and give love.

The Thanksgiving holiday message that I present in my classes is simply about celebrating family and friends, nourishing each other, sharing abundance, connecting with nature, and counting all of our blessings. This month we will be guided by the teachings of the Buddha to inspire gratitude and to be the best versions of ourselves that we can be.

*There are four lessons this month to nurture an "**attitude of gratitude**".*

Om mani Padme Hum,

In Lesson One, we will start with the story and teachings of the Buddha with thought-provoking reflections, discussions, and meditations. You could add these to any of your yoga classes.

In Lesson Two, we will learn how to make journals. We will be doing more fun "attitude for gratitude" journaling and stimulating heartfelt discussions.

In Lesson Three, we will learn about *seva*, *karma*, and reincarnation and engage in activities that promote good energy and positively impact the world. We will learn how our actions, thoughts, and deeds affect everyone and everything.

In Lesson Four, we will celebrate the tradition of Thanksgiving and learn different ways we can come together to rejoice in the connection of food and post-feast yoga flows.

Lesson One –
The Teachings of the Buddha

The Buddha symbolizes selflessness, compassion, and unconditional love. He teaches that peace comes from within, and the more one searches for it outwardly, the more suffering one will find. Peace and unconditional love come from a still place, a place of knowing that you and only you can make yourself happy. There are so many ways to incorporate the teachings of the Buddha into the classroom.

One is to find a picture or bring a little statue to talk with the kids about the Buddha. Kids will most likely have seen pictures or know his face. You can even start an altar and have the kids bring flowers, fruits, rocks or crystals to celebrate the Buddha. Buddha represents courage, and the protection from fear, delusion, and anger. You will also notice that there are different representations of the Buddha. Significant events in the life of the Buddha can be seen in his different postures and hand *mudras*.

The Buddha with hands in his lap symbolizes meditation and contemplation, and the Buddha with one hand up represents peace and serenity. There are also Chinese representations of the laughing Buddha for joy and good luck. There are so many teachings and fun things you can talk about with the statues of the Buddha. Most of all, take in his serene and calm presence. Even though there is so much sadness and strife in this life, the Buddha learned to stay peaceful and present. That is the vision we can all strive for when we glance at his picture.

I love to tell the story of Siddhartha Gautama (the Buddha) as I guide the kids into a yoga flow. They become so interested in the story that yoga becomes like poetry. You can pause into longer stretches like pigeon, dragon, and butterfly as you go deeper into the storyline and then flow through *vinyasas*. It's a nice way of storytelling where the kids can move and flow, but are so interested in what happens next. I like to add more of my own interpretation of what I think the kids need to hear that day when telling the story. For example, the Buddha grew up with many luxuries but was never happy. I like to use that example to show how accumulating things in life won't make up who we are or define us. So, be grateful for your parents, teachers, pets, food, nature, and what you do have in your life rather than what you do not have. Simple teachings like this are so powerful for kids to become mindful of.

The Story of the Buddha

Siddhartha was born a prince. He was born to a queen and king and grew up with all the luxuries in the world. However, despite being royalty, Siddhartha was never truly happy. He wanted to see the world and search for his happiness. So, he ran away from home and went out into the world all by himself.

Alone, Siddhartha experienced suffering in many forms. Even with his privileged upbringing, he realized that his conditioned experiences and protected childhood could not provide long-lasting happiness or protection from suffering. Suffering was inevitable as a human. It was a natural part of life.

After a long, hard, and emotional spiritual search, Siddhartha went into deep meditation under the Bodhi tree, where he realized the true nature of the mind. Through meditation, he achieved a state of unconditional love and happiness. He called this the state of enlightenment, or *Buddhahood*. Siddhartha would then become known as the Buddha.

As Buddha experienced enlightenment, he found freedom from troubling emotions and distracting thoughts and became fearless, joyful, and compassionate. He used the rest of his life to teach others how to reach this same state of enlightenment. These teachings are outlined in the *Buddha's Four Noble Truths*.

The Buddha's life is rich with meaning. He loved and respected the animal kingdom. At the end of his life, when he achieved *samadhi* (or enlightenment) under the Bodhi Tree, he no longer feared the things that once made him fearful. For example, in his earlier life, the Buddha feared snakes. At the end of his life, snakes gathered, crawled, and slithered all around him. He befriended all things and prayed for all beings, creatures, and living things to be freed from suffering.

The Four Noble Truths

The Four Noble Truths are the foundation for the Buddha's teachings. As he meditated under the Bodhi tree, he discovered these four principles and held them as truth.

In the first two Noble Truths, the Buddha recognizes the cause of human suffering. The third Noble Truth is the awareness that a cure exists. The fourth Noble Truth summarizes the heart and core of the Buddha's teachings.

The four noble truths are:

1. **Dukkha**: The truth of suffering
2. **Samudaya**: The truth of the origin of suffering: The Three Poisons
3. **Nirodha**: The truth of the cessation of suffering: Detachment
4. **Magga**: The truth of the path to the cessation of suffering: Eightfold Path

Suffering: *The First Noble Truth*

Humans experience suffering in many ways. Old age, poverty, sickness, and death are the most obvious, and Buddha saw this as a universal truth. The problem of suffering, though, is much deeper than these three simple concepts. As things happen in our lives that fall outside our expectations, we suffer through that feeling of loss.

One of the problems humans face is consumerism. We think we will be happy when we attain things like wants, desires, or cravings. The truth is that even when we satisfy those desires, we do not feel whole or happy. We experience only temporary satisfaction.

While some people think this focus on suffering is pessimistic, Buddhists see it as realistic. This is life as it is at its core. Buddha continues to teach that suffering is not the only thing. There are strategies to manage this suffering.

Discussion on Suffering

In circle time, after you have talked about the Buddha, engage the kids into thinking about things that make them suffer. Have them consider things they have seen or experienced that have brought them deep sadness, anger, and or frustration. This could be like loss, sickness, pain, or sadness. These are realities in life, and eventually, we each feel them all. This discussion allows the children to connect with each other by knowing they have the same emotions and experiences as their peers. For younger children, the experiences might be a friend being mean,

not staying up late, or not having sugar. Whatever it is, have compassion and empathy for people sharing. For older children, have them write down the uneasy emotions they are feeling on a piece of paper, fold it up, and place it on your makeshift classroom altar. By offering these feelings to the Buddha, we ask that he can help ease our pain and suffering and give us the strength and intuition to find goodness in our situations.

Buddha *Meditation*

Sit like the Buddha and imagine your spine is against the Bodhi tree. Feel your spine nice and long, straight, and strong, just like the tree trunk. Close your eyes and imagine your legs and pelvis growing roots down deep into the Earth. Imagine that energy moving up the spine and blossoming upward out from the crown of your head. Imagine, now, that energy turning into the limbs of the tree, expanding out into leaves and flourishing fruits. Imagine the animal kingdom all around you, meditating with you. Know that there is no fear, so invite the animals that sometimes scare you the most to sit beside you. Ask the Buddha to help ease your fears. Open and expand your heart with breath. Expand that love to all living beings. Now with your eyes closed, listen to the sounds in the room. If you get distracted, bring your attention back to your breath. Take five minutes imagining yourself sitting just like the Buddha, receiving all your spiritual powers. What would those powers be? How could you help yourself, others, and this world with those powers? How could your powers make the world better? What will you take away from this experience?

Origin of Suffering: *The Second Noble Truth*

We can often easily identify our daily struggles. We feel thirst, pain when injured, sad when we lose someone or something we love. As the Buddha teaches about suffering, the Second Noble Truth considers that the origin of suffering is much more deeply rooted than these immediately noticeable concerns. The cause of all suffering is desire, wanting more, or being unsatisfied with what we have.

That powerful suffering has a foundation in three deep three roots, known as the Three Poisons, the Three Fires, or the Three Unwholesome Roots[2].

- **Greed** – artistically depicted as a rooster
- **Ignorance or Delusion** – artistically depicted as a pig
- **Hatred** – artistically depicted as a snake

Suffering *Reflection Practice*

During circle time, discuss how desire can create suffering. Desires could be wanting things you don't have, comparing yourself to others' abilities or material possessions, and/or thinking that if you had that one thing, you would finally be happy. Talk about greed and anger and the negativity and suffering they bring. See if you can make it a discussion. Has anyone ever experienced this?

Cessation of Suffering: *The Third Noble Truth*

In order to stop desire, the root of our suffering, the Buddha taught that we need to release ourselves from attachments to material things, people, etc. Those attachments lead to suffering because of their impermanence. Nothing lasts forever. Enjoy things while they last and release expectation. This is a huge lesson for all of us with the cycles of birth and death.

How to End Suffering: *Reflection Practice*

In circle time, discuss a time when you lost something. Talk about how it feels for that to be gone. Then, think about what you still have. Sometimes, we don't recognize the things we have, how truly rich we are, until something is taken from us. Have the kids reflect on their rooms or their closets and notice items that bring great joy and memories. Then think about the things that don't really stimulate any feelings or sensations. Notice the energy attachment to things in our life we think we need. How do we detach from them in a healthy way? One way is to appreciate what you do have and honor the memories and good feelings attached while realizing that they may be gone one day. Can you think of all your things and mentally note what actually brings you joy and what is actually just clutter?

Path to Enlightenment: *The Fourth Noble Truth*

The Fourth Noble Truth is the Buddha's guide for how to end suffering. He created the principles known as the *Eightfold Path*. Also called the Middle Way, the Eightfold Path guides us to avoid indulgence as well as the other extreme of self-flagellation.

The eight stages work to support each other and aren't linear. Notice how they overlap with the Eight Limbs of Yoga.

The Eightfold Path to Enlightenment:

- **Right Understanding** – Making a commitment to a sacred path and sacred studies.

- **Right Intention** – Making a commitment to cultivating the correct attitudes.

- **Right Speech** – Speak with truth alone, avoiding slander, gossip, and abusive speech.

- **Right Action** – Act with peace and harmony; don't steal or kill, and avoid overindulgence in sensual pleasure.

- **Right Livelihood** – Make your living in ways that enhance the world around you without causing harm to the world, animals, or other people.

- **Right Effort** – Stay positive, focusing on freeing your mind from evil and unwholesome thoughts and actions

- **Right Mindfulness** – Be aware of your body, sensations, how you feel, and your state of mind.

- **Right Concentration** – Keep your mental acuity strong and aware.

Lesson Two –
Attitude for Gratitude

*"In the end, only three things matter:
how much you loved, how gently
you lived, and how gracefully you let
go of things not meant for you."*

-Gautama Buddha[3]

I love this quote because it asks for self-reflection. It asks us ultimately if we have loved and lived enough while reconciling the things that don't serve us. These are BIG heartfelt questions. They allow us to have compassion for the past yet gratitude for being able to start living in love and in awareness. Being able to change is a gift we can all practice.

Gratitude is showing thankfulness for the things we have. Different people express gratitude in different ways, including journaling, prayers, giving back time, and charity. It is an expression of thanks for the world around us, acknowledging the simple things like flowers or a friendship or could be bigger like healing from a sickness or overcoming a big challenge. Gratitude helps maintain strong mental health and general well-being. When we are grateful, we are living in a continuous stream of grace.

Attitude for Gratitude *Activities*

There are many different ways to express gratitude:

· Journal, make art, make music, express yourself.

· Recognizing the daily things in your life at a simple level like birds singing and trees swaying.

· Connect with someone to tell them you're grateful for them or something they did.

· Pay kindness forward.

· Meditate on what's positive in your life.

· Pray.

· Appreciate the abundance in your life, like the food on your plate or the clothes in your closet.

Gratitude Journals

Cut up construction paper and make little journals. Let the kids decorate the front with whatever supplies you have: stickers, markers, glue, glitter, etc. Each week for the month of November, let the kids journal what they are grateful for. If they cannot write yet, have them draw pictures and talk it out.

Heart Mandala *Art Project and Journaling Session*

In this art project, inspired by my teacher Shiva Rea, we will discover the full spectrum of self. In this process, we will honor all those who have impacted our lives and talk about our extended families and people in our life that make a difference. We will be thinking of prayers for each individual as well as honoring the people and things most dear to us. We will find gratitude in all the gems that life has brought forth to us through honoring ourselves, our families, friends, teachers, mentors, and Mother Earth. This exercise helps kids become aware of themselves in the world and all the people around them that love and support them the most. It is also a time to send out prayers of peace to those in need or to mend broken relationships.

For younger kids, this can be a gratitude journal project. Draw a heart and three circles around it. In the heart, have the kids write or draw pictures of the things they love about themselves. In one circle, name or draw those they are grateful for in their family (household, pets). In another circle, name or draw those they are grateful for in their circle of friends and or teachers (people who have impacted their lives). In the last circle, give them a choice. They can write or draw their inspirations or heroes, things that they are passionate about or what they love about Mother Earth.

For older kids, follow the steps below. First, make a heart in the middle of your paper and then draw nine circles around it. Make sure you use up all the space on your paper so you have room to write in each ring.

1. In the heart, write down things you love about yourself.

2. In one of the circles, write the names of who is in your home that you are grateful for (parents, caregivers, grandparents, siblings, pets).

3. Move to another circle and write the name of your extended family that you love (aunts, uncles, cousins).

4. In another circle, write the names of your closest friends.

5. Then in the next circle, write the names of your mentors, teachers, colleagues, and collaborators that have impacted your life.

6. Continue with the remaining circles by writing hopes, prayers, or intentions for the world and Mother Earth; then,

7. people in your life that need extra love and attention; next,

8. prayers for people you are in conflict with and or are reconciling and sending peace to; and finally,

9. how you can and will contribute in making this world better. What is your passion? What is your purpose?

Lesson Three –
Selfless Service: Seva

Seva is a Sanskrit word meaning selfless service made without any expectation of reward or repayment. *Seva* was thought to help facilitate spiritual growth as well as contributions to improving the community. The purpose is to give without any need to receive anything. The giving is completely selfless. *Seva* is a blessed action.

Ram Dass explains this, "Helping out is not some special skill. It's not the domain of rare individuals. It's not confined to a single part of our lives. We simply heed the call of that natural impulse within and follow it where it leads us."[5]

"Yoga reminds us that we serve others
because we recognize that the
Divine light in their hearts is the same
essence that lives within us.
Yoga is personal, a way to mend
the fractures within yourself.
But equally important, it's spiritual,
a means to heal that which divides us all
and to bring us back into
union with each other."
-Seane Corn[4]

Seva, Karma & Reincarnation

Seva, *karma*, and reincarnation all affect each other energetically. *Karma* means action, work, or deed. *Karma* also relates to cause and effect, where the individual actions and intent (or cause) lead to a change in the future for that person (effect). The yogic philosophy of *karma* is closely connected to the idea of rebirth or reincarnation.

According to the Hindu and Buddhist philosophies, the lessons we learn and master in this life are intertwined with where we are incarnated in the next life. The more we can act out of love and selfless service, the more we can master life and promote positivity along with our soul's evolution. With **seva**, we can also increase good *karma* or energy through making peace with our past actions, and connecting with the divine or universal consciousness.

Seva *Project*

Have the kids think of things to do for the sake of goodness. Encourage selfless acts of kindness in the home (doing dishes, cleaning their bedroom, appreciating family), at school (helping a friend or teacher), and in the community (Earth clean-up, picking weeds in a garden, planting a tree). If the kids are really compelled to take this on, have them report each week on their random acts of kindness and make a list of all the good deeds, so hopefully, other kids get inspired.

Loving Kindness *Chant*

"This chant reminds us that our relationships with all beings and things should be mutually beneficial if we ourselves desire happiness and liberation from suffering. No true or lasting happiness can come from causing unhappiness to others. No true or lasting freedom can come from depriving others of their freedom. If we say we want every being to be happy and free, then we have to question everything that we do- how we live, how we eat, what we buy, how we speak, and even how we think."[6]

Lokah Samastah Sukhino Bhavantu

My interpretation:

- May all beings be happy and free.
- May all beings be free from suffering.
- May we fill our hearts with loving kindness and see every soul as one.
- May our thoughts, words, and actions be kind, loving, and contribute to the whole.
- May we not dispute with one another.
- May we have spiritual studies.
- May I be loved.
- May I live in joy and gratitude.
- May I know my true self.
- May I be the change I would like to see in the world.

Prayer for Peace *Meditation*

Relax on your back with support under the knees. Inhale and exhale. Feel your body letting go. Honor the breath. Imagine the heart as a very still pond. Imagine tossing a pebble into that pond and feel, from the heart, ripples and vibrations extending outwards. Now offer a prayer for someone or something in your life or world peace. Feel those ripples move outward from the heart into the space that surrounds you. Expand the ripples outside the room, into nature, into your neighborhood, city, country, island, and imagine those ripples blessing every creature, every being on the planet with your prayer. You may take that love and healing to anyone on this planet, specifically, around the globe, or outward and upward into the universe. When you are ready to bring that love back toward yourself, inhale that wave back toward your heart. Sit in this deep state of peace. Honor your heart and its gifts. Honor your power to heal. Honor that compassionate concern for others. Honor the power of prayer.

Loving Kindness Rock *Art Project*

Take a rock and decorate it or paint it as you like. You can write on the rock: '*For you!*' On a separate piece of paper, write down inspirational words that are uplifting and loving. For example: "*You can do this!*" "*You have amazing strength!*" "*You are beautiful and courageous!*"

Fold the paper up and tape it or tie it to the rock. Place the rock in a random place for someone to find. It could be in the house for your parents to find or out in your community. When someone finds this rock, the words of wisdom and positivity will brighten their day and maybe inspire them to do a random act of kindness for someone else.

Prayer Flag *Art Project*

Traditionally, prayer flags promote peace, compassion, strength, and wisdom. The Tibetans believe that the prayers and *mantras* infused into the flags will be blown by the wind and spread goodwill and compassion to all living beings.

Use either strong construction paper or square-cut fabric. Have the kids draw yogic symbols; *yantras*, *mandalas*, *OM* signs, lotuses, or images of the Buddha (animals, nature, trees). Have them bless each flag with a *mantra* or prayer. Some prayers could be for Mother Earth or a specific cause. Have the kids envision that every prayer will blow away in the wind and bless every living being, creature, and person on the planet. If you're using fabric, use a glue gun and glue to string. If you're using paper, then glue the string into a fold in the paper. String them together and put them up in a special place.

Lesson Four –
Yoga at Thanksgiving

Thanksgiving Traditions

The act of giving thanks for food, for life, for a higher power, or for each other is a longstanding tradition that is shared by many cultures around the world. This is especially true both with European explorers and the Tribes that assisted them along the East Coast of North America. More than 400 years ago, in 1621, the Wampanoag Tribe and the Plymouth Colonists shared this tradition, and they gave thanks for a bountiful autumn harvest with a feast. This early feast has since become a traditional national holiday in both the United States and Canada; a Day of Thanksgiving.

Thanksgiving Day can be a time to express your appreciation for those around you and everything they do for you. It can be a time to give thanks to all the people, ancestors, and creatures on the planet that came before you. It can be a time for you to connect to the Divine, to be thankful for your existence and your place in the world. You can have gratitude for the abundance around you and all the things that you have and enjoy every day, everything that makes you feel lucky to be you. Recognize and appreciate the beauty of the Earth, the ocean and the wind; the sky and Moon and the Sun and the stars. What are you thankful for?

The Thanksgiving holiday is also an opportunity for you and your kids to learn more about North America's history and culture and explore Thanksgiving from indigenous traditions and perspectives. Or take Thanksgiving global and find similar traditions around the world, like Pongal in India, Kadazan in Malaysia, Chuseok in Korea, Ghana in Africa, Erntedankfest in Germany and Sukkot in Israel.

Here are some yogic ways I like to share the value of gathering family and friends and using food as a source of healing.

Stimulation for Digestion - *Meridian Points*

Ankle Points

Sit in hero's pose and cross at the ankles. You should feel pressure or even pain sensation on the inner ankle of your bottom foot. This simple pose stimulates an important juncture of meridians with organs that aid in digestion: the spleen, kidneys, and liver.

Wrist Points

Simulate meridian points on your wrist to relieve nausea from over eating. With your right hand, put your four fingers together and lay them across the inside of your left wrist, right below your palm. Find the meridian point by placing all four fingers from your right hand flat across the inside of your left wrist. Line up your pinky to the edge of the palm. Look where your forefinger knuckle is located along your wrist–that's where the meridian point is. Remove your fingers and press firmly on that meridian point with your thumb while supporting your arm. Hold down for one minute or until you feel less nauseous. Repeat with the right arm.

Belly Points

Place peppermint essential oil directly on the belly and navel and massage. Take a drop each of lavender and ginger essential oils and rub clockwise on the belly. Massage from the right side to the left side.

Soothing with Herbal Tea

Brew ginger, fennel, or peppermint tea. Sip and relax.

Restorative Supine Butterfly Pose

Place a bolster or a folded blanket long way against the spine. If you have one, place a block under the blanket where your head would be. Sit with the lower part of the bolster or end of the blanket right against the tailbone and lay back along the bolster or blanket. Bring your legs into a butterfly shape and place a block under each knee for support. Make sure you feel completely supported and able to relax. Send your breath into the lower belly, or just simply let each breath rise and fall naturally as you relax more and more with every exhale.

Food Reflection *Activities*

Food Meditation

Try different foods with the kids. Discuss where that particular food came from (where it was grown and or harvested). Talk about all the ways it traveled to get to the table. Talk about benefits and nutritional value. Use the five senses to experience the food. Slow down and take this opportunity to really soak in that food sensation. Savor every bite.

Sharing Food and Heritage

Bring a healthy dish to share. Bless the food, instilling it with healing and life-giving qualities. Bless all the people in your life who you love and who are important to you. Share your family's culture, heritage and rituals. Share wisdom from your ancestors. Send prayers out to all your teachers and mentors. Send love to this beautiful Mother Earth for sharing her bounty. Talk about what you are grateful for while you share the food.

Yoga Practices *for Digestion and Assimilation*

It's always good to touch base on the motto "*everything in moderation,*" especially when it comes to food. Holidays are times when many of us overindulge and form unhealthy habits when it comes to eating, especially if we are eating out of an emotional or stressful response.

Child's Pose

Come into child's pose. Cross the left big toe over the right big toe. Breathe ten breaths.

Wind Releasing Pose

Lie on your back. Grab your right knee about two inches below the knee cap. Secure your fingers together and pull your knee into your chest, toward the right shoulder, avoiding the rib cage. Take five big belly breaths into that thigh, hip, and lower right side of the belly. This massages the ascending colon. Release and switch to the left side, massaging the descending colon. Release and then take both knees into the chest and grab around the knees, if you can, by the elbows (if not by the hands) and draw shoulders and tailbone down. Try to get the spine nice and flat to the ground. This massages the transverse colon and is a great posture for belly pain, constipation, and helpful for overeating.

Cat Paw Massage

Take the hands or a yoga block, place on the belly, and massage from right to left like a cat kneads with its paws.

Notes:

PART 3

CHAPTER 5 (December)

Celebrating Sacred Ritual

"We'll all get to the same place, but in a timeline that is unique to each being. So, take this with you: know that every person is a teacher and every experience a teaching and that there are angels everywhere guiding us, reminding us, and helping us return home. And when we do come home—and we will—we will know ourselves, we will know each other, and we will know peace."

-Seane Corn[7]

December:
Celebrating Sacred Ritual

December is a time of many holiday traditions and customs. They can become powerful teaching tools for kids. These special moments allow us to pause together and reflect on what is important. Throughout history, December has always been a time to observe nature and the unfolding of the seasons. Creating rituals with kids is one way to bring meaning to these special times.

Like our ancestors before us, we can observe the cycles and the seasons and remember the everchanging flow of life that we are part of. Helping kids welcome these changes in their environment connects them back to the power of nature. Change is inevitable. There is nothing more predictable in life than change. This simple yet powerful idea can be an extremely valuable skill for a child to learn and embrace.

In this month's curriculum, *Lesson One* will focus on learning how to create sacred space by making our own personal altar as well as a group altar. An altar is a special place for objects that have meaning and significance. It's a space to use for prayer, devotion, and organic movement meditation. An altar can help anchor our energy to the present moment and be a ritual place for feeling love and stability.

In Lesson Two, we will learn about the sacred junctures throughout time and space that bring us together and support our highest vision. We will explore an auspicious opportunity to look within during the special astrological event of the winter solstice. We'll also learn practices that support stillness, reflection, renewal, and the retrieval of inner peace.

Lesson Three will build upon the significance of conducting rituals during high-energy times of the year as we build momentum to the new year. The new year's energy is all about shedding old ways and making room for new beginnings. We will learn about the importance of intention setting through meditations and guided journaling.

Lesson Four is all about recognizing what is important in our lives and rejoicing in practices that bring feelings of abundance and joy, like preparing food to share with others and holiday gift-giving. These practices allow our yoga to move outward and bless and bring cheer to our families, friends, and communities.

"May the longtime Sun shine upon you, all love surround you, and the pure light within you, guide your way on."
-Unknown[1]

Lesson One –
Ritual and Sacred Space

Creating rituals for kids helps them anchor their energy into the values and morals most important to them. Rituals also help create consistency in an everchanging world. Any meaningful action we take or event we create can become a ritual. What makes it sacred, though, is the dedication and intention we place in it. Rituals of consistency help kids navigate the holiday season by creating excitement and meaning in the most mundane activities.

Children are happiest and do their best within a routine. They feel safe in the familiar and prefer knowing what comes next. In the face of change, the consistency of giving gifts, uniting over food, singing songs, or simply observing changes in nature can be extremely soothing. Participating in rituals allows us to find meaning in our lives. Rituals honor the seen and unseen parts of life that connect us to each other. When we give strong meaning to an act, we give it dedication and power and make it sacred. Creating rituals around the holiday season and winter solstice is an empowering and meaningful practice to share with your students.

Sacred Space

Connect with your intentions by creating your internal and external sacred spaces. Allow your energy to balance as you prepare to meditate.

- Use music and privacy to create a peaceful environment. Sit comfortably and light a candle as you sit with an altar created to represent your highest self.

- Close your eyes and focus on your breath. Notice how it feels to consciously inhale and exhale.

- Optional to invite your higher power, angels, benevolent spirit guides, or ancestors to be with you.

- Light sage or incense and bless the altar space. Allow your prayers to be offered to the altar and for the universe to hear what is sacred in your life.

How to Make an Altar

An altar is a sacred place for prayer or blessings that represents your true, authentic self. An altar can be used for ritual or simply as a place to feel safe and connected. Religious ceremonies have relied on altars for millennia. Creating your altar based on your inner attunement becomes an outward representation of your whole self. Your altar allows you to honor yourself by representing who you are at your core. Eventually, this altar and the space around it will influence your mood and energy.

Altars also help us maintain a connection to our intentions and what we hope for in our lives. It is important to create your altar to represent what is essential and valuable in your life. You can create an altar with special objects such as elements from nature, photographs, and jewelry. You can also create an altar for someone or something else.

May your altar connect you to the intentions you set. May it also help you feel closer to your divine self and provide a safe and special place for reconnecting with what is sacred in your life.

Pick one to three things in each category:

Winged (bird, insect, feather, claw, sticks from a nest)

Insect (figurine, dead beetle, fly, a bee stinger, butterfly wing)

Reptile (snakeskin, claw, picture, turtle shell, gecko, *Shiva* statue with snake at the neck)

Water Being (shark tooth, seashell, sand dollar, starfish, coral, picture or drawing)

Four-legged Animal (fur from a dog, antler, tooth, claw, picture)

Mineral (rock, gem, crystal)

Shell (seashells, eggshell, turtle shell)

Plant (roots, leaves, flowers, stems, fruit)

Colors, **Symbols**, and **Diminutives** (*OM* symbol, *Ganesh* statue, Buddha statue)

Elements: water/fire/air/earth (sage, candle, a bowl of water, fruit, diamond, or bless the altar with these elements)

Forest/Mountain/Night Sky (constellation, pinecone, leaves, berries)

Fairies, actual beings, manmade (*malas*, photos, idols, ceramics, jewelry, *yantras*, sacred items, statues)

Ritual of Gathering and Blessing your Altar

1. You will need a flat surface and a base cloth that can be made of fur, leather or fabric.

2. When gathering objects, be mindful and respectful. Ask each object where they want to be placed on the altar. Thank them for helping guide universal life flow toward you and your life.

3. Ask all objects to work together when the altar is done. Pick a key object to hold whenever returning to your altar for questions or wishes. Light a candle and ask first to hold the key object before requesting information. Give thanks for the key.

4. Be extremely specific in your requests. Be clear in what you are manifesting.

5. Cleanse the altar often with sage, incense, sound healing, or intention.

6. Lay items out under the full Moon for energizing and harmonizing.

Animal Spirits Altar *Art Project*

You can use animal spirit cards or make some of your own. Place the pictures of the animals or the animal spirit cards in a *mandala* or circle. Have the children close their eyes and ask which animal's energy and power they need right now in their lives. Have each child approach the altar individually, close their eyes, and feel around for which card chooses them. Have all the kids share their animal and think of why that animal picked them today and what energy, power, and lessons that animal will give them. After the discussion, they can draw the animal spirit on a piece of paper.

Group Altar *Art Project*

Have the kids bring in something special to share with the class. Place a cloth down for these objects. Invite everyone to come to the altar, and one by one, have the kids offer their item to the altar with a brief explanation. Once everyone has placed something on the altar, light a candle or incense to create a sacred space. Instruct the kids to slow down their breathing and to bring their focus into their hearts. Have them think of a blessing that they would like to send out. This can be a prayer for themselves, their families and friends or for a worldly benefit. Close the meditation by offering those prayers to the greater good. At the end, you can ask the kids to share their prayers.

Lesson Two –
Sacred Junctures

In yoga, the winter solstice is an auspicious *sandhya*, or sacred time, of transition and transformation. The word *sandhya* literally means dusk, twilight, or junction. Ancient humans knew that the longest night of the year fell on the winter solstice. The Sun would begin its long journey back across the Earth. They knew it was a time of celebration, to be grateful for the return of light, the coming warmth of spring and the return of life to the land. On the winter solstice, the Sun spends its shortest day in the sky, but everyone can feel that change is coming. The winter solstice is about celebrating the end of darkening; inviting in the light as the Sun starts to bless our days, making them longer and warmer.

In yoga, we can celebrate this sacred juncture with reverence for the magic of nature and the unfolding of the seasons in many ways. The practices below are great resources for yourself as well as for the classroom. You can simplify them for younger kids. Intention is everything, and December is a powerful month of reflection and manifestation. We are all blessed with the power to choose to change. We all can create meaning in our lives.

Sandhya *Meditation*

Sandhyas can be located at the sacred unions of rivers or where mountains intersect, or at high-energy vortex spots. *Sandhyas* in the body are found where the *nadis* cross and form *chakras*. *Sandhyas* in the everyday junctures in time and space can be found at sunrise and sunsets, or monthly with the new and full moons, or quarterly like the equinoxes and solstices. These sacred junctures can also be found during rare cosmic cycles such as eclipses and astrological phenomena. These momentous times create space for us to pause and reflect, unite, and breathe together as one. *Sandhyas* are a powerful time for intention setting.

A winter solstice *sandhya* meditation is about turning inward as we honor the darkest night of the year. It's a time for self-inquiry, contemplation, and gentle yoga without judgments or criticism. The energy of the winter solstice calls for reflection and to release things that do not serve our purpose. It's about being open to new possibilities in the new year, a meaningful time of renewal. Our internal clocks reset to this cosmological rhythm as the light slowly begins to increase each day. With the new year's energy on the horizon, it's an exciting time to welcome new seeds of thought and celebrate the lessons learned through out the year. Make peace with the past and move forward with a newfound grace and inner strength.

Intention Setting and Journaling

Setting intentions is different from setting goals. The goal is the destination. It is what you want to achieve. Intention is how you get there and the experience along the way. It is the way that you choose to reach your goals. Intention uses a purposeful balance of feelings, desires, and standards to influence how every event, interaction, and adventure will proceed. With intention, you set the plan from your origin to your goal.

Solstice Yin Yoga Flow

Yin yoga is rooted in the Taoist concept of *Yin* and *Yang*. In this belief, opposite and complementary principles in nature work together. *Yin* provides stability with unmoving, hidden parts of the world. *Yang* leads to change through constant motion and strives to reveal truths. *Yin* and *Yang* manifest in our bodies with stiff connective tissue representing *Yin*, and mobile and supple muscles representing *Yang*.

Yin yoga works by using slow, steady motions to stretch your connective tissues. As you hold your body in a *Yin* pose, those tissues will stretch and grow longer. This is exactly the goal. You want your body to respond to this positive stress and become stronger. *Yin* yoga is excellent for improving energy, enhancing your *chi* in your organs, building strong emotional and mental well-being, and more.

Benefits of a Regular Yin Yoga Practice[2]

- Increased circulation
- Reduced anxiety
- Increased relaxation
- Calm and peaceful mind
- Releases fascia and muscle tension
- Improves flexibility and mobility
- Balances internal organs

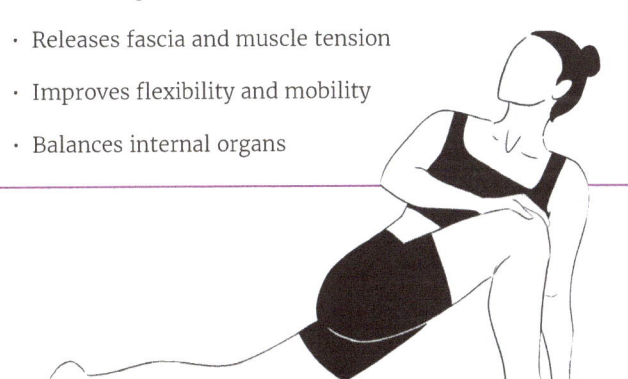

Yin Yoga Poses for kids:

- Butterfly (sitting or lying down)
- Separate leg stretch (one knee bent and one extended)
- Forward fold with legs together or in a V
- Wide knee child's pose (support with bolster under the torso)
- Dragon
- Twisted dragon
- Pigeon
- Sphinx (alternate with one leg frog pose)
- Open wing (support with block under the heart and head)
- Banana
- Thread the needle
- Spinal twist

Elemental *Meditation* — Earth, Water, Air, Fire

This is a great meditation to do with your altar on the solstice. We will be honoring the four elements this peaceful, guided meditation.

Lay down or sit comfortably. See yourself walking barefoot in the sand. Imagine sand squishing between your toes. Honor the Earth with every step. Honor her ability to balance, ground, and stabilize. Feel her energy move up through your body to strengthen the bones, muscles, tissues, and ligaments.

Now, feel the ocean move over your feet. Water splashes all over your body as you submerge yourself. Feel the water's coolness. Feel her ability to nourish, replenish, flow, and circulate. Allow the water to help you release control. Feel the freedom to become spontaneous and go with the flow.

Now feel the air as you walk along the sand once more. Feel the movement of the wind caress the body, surrounding and supporting you. Feel the air begin to cleanse thoughts from your mind. Feel it loosen the rigidity of the body and feel it create a fresh, invigorating sensation.

Lastly, look up into the sky and, as the clouds move away from the Sun, feel the heat of the fire element warming you from the inside out. Feel stress and tension melt away. Feel the relaxing qualities of that warmth create suppleness and mobility. Feel the Sun warm your face. Pull her light into every cell of the body.

Dharana *Meditation*

This is a powerful meditation to do on sacred junctures: holidays, birthdays, or celebrations.

Light a candle and take five to ten minutes to meditate while gazing into the flame. Before and after the meditation, inhale through your nose and exhale through your mouth deeply. Maintain focus. As thoughts come into your mind, acknowledge them, and let them pass. Return to your breath. At the end, honor yourself, your place in this world, and all the gifts you have to share with the world. Honor your light. Breathe in love and send a prayer out for yourself, for someone else in your life, and for the planet.

A Solstice Meditation through the Chakras

This is a solstice and New Year meditation moving through the *chakras*, the seven energy centers in the body. Reflect on or journal new ways to connect with your own truth and consider how you would like to invite revitalizing, renewing energy into the new year. This meditation is good to do with your older kids that are familiar with the *chakra* system. For the younger kids, you can introduce the rainbow body by coloring a *chakra* coloring sheet or guiding them through a *chakra* art project. We will be going over the *chakras* further in April's chapter.

Muladhara Chakra:
Feel into the state of the root *chakra*. This is health and vitality in the physical body. It is also stability in family and home life. What imbalances can be nourished and healed?

Svadhisthana Chakra:
Meditate on the state of your creative process, upon what is being born and manifested by you. What emotions are you feeling stuck in? What could flow a little more easily in your life? What do you want to create? How do you express yourself?

Manipura Chakra:
Breathe into the space of your solar plexus, identity, sense of self, and self-esteem. What can be stoked and ignited? Are you inspired and motivated by your passions? Do you feel connected and empowered by your work and your life? What are you creating?

Anahata Chakra:
Reflect on your own heart-fire. Are you feeling love, receiving love, giving love, and radiating love? How is love being reflected in your home life, relationships, and community? Can you accept compliments easily? What energy is coming in and what is going out? Is it loving, caring, sustainable?

Vishuddha Chakra:
Listen to what needs to be healed from miscommunication and misunderstanding. What are your truths that need to be spoken? How can you use your voice for healing and to be understood? Are you holding anything back? What are you afraid of?

Ajna Chakra and **Sahasrara Chakra:**
Reflect on your highest vision for the next cycle. What limited views must be released? In what ways do you feel disconnected from the source? Reflect upon your unique purpose. How can you realign with your own dharma or righteous path? What do you want to do with your life? How do you connect to a higher power? What rituals are important to you?

Lesson Three – The Year's End

Reflection

When embarking on the yoga path, we will all learn that it's a constant cycle of living, loving, assessing, surrendering, and becoming present. This occurs over and over again. December has many opportunities for the yogi to practice. It's a time of reflection and self-discovery. A time of becoming wise to our old ways of thinking, and opening our minds to how we want to be better, love more, and live a life we are proud to be part of. The new year's energy is about embracing hope. Hope that we can live life gracefully and with ease by learning from past experiences. Hope that every being feels peace and love. Hope that we all can be freed from suffering. Here are some ways to practice and guide a reflection with the kids.

Imaginary Fire Ceremony

Reflect upon the past year. On a piece of paper or in your journal, write about the good and positive moments. What were the gems and the jewels? What are you grateful for receiving? What were the valuable lessons learned?

Now, reflect on the things that you would like to let go of. Think of the things that happened in your life that did not serve you in the highest way. What are you ready to release and let go of?

Reflect on the energy of the new year. What are you ready to manifest? What is your deepest truth that you are willing to live out this year?

Close your eyes and envision a fire right in front of you. Imagine folding your paper of prayers and offering it into the fire. See the smoke rise upwards, into the sky, and disappear. Know that the smoke is carrying your prayers upwards into the ether. Inhale a sense of renewal, peace, and a new start into your heart.

For younger children, make this meditation simple by drawing a picture on one side of a piece of paper something they would like to let go of and release. On the other side, write what they are ready to create. Have them fold their paper up and place it into a collective jar of prayers to hold on your group altar. Guide the children at circle time to use the creative power of their minds to burn up the prayers in the jar and offer the smoke up to the sky.

Journaling with Older Kids

1. Grab your journal and create a sacred space to reflect. Recall your most recent significant experiences (those from the last few weeks or months) and let your body move to express the impact of your memories either through a visualization or an actual physical practice. Journal on this experience.

2. Continue reflecting on the entire year, month by month. Re-experience the important moments of your year. Let your body express through movement how you felt during those times. Again, you can visualize this movement therapy. Journal your discoveries.

3. When you arrive back at the beginning of the year, remember what you were passionate about. What resolutions did you make for yourself last New Year? Do you feel closer to those desires or further away? Write those things down.

4. When you are ready, journey forward, moving clockwise, reliving your past year another time. What new insights come to you?

5. When you arrive back to the present, think of these questions. What did the significant moments of this past year teach you? How did they change you? Allow your insights to inform you as you look toward the year ahead.

Ho'oponopono – *To Make Things Right*[3]

In the Hawaiian language, the word *ho'o* means 'to cause' and *ponopono* means 'perfection.' The term *ho'oponopono* translates as to correct a mistake or make it right. *Ho'oponopono* does not require much teaching to practice, but holds great power to purify your body. It clears bad memories or feelings that we hold in our minds, keeping us in a negative pattern. This prayer is powerful when making peace with the past and inviting new energy in. It's a ritual of forgiveness. It's a potent time to practice this ritual during high-energy times on the planet like solstices, equinoxes, eclipses, full Moon, and new Moon events.

Ihaleakala Hew Len, therapist and teacher, created the term after an experience he had working with a group of mentally ill criminals in Hawaii. Though the therapist thoroughly examined their medical records, not once did he meet any of the patients. Instead, he used the *ho'oponopono* words to alter his mood, which affected the prisoners' mental status.

Through this unique practice, Len was able to heal those around him simply by healing himself. The purpose of *ho'oponopono* is to find forgiveness for yourself and others. In finding that forgiveness, we acknowledge that what happens to us doesn't matter nearly as much as how we respond to what happens. If we have problems within our minds and thoughts, then our minds and thoughts can also solve those problems.

Ho'oponopono *How to Practice*

There are four traditional phrases associated with *ho'oponopono*, which seek to guide us through the steps of repentance, forgiveness, love, and gratitude. As we repeat the words, we release things that block us, negative memories, and traumas that keep us from moving forward. It is a way to reclaim control over our lives. *Ho'oponopono* must happen completely within yourself–it is not an externally driven change.

I like to share this *mantra* with my students as a way to make peace with past. It is a very healing practice to reflect on our own actions and to learn from our mistakes. These four phrases have so much power when we can use them authentically and meaningfully. When we work on ourselves, it affects the whole world.

Set up a sacred space for this *ho'oponopono* meditation. Think about a light of gold in your heart infusing you with compassion, gratitude, and love. Honor everything in your life. What is it that you would like to forgive and find healing through a deeper connection? Think about a person, a relationship or an experience in the past that you would like to make right. Take a moment to center yourself. Bring your breath to your heart. Repeat this *mantra* nine times. You can use the same hand meditation as *Sa-Ta-Na-Ma*.

Ho'oponopono *Meditation*

1. I love you
2. Please forgive me
3. I am sorry
4. Thank you

Lesson Four –
Yoga for the Holidays

Holiday Celebration and Gift Ideas

In this section, I share ideas I have used in the past with my yoga kids. I understand that these activities require extra funding. Sometimes, I ask for donations for these extracurricular holiday gift-giving activities. Please use these ideas if they bring joy to you and your classroom.

Holiday Cards

Bring in paper, pens, markers, and old wrapping paper and allow the kids to make holiday cards to share with friends and family. Encourage kids to write thoughtful and loving messages and add yoga art like *OM* symbols and lotuses.

Holiday Yoga Photo Option

Take photos of the kids at the beginning of the month. Each kid gets to demonstrate their favorite yoga pose. Either send the parents an email with the photo or print it out and have the kids add the photo to their personalized holiday yoga card.

Sugar Scrub Jars

Sugar scrubs are an easy self-care gift to make. You can keep the scrub in the shower or use it in a bath for a refreshing, invigorating experience. The scrub creates extra circulation that exfoliates dead skin cells and replenishes the tissue when applied to the skin. The essential oils relax the nervous system, and coconut oil moisturizes the skin.

What you need:

- ½ cup coconut oil
- ¼ cup sugar (coconut, organic cane, brown sugar, or raw sugar)
- Optional: citrus zest or 10 drops of your favorite essential oil
- Optional: 1 tsp vitamin E oil
- Mini glass jars or small containers of choice
- Spoon and bowl to stir ingredients

How to make: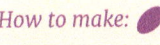

1. Combine room temperature coconut oil with sugar in a small bowl using a spoon or fork.
2. If you're adding citrus zest or essential oils, add them now.
3. Put the mixture in an airtight container, seal tightly and store at room temperature for up to two months. Citrus zest will cause it to have a shorter shelf life.

Holiday Bath Bombs

Essential oils are distilled from plants, taken as a gift from the Earth to be used to bring her power and beauty into your home. Potent chemical compounds from the roots, seeds, flowers, and bark hold medicinal qualities. The oils make the plant smell, protect it from predators and harsh environments, and aid in pollination. These oils are highly beneficial to creating homeostasis within our own environments.

One exciting way to use essential oils in your home is bath bombs.[4] Kids and adults both enjoy using bath bombs and they make great gifts. Even if you do not have a bathtub, these are still fun and great in the shower. The water will dissolve the bath bomb, releasing the therapeutic aroma of the essential oils into the steam. Another great way to use bath bombs is for a decadent foot soak. Try this recipe adapted from Rainbeau Mars.[4]

Ingredients:

- 1 cup citric acid
- 1 cup baking soda
- ½ cup cornstarch
- ½ cup coconut oil
- 8–10 drops favorite essential oil for relaxation: peppermint, lavender, wild orange, eucalyptus, lemon, bergamot, ylang ylang
- Bowl and spoon to stir up ingredients
- Mini cupcake tin or silicone molds

How to make:

1. Put the citric acid, baking soda, cornstarch, and oil in a bowl.
2. Add 8–10 drops of any essential oil you choose.
3. Use a spoon to mix until a soft dough is formed. It will look like damp sand. If it is too wet, add more cornstarch and baksing soda until the texture looks right.
4. If you want, add food coloring, dried herbs, or flower petals to the mixture.
5. Place dough in silicone molds. Let sit for at least 24 hours before removing from the mold.
6. To use, drop it in the bath or shower and watch it dissolve.

Kids Holiday Kitchen Recipes

Introducing the importance of clean, healthy treats is important for kids during this holiday time, where cakes and cookies are an everyday appearance. We are all overwhelmed with sugar and artificial flavors during the holidays, and it's refreshing to know that there are healthy alternatives to candy and sweets. I like to use cooking in my kids' yoga classes to celebrate the ritual of inviting health and healing into our diets.

Cookie Decorating with Chocolate Chip Cookies

What you need:

What you need:

- ¼ cup almond butter (or any nut butter)
- ¼ cup pure maple syrup
- 6 Tbsp applesauce
- 1 ½ cups almond flour (or flour of choice; oat, coconut, buckwheat)
- 3 Tbsp coconut oil
- 1 cup chocolate chips
- Optional: Coarse sea salt to sprinkle on top or cinnamon sugar (before baking)
- Bowl and spoon to stir ingredients
- Lined baking sheet
- Airtight container
- Optional: ½ cup total chopped pecans, walnuts, oats, dried fruit, coconut, chia seed, flax
- Cookie decorations (see below)

How to make:

1. Mix everything in a bowl and spoon onto a lined baking sheet.
2. Bake at for 350° Fahrenheit for fifteen minutes until the edges are golden brown.
3. Let cool completely.
4. Decorate with the kids with vegan frosting, healthy gummy bears, dried fruit, vegan chocolate chips, banana or coconut chips.
5. Store in an airtight container.

Holiday Vegan Cookie Dough

What you need:

- ½ cup coconut flour
- ½ cup almond flour
- 1 Tbsp ground organic flax
- 1 Tbsp raw cacao powder
- 1 tsp chia seeds
- 3 Tbsp coconut oil organic, refined and melted
- 3 Tbsp brown sugar
- 3 Tbsp pure maple syrup
- 1 tsp pure vanilla extract
- 3 Tbsp preferred dairy-free milk (almond, coconut, rice milk)
- ¼ tsp sea salt
- ½ cup mini vegan chocolate chips
- Bowl and spoon to stir ingredients
- Airtight container

How to make:

1. Combine all ingredients except chocolate chips into a bowl or mixer and mix well until a smooth dough forms.
2. Stir in the chocolate chips and chill the dough for at least 15 minutes to an hour.
3. Roll into balls or eat with a spoon!

Chocolate Chip Energy Balls[5]

What you need:

- 1 ½ cups rolled oats
- ½ cup pure maple syrup
- ½ cup natural peanut butter
- 1 tsp vanilla
- ¼ cup vegan protein powder
- ½ cup vegan chocolate chips
- Bowl and spoon to stir ingredients
- Airtight container

How to make:

1. Mix the maple syrup and peanut butter until well combined.
2. Add in the remaining ingredients and mix them together.
3. Roll into balls and store in an airtight container.

Macadamia Nut Energy Balls[5]

What you need:

- 2 cups old-fashioned oats
- ½ cup pure maple syrup
- ½ cup nut butter
- ¼ cup hemp hearts
- 1 cup chopped macadamia nuts
- ½ cup unsweetened shredded coconut
- Bowl and spoon to stir
- Airtight container

How to make:

1. Mix the maple syrup and nut butter until smooth.
2. Stir in the rest of the ingredients until well combined.
3. Roll into balls and store in an airtight container.

Holiday Healthy Fudge[5]

What you need:

- 1 cup coconut oil
- ¾ cup honey
- 1 cup cocoa powder
- Bowl and whisk to stir up ingredients or use a blender
- Loaf pan or glass dish to store in the refrigerator

How to make:

1. Melt coconut oil.
2. Put melted oil, honey, and cocoa powder in a blender, blend on high.
3. Pour into wax-paper lined pan (9 x 5-inch loaf pan)
4. Chill in the fridge or freezer. Once firm, cut and serve. Store in the fridge.

Variations: Add vanilla, coffee beans, 2–3 drops peppermint essential oil, wild orange essential oil, nuts, ¼ tsp sea salt

Blueberry Almond Butter Energy Balls[5]

What you need:

- 1 cup almond butter
- ½ cup pure maple syrup
- 2 ¼ cup sprouted rolled oats
- ¼ cup hemp hearts
- ½ cup chopped pecans
- ½ cup dried organic blueberries
- Bowl and spoon to stir ingredients
- Airtight container

How to make:

1. In a medium-size bowl, blend together the almond butter and maple syrup.
2. Add the rest of the ingredients and stir. It should resemble a sticky, crumbly texture.
3. Roll into balls and store in an airtight container.

PART **4**

CHAPTER **6** (January)

New Year,
New Beginnings

*"Every great dream begins with a dreamer.
Always remember you have within you the
strength, the patience, the passion to reach
for the stars to change the world."*
-Harriet Tubman[1]

January:
New Year, New Beginnings

January is a wonderful time to start afresh. The energy of the New Year holds so much hope and promise. New beginnings can inspire new intentions. But sometimes, those expectations fall short if we have unrealistic dreams. Usually, we won't stick to our plans because our resolution starts with the words: *I want.* We create New Year's resolutions based on our ego—misguided by what the material world tells us we should want or need. We set these resolutions based on the mistaken idea that we will only find true happiness when we acquire our every desire. We falsely believe we are not good enough. We call upon ourselves to change what we do and who we really are to get what we think we need.

One of the most important things yoga can teach us is that there is a difference between what we desire and what the universe desires for us. *Yoga* offers us this teaching through *sankalpa*. The phrase *san* means our connection with the highest truth, while *kalpa* refers to the rule we must follow above all others. Combined, *sankalpa* becomes a commitment we make to ourselves only to seek our highest truths. We must honor the true, deep, core meaning of our life. *Sankalpa* points us to our *dharma*—the spiritual and moral law that governs our life—and reminds us to focus on our purpose for being. As I learned from one of my *yoga nidra* instructors, Rod Stryker, "A *sankalpa* practice starts from the radical premise that you already are who you need to be to fulfill your life's *dharma*. All you need to do is focus your mind, connect to your most heartfelt desires, and channel the divine energy within."[2]

In general, when we are on the right path, it feels like the universe's energy is working for us and that we are actually manifesting who we truly are. Our divine nature already has an inherent knowledge of how we can make an impact on planet Earth. Turning to our yoga and meditation practice can help us discover what that action looks like. Encouraging kids to be excited about what they are learning and finding recognizable moments where they feel connected is important in their growth.

As we practice what we preach and honor those moments where we feel totally in sync with the universe, we are living out our personal *dharmas* and, like messengers and role models, impacting our communities and the world because we align with our soul's purpose. That knowledge helps share this elation and joy for living with others and the world.

"The future belongs to those who believe in the beauty of their dreams."
-Eleanor Roosevelt[5]

This month, we will explore our individual intentions by aligning with who we are at the core. We will be discerning our likes and dislikes, learning about our horoscopes and personalities, becoming curious about what moves us, and discovering who and what we want to devote our time and energy to. We can use the practice of *sankalpa* to empower our life's mission through prayer and intention setting.

In Lesson One, we will be learning about 'Earth Messengers', people in history who have done great things. I'll discuss two extraordinary individuals that I like to share in my classroom setting. Encourage the kids to reflect on thinkers and innovators who have impacted them in their lives thus far and talk about the people who inspire them to be their very best. This can be simply family, friends, and teachers who have already made huge impacts.

In Lesson Two, we dive into the meaning of *namaste* on a global level. We will learn the philosophy beyond the idea that we are all one. When we can see each other as equal, the ego dissolves. We are all born into our bodies with special *karmas* to play out. We all need to learn how to love and support each other instead of turning against one another. When we can drop self-entitlement and become humble to the fact that we are all flesh and bone, we can learn to accept more and be less judgmental.

In Lesson Three, we will be learning about *sadhanas* or peace practices that cultivate consistency through repetition. We will tune into what our bodies, minds, and lives are speaking to and create a fulfilling and meaningful practice. A *sadhana* can stem from what energy or *sankalpa* you are aligning with. Anchoring your intention into practice with a purpose can be both fulfilling and supportive to your evolution.

In Lesson Four, we will learn more about our individual self through the lens of astrology, horoscopes, and the Chinese zodiac. We will learn more about those personality traits that support our highest endeavors.

In Lesson Five, we will dive into Chinese philosophy by learning about the *Yin* and *Yang* symbol through art explorations.

In Lesson Six, we will learn a little more of Chinese medicine basics with some profound movement practices that are wonderful to do with the kids. I love introducing these concepts into my classroom because we can see the connection between our emotions and our physical bodies. We can introduce practices that stimulate energy as well as wind-down energy. We can learn a lot about our inner and outer nature through Chinese medicine. **Let's get started!**

Lesson One –
Earth Messengers

There are wonderful examples in history of people living out their *dharmas* and spreading valuable messages. Mahatma Gandhi is one of them. He coined the powerful saying, "*Be the change you would like to see in the world.*" It all starts with us on an individual level. If we don't practice what we preach, we are not living in line with our truths. Being the change starts with embodying what we want to see and how we want to live in the world.

"My life is my message."
-Mahatma Gandhi[3]

Mahatma Gandhi is widely recognized as the world's greatest social revolutionary. He lived by the primary yogic principle of *ahimsa*, or to do no harm. His social revolution used non-violence as its core value because Gandhi knew that we could not affect lasting change by behaving like oppressors. Gandhi emphasized that we couldn't stop the violence or hate with more violence and hate. *Ahimsa* was Gandhi's entire strategy for liberating India from the British Empire. Gandhi advocated for meditation and prayer in combating oppression and real-life issues such as poverty, famine, sickness, and pain.

Another especially important messenger was Dr. Martin Luther King Jr. Jr. The third Monday in January is dedicated to his memory. The most visible leader of the Civil Rights Movement, Dr. King was a Christian minister and activist. He led the Civil Rights Movement in America from 1955 until he was assassinated in 1968. Like Gandhi, King believed that nonviolence and civil disobedience were the best ways to begin a revolution for good. I like to refer to Dr. King's 1963 "*I have a dream*" speech. His message that day was a powerful call for equality and justice that offered a vision of a better future where all people will prosper together in unity. I also like to highlight that we are all messengers and have the right to dream and share our vision for a better world. We are all equal, we all have

the power of expression, and we all have the ability to inspire each other. When we can see the oneness in all creation and treat each other with respect and love, we are truly practicing our own yoga.

"If I cannot do great things, I can do small things in a great way."
-Dr. Martin Luther King Jr.[4]

'I Am a Dream' Board *Art Project*

This month we will be creating art inspired by our own true nature. Living each day with purpose allows us to feel more connected, grounded, and inspired. We, essentially, are the dream. Our dreams are a reality because we are living them out day to day. A dream board is a place to start manifesting that which we already are, reflecting who we are at our core. Images of love, peace, uniqueness, hobbies, excitement, birthdays, all reflect our divine self. This is a practice of rejoicing in who we are rather than who we are not.

First, through *asana* and meditation practice, reflect on what is true in your life. Reflect on the values, strengths, talents, beauties, gifts, passions, interests, and other attributes of your divine nature.

Use magazines to find inspiring images, phrases, or words. Cut them out and glue them onto a strong canvas or large piece of paper. Incorporate pictures that emulate the peaceful and powerful nature we all hold within. You are living the dream. Journal how it feels to be in balance with life and in tune with universal energy. What is your message? What is your dream?

If you don't have a canvas or paper for a dream board, then journal these questions: What are your likes and dislikes? What brings you joy and peace? What change would you like to see in the world? What is your passion?

Lesson Two –
Namaste

Namaste is a Sanskrit word that is traditionally used as a greeting or salutation. So instead of hello or goodbye, they'll say *namaste* or *namaskar*. This translates to the 'divine in me recognizes and bows to the divine in you.' Beyond skin color, ethnicity, religion, occupation, any and all of the facts and facets of our individual lives, you and I are one. This idea of oneness is a theme central to ancient Vedic culture.

The Namaste *Meditation*

Have the kids sit in a circle and talk about practicing seeing each other as the same. Beyond gender, skin, age, and culture, see if you can just witness the light within each other. Now take this practice out into the world. See if you can see people in your community this way. See if you can have a soul-to-soul connection.

The Butterfly Effect

Class Discussion

Introduce the idea of the butterfly effect; how the smallest single action, word, thought, or deed can influence something else, perhaps something unexpected, unseen, or seemingly unrelated. The consequences of the beat of a butterfly's wing may be felt across the world. Talk about this message, how one good thought can ripple across the world, how an act of kindness can have an enormous impact beyond that which is immediately obvious.

Art Project

Draw a picture of a butterfly (you may wish to paint half of a butterfly on paper before folding it in half to create a mirror image). What would you like to let ripple out into the world? How can one act of kindness affect the other side of the planet? What change would you like to see in the world?

Yoga Asana

Have your students come into butterfly pose and ask them where they want to fly to today? Ask them who are they going to bless? Who will they be helping? Where will they be sharing their beauty?

Lesson Three –
Sadhana: *Peace Practice*

Creating a Living Sadhana

One way to cultivate everyday awareness of our actions is through *Sadhana*. This practice was introduced to me by my teacher Shiva Rea and has profoundly impacted my yoga experience. I received these teachings below from her.

Sadhana is derived from the Sanskrit root *sadh*, which means to accomplish or to succeed. *Sadhana* holds the power to transform and bring one fulfillment through mindful practice and repetition. Essentially, *sadhana* translates into a practice of peace. The only problem with practice is that it can often be something we do, rather than a being a natural part of daily life.

Gradually, through daily practice, a *sadhana* creates transformational momentum that can develop into a pathway within. This pathway embodies the flow in yoga, entering us into the continuous stream of living yoga. A *sadhana*, then, becomes a way of being. A living yoga *sadhana* shines on all aspects of our life as a constant light of awareness that also changes according to the seasons of our lives and what we are passionate about seeking and fulfilling.

The primary goal of a daily, weekly or monthly practice is to develop an appropriate and effective ritual that will sustain us throughout our lives. Our *sadhana* becomes a natural support. It can reveal self-realization and a self-recognition of our innermost essence. The goal is to achieve a meditative, unhurried, and purposeful grace to living through yoga.

To start, from the list of sample *sadhanas* below, choose a *sadhana* that moves you most at that specific and important time in your life and create a timeframe that is realistic to practice. Suggestions like going from new Moon to full Moon or practicing for a calendar month may be realistic timeframes to dedicate.

> *"I've learned that people will forget what you did, forget what you said, but people will never forget how you made them feel."*
> -Maya Angelou[6]

Sample Sadhanas

- Where can I bring more balance into my life? A *balance sadhana* is about picking one thing in your life that you would like to bring into balance. For example, if you need more sleep, practice *yoga nidra*. If you have been feeling stressed, add some breathing and relaxation practices into your day.

- Where in my life can I feel healthier? A *health sadhana* could be cultivating vitality through practices of nourishing, cleansing, diet, exercise, and or sleep. It can be practices that ignite, purify, and expand, like starting up a daily power yoga class or making an effort to hike each week. It can also look just the opposite. It may be rejuvenating practices that replenish and coil in, like daily meditation, restorative yoga and or *nadi shodhana*.

- Where in my life can I be more of service? A *service sadhana* is a practice that can help better your home, work, community, and the planet. It can be as simple as helping out at home or organizing the office for better work production. It can also be deeper, like volunteering or devoting time to a higher purpose.

- Am I living out my real dreams? A *creative flow sadhana* is becoming an instrument of creative energy, like writing a book, singing a song or learning a new interest or hobby.

- How are my relationships? A *relationship sadhana* is about cultivating inner and outer connections with people and or current relationships. How can we heal those relationships we see important to tend to?

- Lastly, a *love sadhana* is about choosing love over fear in all aspects of life. It could be cultivating self-love or extending that love out to someone or something in need.

Individual Sadhana

Have the kids pick a personal *sadhana*. Have them share how they are cultivating, nourishing, adding to, and caring for their own unique mission each week. This could be, for example, an ocean or land clean-up *sadhana*, where one picks up trash or tends to plants or the Earth every day. It could be a personal *sadhana*, where they are learning how to cook nourishing food, or perhaps practicing yoga with a specific goal in their personal *asana* practice. It could also be reflective like daily journaling, a rejuvenating yoga practice, or just working on emotions and being aware of negativity or harmful behavior.

Group Sadhana

You can also choose a *sadhana* for the class and have everyone contribute in their own way. For example, you can do an *aparigraha sadhana*, where everyone goes through their toys and gives up one thing to add to a collection to be donated. Another example is an earth *sadhana*. Create a community garden with your class, where everyone gets to bring seeds to plant, and everyone is assigned jobs to care for the new garden. Another example is a kindness *sadhana* where everyone does random acts of kindness each day. Whatever it is, it's important that the kids keep each other accountable, reliable, recognized, and inspired.

Sadhana Yoga Practice

Pick a theme for the month. It could be back bending, handstands, leg stretching, whatever you want. Every week, contribute to that sequencing of building up to that specific goal.

Pick a warm-up arm meditation, a breathing technique, a yoga flow, a *mantra*, and end with a meditation. Adding a *sankalpa* at the end, reminding yourself of your highest truths and divine nature, is a great way to close out the practice.

Lesson Four – Unique in the Universe

Astrology, Horoscopes, Constellations and the Zodiac

The word astrology literally means the 'study of the stars.' For millennia, astrologers have studied the movement of the planets around the Sun as well as the movement of the Moon around the Earth. The positioning and movements of the Sun, Moon, planets, and fixed stars profoundly impact what happens here on Earth and in our lives. Together, we have a magnificent relationship and our astrological chart can provide an array of wisdom, motivations, personality traits, past and future predictions just based on the alignment of the Sun, Moon, and planets in the sky on the day we were born.

When studying the stars, astrologers look for the movement of the Sun, Moon and planets around the zodiac. The zodiac is an imaginary band around the sky that is divided into twelve equal sections that consist of the astrological signs: Aries, Taurus, Gemini, Cancer, Leo, Virgo, Libra, Scorpio, Sagittarius, Capricorn, Aquarius, and Pisces. An astrological chart is basically a snapshot of the celestial positioning at the time and place that you were born.

A horoscope can shed light, insight, and awareness on our potential, our challenges, and personal prerogative. With the kids, I like to start with their sun sign. The sun sign simply tells us in which zodiac sign the Sun was positioned at the time of one's birth. Your sun sign can shed plenty of light on both positive and negative traits of your personality.

Learning about the unique times in which we were born can help us see ourselves more clearly and allow a celebration of life to unfold. It is a fun investigation. This section is great to introduce to kids because once you get savvy in astrology, you can see how and why people are the way they are. It is all in the stars!

Sun Signs and Constellations

Explore the different shapes and symbols associated with kids' sun signs and constellations.
You can draw out their specific horoscopes symbol, or recreate the astrological constellations.

22 Dec-20 Jan	21 Jan-19 Feb	20 Feb-20 Mar	21 Mar-19 Apr
♑	♒	♓	♈
Capricorn	**Aquarius**	**Pisces**	**Aries**
Earth·Cardinal·Saturn	Air·Fixed·Uranus	Water·Mutable·Neptune	Fire·Cardinal·Mars
The Goat	**The Water Bearer**	**The Fish**	**The Ram**

20 Apr-20 May	21 May-21 Jun	22 Jun-23 Jul	24 Jul-23 Aug
♉	♊	♋	♌
Taurus	**Gemini**	**Cancer**	**Leo**
Earth·Fixed·Venus	Air·Mutable·Mercury	Water·Cardinal. Moon	Fire·Fixed·The Sun
The Bull	**The Twins**	**The Crab**	**The Lion**

24 Aug-22 sept	23 Sept-22 Oct	23 Oct-22 Nov	23 Nov-20 Dec
♍	♎	♏	♐
Virgo	**Libra**	**Scorpio**	**Sagittarius**
Earth·Mutable·Mercury	Air·Cardinal·Venus	Water·Fixed·Pluto	Fire·Mutable·Jupiter
The Virgin	**The Scales**	**The Scorpion**	**The Archer**

Celebrating our Birth *Activity*

Make a chart with all the kids' names and add their birthdates, specific horoscopes, and their unique elements. From there, share with your students the individual personality traits and qualities when in balance and when out of balance. You can also add their animals from the Chinese calendar. Have the kids make homemade journals, an '*all about me*' book, where they can also go home and research more on their individual signs and traits.

Astrology Rock *Activity*

Start with a smooth rock, and you can either paint it first and or use glitter glue or markers to draw their symbol or constellation on the rock. .

The Elements

In Greek theory, the four elements associated with one's Sun sign, have been used to classify behavioral tendencies throughout thousands of years. These elements are reflective to a person's personal constitution. For instance, water people tend to be more emotional, earth people more grounded, fire people more independent, and air people more social.

Chinese Astrology

Your Chinese zodiac sign depends on the year you were born. The Chinese believe the animal that rules your birth year can significantly influence both your personality and destiny. There are twelve different animals associated with the Chinese zodiac. The Chinese say, "*These animals hide in your heart.*"[7] Legend has it that each of these twelve animals said goodbye to the Buddha when he left the Earth, so he gave them a special place of honor in the years they represent.

Chinese Zodiac Animal *Art Project*

Draw the animal of your Chinese zodiac sign. Read about the different traits of that animal; these could be your strengths and weaknesses.

In the chart below, different elements are mapped out with their correlating Sun signs and positive traits. Help your students get to know their themselves better by journaling or drawing out their specific elements. Use dance, creative movement or a yoga flow to express these dynamic forces of nature.

Water Element:
Cancer, Scorpio, Pisces

Characteristics: Dreamers, heartful, family-oriented, soul of humanity, intuitive, imaginative, psychic, great at speaking and reading between the lines, sweet, empathetic, dramatic, caring, nurturing, detectives, poets, doctors, therapists, filmmakers, soothing, in touch emotionally, healers, would do anything to help anyone.

Earth Element:
Taurus, Virgo, Capricorn

Characteristics: Grounded, secure, brave, down-to-earth, helpful, connected, wise, practical, stable, gardeners, cooks, great friends and lovers of life, great business people and organizers, professional, reliable, caring, value nature, trusting.

Fire Element:
Aries, Leo, Sagittarius

Characteristics: High-energy, leaders, performers, teachers, creative, courageous, confident, gregarious, social, bright, warm, loving, passionate, goal setting, brave, artistic, overachievers, popular, big hearts.

Air Element:
Gemini, Libra, Aquarius

Characteristics: The 'cool kids.' Great writers, artists, communicators, charmers, light workers, intellectual, high vocabulary, smart, mentally quick, witty, curious, social, flirty, wise, balanced, good listener, big friend group, likable.

Lesson Five –
Yin and Yang

Yin and *Yang* represent a duality in the cosmos—two opposing and complementary principles guide all that exists in nature. The *Yin/Yang* philosophy tells us that everything has duality. We see duality all around us—the Sun and Moon, day and night, dark and light, male and female—and notice that they are opposites yet they work together. *Yin* energy is characterized as feminine, reflective, cooling, and quiet. *Yang* represents a masculine, energetic, and heating energy.

Yin/Yang Symbol

This concept is symbolized by the Chinese *Tai Chi* or *taijitu*—a circle divided in half by a curved line. One half of this circle is black for *Yin*; the other is white for *Yang*. A small circle of each color sits within the other half, and as they merge together in a spiraled curve, the whole image represents the concept that *Yin* and *Yang* are not separate but parts of each other. The *Yin/Yang* symbol embraces both sides: duality, paradox, and union.

陽 Yang

Sun/light/bright
Assertive/strong
Dry/fire/hot
Male
Positive charge
Heaven
Spring and
summer

陰 Yin

Moon/dark
Recessive/nurturing
Cool/water/damp
Female
Negative charge
Earth
Autumn and winter

Yin/Yang *Art Project*

Draw the *Yin/Yang* symbol. Discuss dualities (day and night, light and dark, hot and cold, etc.) and how they make up our world and our perceptions. Talk about all the opposites the kids can think of.

Creative Doodling *Art Project*

Create *mandalas* within each half circle. Have the children create their own artwork or creative doodling inside the outline of the *Yin/Yang* symbol.

Yin/Yang *Rock Art*

Take a smooth rock and paint the *Yin/Yang* symbol on it. Use the rock for putting good energy and positive intentions to wherever you place the rock: your room, garden, yoga space, altar, or kitchen. Create a happy home for this good luck charm.

Lesson Six –
Yin/Yang and Chinese Medicine

Introduction to Chinese Medicine

Chinese medicine recognizes the concepts of *Yin* and *Yang* and the concept of *qi* (also known as *chi*), the vital force of life. All our vital organs are either *Yin* or *Yang*. The *Yin* organs exist to produce, transform, and regulate the body. They focus on *chi*, blood, and body fluids, and include the liver, heart, spleen, lungs, kidneys, and the pericardium.

Yang organs work to digest food and spread nutrients through the body. These organs include the gallbladder, stomach, small intestine, large intestine, and san jiao also known as the 'triple burner.' The triple burner is not associated with a physical organ but is the body's most powerful energetic pathway for metabolism function.

In Chinese medicine, the body's physiological functions are based on harmonious relationships between *Yin* and *Yang* organs. Each organ has a male and female pair. The energy and health of one organ can affect the energy and health of the paired organ. Each pair, when blocked or stagnant, holds a certain emotion. With sound therapy, we can energize the organs and release old, stale, and blocked energy.

Each organ in traditional Chinese medicine also associated with five elements: earth, fire, water, metal, and wood. These five elements are related to the phases of nature and the life force that flows through them. These elements are basic foundation on how to bring balance back to the body, mind, and spirit.

I like to lead the kids through a visualization that includes the elements, sound, color, and orientation of the specific organs in the body and the associated emotions. I also love to use tapping and other *qigong* movements to enhance energy flow. Yoga naturally stimulates the internal systems, but it's also nice to go over which areas are stimulated to create further circulation and respiration.

Start orienting kids to their own anatomy. It is also valuable to learn about our different emotions and how they are associated to specific organs. Knowing this, we can learn how to energize with sound, stimulate through yoga, and release blocked or negative energy through stimulating the meridians.

Below is a chart that maps out each *Yin* and *Yang* organ according to their specific element, season, sound and emotions in traditional Chinese medicine. There are great yoga practices to help bring harmony back to the body and mind.

Element: Wood

Organs: Liver, gallbladder, eyes, muscles, fingernails

Season: Spring

Direction: East

Sound: xxuuueee

Emotions In Balance: Patience, tolerance, flexibility, and creativity

Emotions Out of Balance: Anger, frustration, irritability

Yoga for Organs: Half-moon, twisting, breathing, inversions, seated postures, side body-opening, detoxing flow, leg stretching with strap, detoxing breathing, stomach compression with bow pose, long *savasana*

Element: Fire

Organs: Heart, small intestine, tongue, blood vessels

Season: Summer

Direction: South

Sound: huhhhhu

Emotions in Balance: Mental clarity, a peace-loving temper, curiosity, and enthusiasm

Emotions Out of Balance: Anxiety, tension, desire, confusion, excessive excitement, insomnia, and hysterical behavior

Yoga for Organs: Restorative yoga, inversions, heart openers, shoulder openers, forward folds, back opening postures, guided meditation

Element: Extension of the Fire element

Organs: Pericardium, san jiao /triple burner

Season: All seasons

Sound: seeeaaaa

Emotions in Balance: Peace, harmony, serenity, contentment

Emotions Out of Balance: Hypertension, stress

Yoga for Organs: Chin to chest postures with compression, neck stretches, inversions, heart opening, back bending with supportive props, acupressure flow yoga, deep breathing, guided meditation

Element: Earth

Organs: Spleen, stomach, pancreas, connective tissue, mouth, flesh

Season: Late Summer

Direction: Center

Sound: hooooo

Emotions In Balance: Caring, rationality, concentration

Emotions Out of Balance: Worry, doubt, fanaticism

Yoga for Organs: Half-moon, twisting, forward folds, restorative yoga, inner leg stretching, side-body opening, *chandra namaskars, yoga nidra*

Element: Metal

Organs: Lungs, large intestine, skin, hair, nose

Season: Fall

Direction: West

Sound: ppffuuuu

Emotions In Balance: Selfless and just actions, generosity

Emotions Out of Balance: Grief, sadness, inability to let go, hopelessness, dependency, egoism

Yoga for Organs: Breathing, twisting, forward folds, detox *surya namaskars*, arm stretching like eagle arms, or palm stretching

Element: Water

Organs: Kidney, bladder, bones, hair, ears

Season: Winter

Direction: North

Sound: twweeee

Emotions In Balance: Fearlessness, strength of will, wisdom

Emotions Out of Balance: Fear, obsession of power

Yoga for Organs: Backbends, forward bends, breathing into back body, detoxing breaths, restorative yoga, *chandra namaskars*

Qigong for the Chinese Elements

These movements are held for about thirty seconds each.

- **Earth** – Take the arms in front of you in the shape of hugging a big tree right in front of you.

- **Metal** – Take the arms parallel with each other and to the floor and straightforward in line with your shoulders.

- **Water** – Take the elbows straight back behind the armpits with the elbows bent.

- **Wood** – Take the arms straight out to each side with fingertips in line with your shoulders.

- **Fire** – Take the arms up overhead with bent elbows and the palms facing up toward the sky and gaze through the diamond shape you make by bringing the thumbs and forefingers together. Keep the chest and heart lifting upward toward the Sun.

Meridian Movement *Practices*

These are great practices that stimulate the meridians and are fun to do with the kids.

Drawing Sky Energy Down: Inhale while sweeping the arms out and up, and reaching up to grab the sky energy. As you exhale, drawing that energy down through the crown and downwards toward the Earth, feel it move throughout your entire body. Inhale once again, sweeping the arms outward and up, palms or fingertips reaching up to the universal and or sky energy. Exhale as you bring that energy down through the body as grounding energy. Imagine a shield of protecting light cascading down in front of you.

Drawing Earth Energy Upward: Reverse and sweep the arms and hands from the Earth up the front of the body, following the spine up toward the crown of the head. Exhale and extend the arms outward and down like painting a bubble of light around the body. Inhale, imagine gathering that grounding energy from the Earth and scooping it up through the body as the arms reach up to the sky. Exhale, and extend the arms outward and down as if you were drawing a shield of light around the body. Repeat three times in each direction.

Kidney Tap: Place the feet wider than hip-distance apart. Swing the arms from side to side, kind of like a helicopter motion. Feel the arms and hands start to sway and wrap around the body as you twist from right to left, keeping the knees bent and easy.

Now make fists, allowing those fists to gently tap on the back of each kidney as the hands wrap around the back with each twist. Now feel as one fist taps the back kidney, and the front fist gently taps at the opposite chest. These are two kidney points in Chinese medicine and, when tapped, they help increase natural energy to all systems of the body without any stress to the adrenal glands.

Whole Body Meridian Tap:

- Standing easily, take your right hand and tap down the left (*Yin*) side of the arm, from on the inside from shoulder to hand. This stimulates the lungs, heart, and pericardium.

- Then, turn the left palm down and take the right hand and tap the outside (*Yang*) side of the arm all the way up toward the shoulder and trapezius muscle. This stimulates the small intestine, large intestine, and thyroid. Repeat on the right side.

- Next, take the fingers and massage the tops of each shoulder to stimulate the gallbladder meridian. Using the fingertips, tap the outside of the face, jaw, temples, head, and forehead. Massage the ears from top to bottom. Take your two fists and tap on the points like a gorilla right below the clavicle bones. These are important kidney points that help boost energy naturally.

- When you are done tapping, take the fingertips or knuckles and zig-zag down the front of the sternum to stimulate the thymus gland, which helps stimulate the immune system. Keep zig-zagging down till you reach the navel and massage around the belly button. Then, put your hands on the right side of the belly and tap up and over to the left and back down over to the right in a circle, stimulating the digestive fire and the large intestine.

- Finally, tap down the front of the legs, bending forward in the knees, stimulating the stomach meridian. Stay low as you tap up the back of the legs, which is the bladder meridian. Tap down the outside of the legs, which is the gallbladder meridian, and then tap up on the inside of the legs, which is the liver, kidneys, and spleen meridian. Relax your hands down by your side and feel the vibration of *chi* move throughout the whole body.

Ha Kriya Breath in Horse Stance

Inhale, arms going up, fingers and hands spreading, and then exhale from the mouth and bring the elbows into your sides with a little force. This gentle tapping of elbows to ribs helps release all the stale air trapped at the bottom of the lungs. Repeat these ten to twenty times. This is great for stimulating the gallbladder meridian, replenishing the lungs, good for digestion, and a big release of emotion, like anger and frustration.

Switch arm positions, taking arms forward away from the body at shoulder height. With hands forward, palms down, spread the fingers wide, and exhale from the mouth with force as you bring the elbows into the sides of lower ribs, making fists with the hands during a strong exhale. Repeat ten to twenty times. Make sure you feel the elbows snap around the lower side ribs to force stale air out with each exhalation.

Internal Organ Rejuvenation *Meditation*

Lie on your back with support under your knees. Feel the natural flow of breath. Next, inhale for four counts, hold your breath for four counts, exhale for four counts, and hold your breath out for four counts. Take about five more rounds of breaths to fill up, expand, release, and let go. It takes six long, slow, deep breaths to shift us from the sympathetic nervous system (fight or flight) to the parasympathetic nervous system (rest and digest). Plus, all the magic happens in breath retention. Pausing at the top and bottom of each breath is when the body can actually process and absorb the oxygen. The conscious exhale gives the body time to eliminate physical toxins and gently allow emotional and mental releases. Honor these breaths as an opportunity to give back to the body. Giving the body time to deeply restore is one of the most important things we can do on a daily basis to keep all systems alive and vibrant. Feel this breath for another minute or so.

Now we are going to take our consciousness through the different internal organs. In Chinese Medicine, each organ has a pair, a *Yin/Yang*, male/female counterpart. Each pair also has a color, vibration, sound, and a negative emotion that can arise when out of balance. We will be taking a journey through the vital organs and reclaiming their power with affirmations. Release the breath to normal, moving in and out with ease. Feel your body relax.

- Bring your attention to the right side of your chest, beneath the right rib cage. Here you will find the liver and gallbladder. The color is green. When out of balance, they hold emotions of anger, resentment, irritability, and frustration. Take a deep breath into any of those emotions you may feel and exhale out all that negativity. Now picture the vibrant color of green and inhale a green light into those organs. Inhale love, happiness, peacefulness, and patience.

- Bring your attention to the left side of your chest and picture the stomach and the spleen. The color of these organs is yellow or orange. When out of balance, the emotions they hold are worry, doubt, and apathy. Inhale into these organs and exhale to release any of those emotions you may have been feeling. Inhale a bright yellow color into these two organs and feel hope, balance, faith, and positivity.

- Bring your awareness to your heart and small intestines. The color is red and, when blocked, these organs hold the emotions of anxiety, nervousness, and an inability to process and renew. Inhale into these organs and exhale to release any of those emotions you may have been feeling. Inhale a red light into the heart and small intestines and feel the energy of love, relaxation, and ease that everything is good.

- Bring your awareness into your lungs and large intestine. These organs are the color gray. When blocked, these organs hold the inability to let go, change, transform, or move forward as well as cause deep depression and insomnia. You might be feeling stuck, unable to change and or having a hard time moving on. Inhale into these organs and exhale to release any of those emotions you may have been feeling. Inhale the color gray into those organs and feel a sense of change, transformation, metamorphosis, adaptability, reassurance, and the ability to move on.

- Bring your awareness to your back and picture the kidneys and bladder. The color is blue and, when out of balance, you might feel fear, unease, nervous tension, and scared for the future. Inhale into these organs and exhale to release any of those emotions you may have been feeling. Now inhale into those organs, picture the brilliant color blue, and breathe in peace, faith, comfort, contentment, positivity, and love.

- Now send the breath to all the vital organs inviting love and harmony, health, and healing. As you exhale, release anything that doesn't serve you in the highest. Inhale peace and balance and exhale, feeling more relaxed and renewed. Feel gratitude for all the simple, wonderful things in your life that are positive. Breathe into all the vital organs and give thanks to them for working for you every moment of the day. Honor yourself in the highest regard and bask in that sensation of presence and bliss.

Emotional Freedom Technique

Tapping, otherwise known as EFT or Emotional Freedom Technique, developed by Gary Craig, synthesizes ancient Chinese acupressure and modern psychology and "has been called a psychological version of acupuncture."[8] It's known as 'tapping' because we are literally tapping on end points of the meridians of our body. At the same time while tapping, we are also taking ourselves through an assessment of emotions. Certain statements are voiced to encourage the mind to be in the now, ready to let go of the old, unwanted thoughts. In the end, our voice clearly speaks to what truths we are inviting into our consciousness.

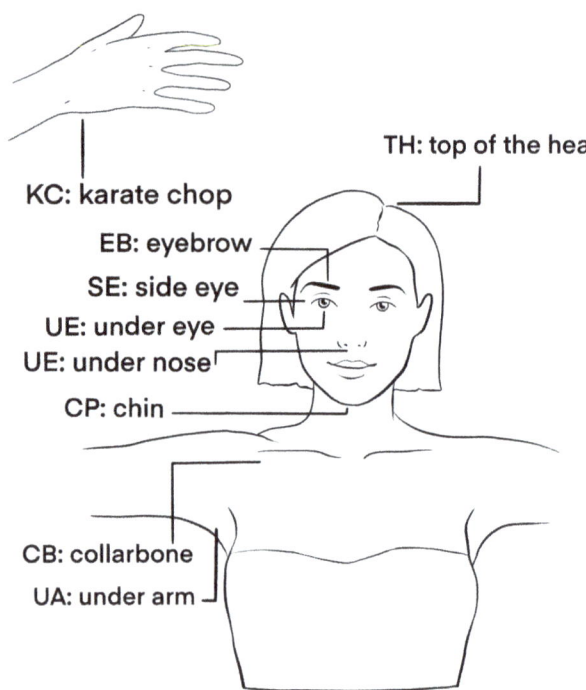

TH: top of the head
KC: karate chop
EB: eyebrow
SE: side eye
UE: under eye
UE: under nose
CP: chin
CB: collarbone
UA: under arm

The purpose of tapping is to physically alter the brain, energy system, and body at the same time. The exercise consists of tapping your fingertips on specific points acknowledging all your feelings in the now, while breathing out the old stuck feelings. Tapping is a terrific modality for relieving anxiety, easing tension in the body, and creating new positive affirmations in the mind. You can tap with a specific goal or to welcome a positive phrase or statement. If you are interested in sharing this practice below, please learn with a certified teacher first who has been trained through Gary Craig and his EFT technique and practice before you teach. I have found this technique to be very effective in clearing out the old and creating new positive neural pathways and energy. It is a powerful practice to do with your students.

EFT *Practice*

- Sit comfortably. Think of the truth you are feeling right now. It could be stress, pain, irritability, nerves, etc. It could also be feeling the weight of the world. Whatever it is, it's alright to feel those feelings and acknowledge that whatever you are feeling is OK.

- Start tapping your fingertips, ten to twenty times, on the outside of your hand, the part you'd use in a karate chop. Acknowledge what you are feeling. Then, bring the fingertips up to the inner brow and tap there to repeat the same statement but add *even though I feel those feelings, it's alright, and I accept myself unconditionally.* Then come to the temples on each side to tap with the same *mantra,* then to the upper cheeks, below the nose, on the chin, under the two clavicles, under the armpits on each side, and, lastly, on the top of the head.

- In this second round, we will be shifting into a more positive phrase or statement such as, *even though I feel those feelings, I love myself unconditionally* and be more specific about what those feelings, memories, and emotions are. Repeat the tapping on all the areas, really feeling what you are ready to heal from or let go of.

- Now, in the final tapping cycle, add more positive phrases and statements about what you want in return. What are you healing, bringing into balance, or wanting with your life, your health, your livelihood? Repeat the third round of tapping with that positive *mantra.* At the end of the tapping, take a deep breath in and hold it. Exhale and release. Feel the stress melt away.

Tapping Simplified for Children

This is a great way to modify the tapping sequence for younger kids. One of my intuitive healers taught me this modified healing tapping technique that can help process negative energy and transmute it into a positive message for the body and mind.

- Tapping on the chest with both hands.

- Tapping on each side edge of the hands, do one and then the other.

- Tapping on the back of the neck with one hand.

As you start tapping about seven times on each of these spots, repeat these phrases and encourage the kids to fill in the blanks:

- State exactly how you feel.

- But then say, "but things can change."

- Lastly, I want to change to . . .

PART **4**

CHAPTER **7** (February)

Individuality & Conscious Leadership

*"Our personal practices and our communal
presence are extensions of one another.
If we have the resources and the tools to show up for
ourselves, then we have the responsibility
to show up in ways within our families and
communities that engage and unite."*
-Seane Corn[1]

February: Individuality & Conscious Leadership

Stepping Into Our Power

Yoga means to unite and to come together. In this process, everything is connected. However, this connection does not mean we are the same. We are connected by our individuality. Like puzzle pieces, we are all different, but we can fit together perfectly, united. We each have our own part and a unique role to play.

As we become aligned with our own personal *dharma* (our uniquely designed purpose), yoga becomes an opportunity to rise up and fight for what we believe to be true. It becomes a mission to find our 'tribe'—the people we feel compelled to work with, to join and unite with, to make this world a better place.

We all have passions in our hearts that we can transform into purposeful action. Some might be compelled to fight for social justice and human rights. For others, it could be standing up for animal rights or the environment. What we choose to advocate for can be greatly influenced by our upbringing, experiences and hardships. Sometimes the pain in our lives or the suffering we see in the world fuels our purpose. It is incredibly valuable to teach children that the hard lessons in life can actually be a significant gift.

Aligning ourselves with our values and beliefs is an important part of process. When we become advocates for what we believe in, not only can we do great things, but we can lead others to great things. Developing our conscious leadership potential begins with accepting who we are, why we are here and what can we do to make this world better. We can encourage conscious leadership in our kids by fostering their curiosity and passion for learning. Essentially, they are the future leaders of tomorrow.

In Lesson One, we will dive into fostering leadership skills within our youth.

In Lesson Two, the story of *Hanuman* will inspire the kids to follow their hearts and take action. This section has some great yoga *asana* ideas.

Lastly, *In Lesson Three*, we will learn about the energies behind creation according to yoga philosophy. When we work with the natural forces of the universe, we learn how to plan our life goals successfully and efficiently.

"Don't forget that little successes turn into huge triumphs."

-Baron Baptiste[3]

"Imagination is the greatest gift you have ever been given."
-Wayne Dyer[2]

Lesson One –
Cultivating Leadership Skills

When talking about leadership, it's important to give kids strategy, structure, and a plan on how to cultivate a vision that feels grounded, empowered, and impactful. To teach kids to be conscious leaders, they first need to be aligned with their hearts, curious about their own beliefs and supported within their interests and aspirations. Helping them organize their thoughts and make a plan to carry out their missions in a clear and structured way is a great way to support their missions. Supporting tasks that they can follow through with is also beneficial to their self-esteem and their love for learning. By inspiring imagination, we can foster the activist, the healer, and the inventor within our children.

Trust Intuition

When something doesn't feel good, try not to overthink it. That strong sensation in your 'feeling' body tells you all the answers. Trust your intuition, that inner knowing. Notice the difference between thinking and feeling. Try to align the heart with the mind when it comes to decision-making. Trust your gut reaction. Journal these emotions around a choice or a cause. Are you 100% in? Where do you feel it in your body? Does it feel tense or at ease?

Buzzing the Third Eye *Practice*

Sit or lay down comfortably. Take a deep breath in and a long exhale, humming *Mmmm*. Feel the forehead vibrate. Repeat three more times. Take time to soak that sensation in with a quiet mind. This is a great sound to increase intuition and connect to our highest self. When we can slow down and tune in, our intuition naturally heightens. Intuition is not a gift but rather a skill we can all work on.

Be Courageous

Self-doubt can make you feel trapped or prevent you from reaching for what you want. Self-doubt can be shifted into courage when we connect with that inner strength and knowledge. Connect with that sense of purpose and know that greater energy from the universe will be there to support you. When you have faith in yourself and the bigger impact of your mission, the universe will support you. Journal the feelings that are holding you back. Are they accurate and true? Breathe faith into the fear, courage into doubt.

Drum Breath *Practice*

This is a great breathing technique for focus, inspiration, and energy. Once you have a vision for yourself, keep that thought in your mind's eye. Use this breathing to stoke fuel for the fire in manifesting your dreams. Inhale swiftly twice through the nose and exhale through the mouth once with a big *HAAA* sound. Repeat over and over until it sounds like the beating of a drum.

Powerful Breath of Fire *Practice*

This is a great breathing technique for courage and bravery. With the kids I call it 'dragon breathing.' In yoga, it is called *kapalabhati* breath of fire. Exhaling deeply and getting all that stale air out helps replenish the lungs, and creates vitality and energy to do great things. It gets you gets fired up!

To practice: Concentrate on the exhales as the belly draws in. Do not think of the inhales; they will just naturally happen. Exhale with a bit of force either out through the nose (imagine you have a fluff ball under each nostril that you are trying to blow away) or out through the mouth (imagine you're trying to blow out candles a few inches from your mouth). Start with twenty. Work up to sixty per session. This is great for releasing pentup emotion, physical detox, and increasing energy.

Power Yoga *Practice*

Design a class that is empowering and liberating. Find poses that have strength and energy (warriors, active sun salutations) with fun jumpbacks into downward facing dog or plank pose, *kapalabhati* (breath of fire) within the *asanas*, handstand, donkey kicks, and dynamic flow sequencing. Core strengthening is great for the *manipura chakra* that is all about self-empowerment and courage. Use your strong voice to lead with conviction, awareness, clarity, and ease.

Find Your Voice

Before we can communicate clearly, or learn to use our voices for speaking our truth, we must first find what is holding us back—keeping us quiet. Do you care about what other people think of you? Do you fear your imperfections? How do those blocks affect you in your mind and body?

Now, try pushing aside all your fears of failure. Reclaim the power from your insecurities. Think about a time in your life where you've taken a risk to speak up about what matters to you without being held back by fear or ego. Journal how it feels to find your voice and let the universe know your truth.

Lion's Breath *Practice*

Lion's breath is a great breathing technique to enhance clear communication and speaking the truth. It stimulates the fifth *chakra* in the throat area, which helps one get their voice out into the universe. Inhale big and exhale, tongue to chin, with the optional lion's roar. This is a great breathing technique to do in a cat posture or downward facing dog posture. Lion's breath opens the jaw and mouth and is good for releasing tension in the ears, face, cheeks, jaw, and throat.

Leadership Traits

Talk about the issues your students are passionate about: the homeless, the hungry, the oceans, littering, animal rights, bullying, mental health, endangered animals. What leadership traits are important in advocating for these issues? For example, being a conscious leader involves being mindful, trustworthy, honest, and loyal. Practicing what you preach is also an important trait. Other traits could include following certain morals and codes of ethic. Invite the kids to discuss further leadership traits. How do they make us stronger leaders and better people?

Collage *Project*

Creating a collage of pictures that represents your missions in this world is a great way to put all your interests and passions in one place. If it's a vision you have in this world to heal, fight for, stand up for, and to contribute to in any way, draw a representation of that mission or cut out pictures that inspire you to be the very best.

Seva – *Selfless Service*

Take this month to explore ways in which we all can contribute selfless service to a greater cause either by prayer, devotion in action, our voices, and/or creating a support group. Talk about ways in which they can be a leader in making great change and awareness. Little successes add up to big changes, so start small and be realistic with the goals. Encourage the kids to ask questions. Encourage them to think and strategize.

Leadership *Game*

Yogi Says: This game is like "Simon Says," in which the one person gets to lead the group through yoga postures or fun positions, cueing their friends in a way that one has to listen very carefully. The kids only do what the Yogi says. If they say, "Yogi says 'Do tree pose'" for example, all the kids do tree pose. If the leader just says, "do tree pose," and you do it, then you have to sit down until the last yogi is standing. This is a fun game of using our listening skills.

Set Healthy Boundaries

Talk about protecting your energy and only say yes to the things you can stay accountable to. Ground down and stay true to your core values. What are they? What do you need to protect your energy? Do you need rest, more water, more connection with nature? Attract friends that have the same visions. Look for support to gain momentum in your mission. Be true to yourself. Journal the grounding techniques you need to protect your energy. What do healthy boundaries look like to you? How does setting these boundaries inform others about how to treat you?

Energy Protection *Meditation*

This is a meditation for protecting one's energy and creating clear and concise boundaries. Once you envision what you are protecting yourself from, begin this meditation with that exact intention.

Sit or lie down. Imagine a circle of light around you. Color the circle with all the colors of the rainbow. Know that this circle of light is protecting your peace so no one can steal it. Perform this practice every morning before you go out into the world. Know you are safe and protected.

Empathy

It's important to have empathy when you are connecting to other people. Kids who are more empathetic build, create, and sustain stronger relationships. Can you imagine for a moment a world where everyone was capable of seeing the perspective of the other side? Can you imagine a world where people acted more from their hearts rather than their minds?

Listening *Practice*

Be present and soak in the moment. If you are by yourself, immerse yourself in the sounds, feelings and vibrations of your surroundings. If you are with a friend, listen unconditionally to their words. If you are with a group of people, practice having compassion and empathy for what they are saying. Release the judgements. Listen from the heart.

Lesson Two – The Story of Hanuman

Hanuman: An Epic Tale in Courage

"It was the greatest leap ever taken. The speed of Hanuman's jump pulled blossoms and flowers into the air after him, and they fell like little stars on the waving treetops. The animals on the beach had never seen such a thing; they cheered Hanuman, then the air burned from his passage, and red clouds flamed over the sky." -William Buck[4]

In India, there are many epic tales of leadership. One of them is the story of *Hanuman*, the part human, part monkey God, who showed great leadership and confidence in his story of saving his beloved Sita. *Hanuman* is one of the most revered Gods in India because of his selfless service and courageous heart. His name symbolizes the yoga posture (split pose) he took in conquering good over evil.

Hanuman is a central character in the Hindu *Ramayana*. Stories tell of him as a man with the face of a monkey and a long tail. He is the son of the Hindu wind God *Pawan* and is known for his daring acts of strength, fearlessness and loyalty. *Hanuman* has many attributes. He symbolizes perseverance, pragmatism, strength, sense of humor, selflessness, and humility. He possesses great knowledge, intellect, and wisdom. *Hanuman* is the ideal yogi, as he has obtained perfect mastery over his senses. He controls his own mind through his disciplined lifestyle and selfless devotion (*bhakti*).

Hanuman's love is always turned inward toward *Ram* (God). Anything that approaches *Hanuman* feels that great love. *Hanuman* tells us that to enter into that flow of grace, we must leave some of that baggage behind. It's not always pleasant to face that which bogs us down, but we feel lighter, more resilient if we do so. *Hanuman* shows us how to overcome fear, break attachments, eliminate suffering and destruction from our lives, and how to let go of everything that holds us back. He embodies the concept of hard love.

Hanuman acts as though driven by destiny instead of selfishness. This ability to do things without attachment makes him the perfect *karma* yogi. In his epic story, he saves his beloved *Sita* (*Lord Rama's* wife) from the evil *King Ravana* by leaping from the southern tip of India to Sri Lanka. He does the splits, which is why he gets the glorious name *Hanuman*.

Hanumanasana is an *asana* that represents the leap *Hanuman* made from the southern tip of India to Sri Lanka. Flexible hips, groin, and legs are essential. As you reach the fullness of the pose, the legs are in a front split position, with one leg extended in front of the torso and the other behind you. Place your hands and arms in a prayer position, stretched to the sky.

Hanuman teaches us of the untapped power each of us holds within. His devotion was carried out with great courage and heart. His legacy inspires others to seek the truth, follow the heart, and act from a place of divine courage and inner strength.

Hanuman Inspired Yoga *Practices*

All the hip and leg-opening practices below set us up for the ultimate split pose, hanumanasana!

Wall Yoga
Downward dog to the wall, one leg up to the wall, then walk the hands back to do the splits against the wall. Rest before repeating on the other side.

Yoga with a Strap
Lie on your back. Take one leg up and place the strap around the ball of the foot. See if you can make that leg straight as possible, engaging the quad and flexing back all five toes. Breathe ten breaths and repeat on the other side. Then, take both feet up to the strap and open the legs into a V, allowing the feet to slide open along the strap. Breathe ten breaths and release.

Standing Separate Leg Stretch
While standing, take your feet wide on your mat with your heels in one line, toes forward. Arms out to the side and inhale, lift the chest and exhale, forward fold and bring the hands to the floor. If you can, keep your legs nice and straight, engaging the quads, so the hamstrings safely stretch. If the knees bend, take a block under the hands, so the spine extends nice and straight. Breathe into the sensation.

Lunges
Take dragon pose or lizard pose, then move the front leg straight and take half *Hanuman* pose. Forward fold over that front leg and then into full *hanumanasana*, full split pose, and repeat on the other side.

Full Hanumanasana
Split Pose: Use a block under the sitz bones to make this posture easier to relax into.

Lesson Three –
Leaders of Creation

The Trinity: Brahma, Vishnu, and Shiva

Another commonly known story in India tells us of creation. The tales of creation help us unveil the energy behind all of life. According to Hindu beliefs, the trinity of *Brahma*, *Vishnu*, and *Shiva* are the three forces that sparked all of creation:

Brahma	**Vishnu**	**Shiva**
is the creator of the universe.	is the preserver of all life.	is the destroyer of ignorance.

These three magnificent energies make the world go around and are powerful forces to learn from. Working with this energy can help us be better leaders, innovators, guides, visionaries, and creators.

In India, there is a deep reverence for these life cycles and the energies that created them. These energies can be a pillar to almost everything that exists. In essence, the trinity represents the power of vision and sustainability. It also honors the cycles of death and rebirth and the power of transformation.

When becoming a leader of anything, there are cycles to our mission. We must recognize and honor these forces in everything that we create. Nothing can last forever. Change is the only constant, and so must be our adaptability to the ever-present Om Namash Shivaya forces of the universe.

Trinity Discussion & The Sound of OM

Brahma is the creator of all things. This energy is about ideas and values as well as our mission and purpose in this lifetime. *Brahma* helps us sow the seeds that can turn into great things. What would you like to create in the world? Where does your heart go out to? What moves you? Where are your values placed? Is it the health of our oceans and marine life? Is it saving endangered animals? Is it picking up trash and plastics that are polluting our Earth? Is it helping the sick? The impoverished? Homeless? The hungry? *Brahma is the sound of AHHHHHH.*

Vishnu is the preserver. He is known for his powerful, peaceful presence. He is the sustainer of all of life. He is about balance and peace. We have to find that happy medium of preserving our energy and maintaining good health and strength. Where in your life do you feel balanced? How do you replenish your energy? *Vishnu is the sound of OOOOOOO.*

Shiva is the lord of destruction. He is a powerful deity, destroying the things in life that do not serve anymore to make room for renewal, new creation, and higher levels of consciousness. He destroys negativity and illusion. An example of the natural process of this destruction is that the body completely transforms every single cell every seven years. Another example is forest fires. Fires deplete the forest yet allow the soil to become more fertile for new growth and beginnings. Sometimes destruction brings about new growth and positive change in our lives. Where do you see this in your life? What is not working? What is falling apart? *Shiva is the sound of MMMMM.*

Trinity *Practices*

Trinity Movement Meditation: Energy of the Universe

Make up a fiery sequence of dynamic yoga postures related to nature. Make up different movement meditations like the energies of the Gods—for example, *Shiva* dances in the ring of fire. Or become *Lord Shiva* and use your arms to dance in the ring of fire. How would *Vishnu* look in a yoga posture? *Brahma*? Listen to music, dancing and moving as though you were about to create the universe. Channel these incredible energies into your movement meditation.

Trinity Freeze Game

Have the kids move and dance freely to a song. When the song stops, you call out 'Three Elbows,' and three of the kids have to come together and touch elbows. Then play the music and allow them to be free and wild, stop the music and call out 'Three Knees,' and they have to connect three knees peacefully. Continue with different body parts.

Cycle of Life Meditation

Notice how our thoughts and feelings can change. Sometimes they are influenced by an experience or something someone has said. Sometimes they are something we see or feel directly. Sometimes it's time that changes the way we think with new information always coming in. These are the energies of *Brahma*, *Vishnu*, and *Shiva*. It's the cycle of life. A new thought comes in; we feed it and preserve it, and then it dies, just like nature. Reflect on those things you can see in your life that have also gone through this cycle of life. Now reflect on nature and see how she is in a constant state of transition.

Trinity Vision Meditation

Think of a goal or dream you have. Now, plan out how you will achieve that dream. Understand that the trinity energy is at work in this process—first, the idea (*Brahma*). Second, the means to get to the end (*Vishnu*). Then, the end result and perhaps the dissolving, shifting, destroying energy (*Shiva*). Maybe the end result is different from what you thought it might be.

Art Meditation with Brahma, Vishnu, and Shiva

Talk about the beginning of the universe and these compelling energies coming together to form planet Earth and all life as we know it. Find coloring sheets of these deities on the web and print them out for the younger kids to color. For older kids, it is nice to have a visual. Talk about the symbolism in the art and what these deities represent and hold in their hands.

Notes:

PART **4**

CHAPTER **8** (March)

Removing
the Obstacles

"In the middle of every difficulty lies an opportunity"
-Albert Einstein[1]

March: Removing the Obstacles, Ode to Ganesh

The Healing Practice of Yoga

Do your practice, and all is coming.
-B.K.S. Iyengar[2]

I love this quote by the yoga master, B.K.S. Iyengar. In my eyes, you can interpret it in many ways. First, with repetition and consistency, you can reap the benefits of your practice. As yoga practitioners, we know there are poses and perhaps elements of the physical practice that come more easily than others. Some of us may be naturally flexible, and some may have to work on it. Regardless of what you bring to the yoga mat, we can all experience lasting benefits with an open mind and steady practice. We cannot expect to touch our toes or still our thoughts within one day or one experience. It might take many. It might take lifetimes.

Another interpretation is that all is coming with a steady practice: the good, the bad, the crazy, and the chaotic. Once we begin our journey back to ourselves, the stories we have been telling ourselves, denial, untruths, past trauma can all resurface. The things in our lives we have never dealt with or healed from could also arise. Our past regrets, things left unfinished, might also bubble up as emotion, pain, and sensation in the body. As the mind stores memory, the body stores emotions, and when activated with breath and movement, old feelings can come to the forefront to be addressed. This is an incredible benefit of yoga, even though it may feel extremely uncomfortable and scary.

One of the many things that yoga does is connect us to our sensations. Embodied practices can be an incredible mirror to ourselves and our healing. These intentional movements can help us cultivate an awareness of our sensations, emotions, impulses, and the present moment. Connecting to our sensations and the parts of us that feel out of control is the real key to healing. It's the key on a physiological level.

If we refuse to feel and acknowledge those feelings, we cannot transform ourselves. If we can't feel our big emotions, we can't heal ourselves. Once we can connect to the intense feelings, we can use the breath and intentional movements to release the energy trapped in our bodies. Our capability for transformation is a direct outcome of the ability to face our stuff. When we take something uncomfortable and make it our own, we gain significant strength, knowledge, and power from it. With a willingness to stay present and bear witness to the unrefined attributes of ourselves, we enable transformation and healing.

This month we are dedicating ourselves to learning more about our beautiful and brilliant design. Our bodies and minds were built to deal with and heal from stress. Once we find resources to breathe into the wild rollercoaster of emotions, we will learn embodied ways to calm ourselves and create deep peace. Yoga gives us a matrix of solutions that feed, nourish, and support every stage of our lives. Yoga is a resource to transmute negativity into positivity. It's the action of regenerating love. It's also a constant remembrance of that true, divine self. Ultimately, the many practices of yoga give us powerful ways to remove the obstacles upon our paths.

In Lesson One, we look at the story of *Ganesh. Ganesh* is a symbol of strength and perseverance. He is the remover of all obstacles and has the power to help us rediscover our own inner power and resilience to move through tough times. In this lesson, there are breathing and movement practices that engage and ignite as well as art projects that are mindful and meditative.

In Lesson Two, we will uncover how stress can chip away at our health and well-being. There are wonderful practices and activities to introduce to your classroom that can help balance the nervous system and keep the mind and body connection present and peaceful.

In Lesson Three, we will learn about the amazing benefits of *yoga nidra* and how to teach this to your kids, your families, and your friends. We all need more relaxation in our lives!

In Lesson Four will uncover practices to actively dispel unwanted energy to clear the mind and feel deep, long-lasting peace, practicing equanimity

In Lesson Five, we honor the spring equinox in a sacred, intentional way. Enjoy!

Lesson One –
The Story of Ganesh

Ode to Ganesh: The Remover of Obstacles

The Lord of Good Fortune, *Ganesh* is one of the best known and beloved deities in the Hindu pantheon of Gods. *Ganesh* provides prosperity, luck, success, and abundance. He removes obstacles when they need to be and is willing to place obstacles to block those who need to be reminded of their humility. Also known as the Lord of Beginnings and the Remover of Obstacles, he symbolizes intellect and wisdom and highlights the growth that comes with every challenge. Followers of *Ganesh* believe that if you revere him, you'll find success, prosperity, and protection from hardship. *Ganesh* destroys vanity, selfishness, and pride. He can be used as a resource to ask for help in hard times. He is a symbol of letting things go that do not serve.

Yoga is about being in a relationship with all aspects of ourselves, learning our own individual lessons so we can be free from that which binds us. The energy of *Ganesh* is a resource for kids to use. There are valuable teachings and wisdom in every *Ganesh* experience. The lessons of *Ganesh* can help us confront anything blocking us from our highest potential. The teacher is everywhere. *Ganesh* can help us find meaning and symbolism in the most challenging of times.

Ganesh

Om Gam Ganapataye Namaha

The Story of Ganesh

There are many versions of this epic tale. This is the one I like to share with the children.

Once upon a time, there lived *Lord Shiva* and his wife the beloved Goddess, *Parvathi*. They lived in a beautiful palace with all the luxuries in the world. Despite this, *Parvathi* wasn't completely happy. She wanted to have a baby. *Lord Shiva* said they could not have a baby because he had to go to war. The next day, *Lord Shiva* was called to war and left the palace. *Parvathi* was very lonely and very desperate for a companion.

One day, *Parvathi* was getting ready for her bath and needed someone to guard her chamber. She made a beautiful young boy from clay and gave him life by sprinkling the holy water of the Ganges on him. She blew the breath of life into him, and, magically, the boy came to life. She entrusted him with guarding the door so she could take a luxurious bath in peace. As she soaked in her bath, *Lord Shiva* returned. A boy stood at the door to her room, blocking the entry.

Lord Shiva demanded, "Who are you, and why are you in my way?"

"This is my mother's chamber; no one may enter," the boy said.

Lord Shiva was shocked. "Get out of my way. This is my wife's room, and I have every right to be here."

The boy wouldn't move. He stood his ground with dignity, enraging *Lord Shiva*, who did not like to be disobeyed. *Lord Shiva* took his sword and cut off the boy's head.

When *Parvathi* finished her bath, she saw her dead son on the floor. Grief overtook her, and she cried out, "How could you do this to our son?"

"Our son? I did not know he was our son!" *Lord Shiva* sent out his soldiers to find the head of the first creature they could find. They rushed away.

Soon, they found a dead elephant. They removed its head and brought it to *Lord Shiva*, who attached it to the boy's body.

Parvathi breathed life back into the boy, and he magically drew in the life force, becoming alive again. Now he was part boy and part elephant. *Parvathi* named him *Ganesh*.

In an attempt to make up for his error, *Lord Shiva* promised *Parvathi* that *Ganesh* would be worshipped before all other Gods.

Even today, the idol of *Lord Ganesh*, the elephant-headed God, sits at the entrance to all temples. *Ganesh* is the Hindu God of beginnings and is revered all over India for his lighthearted ways, ambient being, intoxicating laugh, good nature, and immeasurable love of sweets. He is the most well-revered, benevolent God all over the world. Everyone loves *Ganesh* because he removes the obstacles and challenges in our way. He helps us see the antidote to our problems and gives us a light hearted sense to try and release struggle and control.

Ganesh *Practices*

Chant: *Om Gam Ganapataye Namaha*

Meditate with this *mantra* and allow all inner and outer obstacles to be removed from your divine path.

Sitting in a circle, guide the kids through an easy chant invoking the power of *Ganesh*. You can use a drum or any other musical instrument to enhance the experience. Chanting might seem intimidating at first, but don't worry! Chanting with kids is fun, and you will get over your fear of singing and doing something different quickly as they join in.

Ganesh Art

Draw, paint, and get creative with *Ganesh* art (use your imagination and make anything elephant-inspired).

Ganesh Story Time

There are so many wonderful and meaningful stories about *Ganesh*. The symbolism within these mythological tales is so rich for the kids. Dedicate a month to the wonderful and fun stories of *Ganesh* and honor his sweet, playful, and loving ways.

Yoga Flow

Start a yoga practice with the kids and introduce the story of *Ganesh*. Move, flow, and breathe through this exciting drama during story time yoga.

Ganesh Altar Meditation

Revisit the altar created in December LESSON ONE. Refresh it with the energy of *Ganesh*. Since he is the remover of obstacles, we can honor *Ganesh* when we sit down and reflect on the things that might be blocking us from our ultimate potential. *Ganesh* is also very grounding and can help clear the mind and balance our energies. He reminds us to take ourselves lightly and to have fun.

Place items on the altar that bring great peace and joy like a picture of *Ganesh*, a sentimental item, or even a fresh piece of fruit or some flowers. The kids can bring in a special item from home for their makeshift altar in the yoga classroom. They could also go outside and grab something from the Earth.

Sit facing the altar and clear the mind for three to five minutes. If the mind feels busy, then ask these questions: How can I serve? What do I need to know today? What are my body and mind craving? What needs nourishing? What needs releasing? After sitting in meditation and contemplation, send prayers and blessings out to all living beings. Thank your altar and *Ganesh* for listening to your heart.

Lesson Two – Stress Less

Stress and our Nervous System

Stress, a part of life, is a reaction we all can learn from. We all handle stress differently. It's how we deal with it that matters. Giving children the tools to deal with life's stressful situations is one of the most important things we can share with them. To do this, we must understand how our nervous system works within our body and what we can do to control it.

In a well-regulated central nervous system, we experience activation in the (sympathetic nervous system or SNS) and discharge (parasympathetic nervous system or PNS) on a continuum. However, most of us either get caught up on the high end of stress, where we can't sit still and are anxious, or the low end of stress, where we feel depressed and can't motivate ourselves to get going. When we are constantly stimulated by stress, the SNS is on high alert all the time. We begin to experience fearbased impulses: fight, flight, or freeze.

As the SNS guides our involuntary responses to stressful or dangerous situations, a flood of hormones rushes through our bodies, increasing alertness, heart rate, and blood flow to muscles. Other effects of this system include an opening of bronchial airways, decreased digestion, constricted blood vessels, dilated pupils, goose bumps, sweating, and increased blood pressure. All these stress responses plus an increase in stress hormones like cortisol and adrenaline can, over time, wreak havoc on the body's internal organs and the mind's ability to relax and come back into balance.

The PNS works to undo the responses triggered by the SNS. It calms the body and restores normal function. The PNS decreases respiration and heart rate and increases digestion. It also conserves energy to be used at a later time. Embodied practices that restore and replenish the PNS can help keep the body regulated. With tools like breathing, centering, grounding, and working through the discomfort, we have ways to release and discharge the energy so it doesn't get stuck. Ultimately, we become more resilient and conditioned, better prepared for the next stressors that come our way.

Balancing the Nervous System

Conscious breathing is one of the best ways to affect the nervous system. Breathing not only helps to increase energy and vitality but to calm and soothe the mind and body. Breathing can instantly help us feel better and can shift our mood as well as fatigue and achiness in the body. The amount of oxygen we inhale through our breathing influences the amount of energy released into our cells. The more we breathe deeply, the better we feel because the cells are being nourished and saturated with life. These stress reducing breathing techniques also help strengthen the elasticity in the lungs and can help boost the immune system and help with overall energy to feel clear and focused.

Balancing the Nervous System *Practices*

Boxed Breathing

The breath is a reflection of the mind. The slower we breathe, the calmer the mind.

Inhale four counts in and hold for four, exhale for four counts and hold for four. This breathing technique slows the mind and emotions down and creates focus and determination. It also relaxes the body and helps release anxiety. This great breathing technique to replenish the lungs and the lung tissue.

Nervous System Reset

You can use as many equally inhaled and exhaled breath counts as you wish. I like to use between four to seven counts with the kids. In this practice below, I will be using five.

Inhale five counts in and exhale five counts out. Do this breathing for five minutes in the morning when you first wake up. Do it for five minutes before you go to sleep and five minutes somewhere in the day. Over time, this breathing really calms the central nervous system and gives the body a chance to come back into balance

Six Belly Breaths

Sit or lie down and get comfortable. Feel the breath move into the lower belly. Take six deep, slow, low, belly breaths. This breathing technique helps relax the vagus nerve, the primary nerve from the belly to the brain, and enables tension to release from the heart. It also allows the organs to become saturated with breath and helps turn on the parasympathetic nervous system. Great for stress reduction, anxiety, and overwhelming feelings. Deep breathing reduces cortisol levels in the body.

Lesson Three – Yoga Nidra

The Power of Yoga Nidra

Another way we can move through blockages and shift our energy at will is through the powerful practice of *yoga nidra*. *Yoga nidra* is an ancient method of relaxation and meditation. It is practice using breath, visualization, and awareness techniques to restore and reset the body physically, mentally, and spiritually, returning us to a sense of wholeness. *Yoga nidra* can help to dispel our old beliefs and negative patterning in the subconscious mind, as well as restore and revitalize our very nature. Designed by yogic sages to purify the *samskaras*—the imprints left on the subconscious mind by experience—*yoga nidra* provides the opportunity to observe the subconscious mind consciously.

Yoga nidra can be a powerful and effective practice for everyone, and a wonderful way to introduce meditation to kids. Through a guided awareness of the physical body, you are ushered toward a state of deep relaxation while remaining completely aware of all that is occurring within you and around you. In this type of meditation, you are guided on a journey through different layers (*koshas*) of consciousness. You move through different brain states from beta into alpha and essentially, into theta. Some people fall asleep as they enter into the delta state. This is perfectly fine because your body needs the sleep and your subconscious is still listening.

In Sanskrit, *nidra* means sleep. *Yoga nidra* translates as yogic sleep or psychic sleep. When the mind starts to focus on the meditation itself, relaxation takes place. Remaining aware and awake while progressing through all states of consciousness has many therapeutic benefits and is a key tool to develop self-awareness. It is said that twenty minutes of practice is equivalent to four hours of restful sleep. Over time, *yoga nidra* practice is a resource to feel more energy and balance in your life.

Yoga nidra is a meditation exercise that trains the brain to focus and pay attention. Practicing *yoga nidra* is a powerful way to set intentions. Your intention becomes anchored as positive statement is recited at the beginning and the end of *yoga nidra* practice. Ultimately, *yoga nidra* practice becomes a place to clarify, strengthen, and manifest your highest intention as you release old, debilitating thoughts and beliefs. All of this is achieved through the development of a clear intention or a *sankalpa*. As you move through the various levels of consciousness, the power of the intention will make an imprint on your psyche.

The Sutras of Patanjali discussed *yoga nidra*. Patanjali said, "The purpose of yoga is to still the wave of the mind. Then the seer is established in his/her true nature. At other times, the seer takes on the form of the fluctuations. The cause of our suffering is forgetting our true nature."[3]

The Benefits of Yoga Nidra

- Calms the nervous system by turning on the PNS
- Slows heart rate
- Regulates breath
- Dilates blood vessels
- Sends blood to the digestive system and brain
- Lowers cortisol levels
- Decreases lactic acid levels and reduces muscle tension
- A twenty minute *yoga nidra* practice is equivalent to four to five hours of deep sleep
- Helps with insomnia, chronic pain, chemical dependency, anxiety, depression, post-traumatic stress disorder (PTSD)
- *Yoga nidra* boosts these hormones: serotonin (feel good), dopamine (pleasure and reward), GABA (brain calming, memory boosting), melatonin
- *Yoga nidra* boosts t-cells (immune defense)
- Adds a deep calm to everyday life
- Encourages positive perspective
- Awakens inner intelligence
- Increases intuition and self-confidence
- Repairs negative thought patterns and perspectives
- Moves through the brain states of Beta (awake state), into Alpha (brain slows), into Theta (where all the magic and healing happen), and sometimes Delta (deep sleep)
- Every time we go into a relaxed space, healing takes place

Yoga Nidra Script for Kids Ages 3—6

- Focus on the breath.
- Focus on the breath moving to different body parts: face, brain, head, eyes, nose, ears, mouth, chin, neck, heart, shoulders, elbows, hands, belly, back, hips, knees, ankles, and feet.
- Feel the body rise like a feather blowing in the wind.
- Feel the body melt like a chocolate bar on a sidewalk on a hot sunny day.
- Use a stuffed animal or block and feel the belly lift that object up and feel it relax and release.
- Count backward from ten all the way down to one.
- Now see yourself doing something that you love: skating, swimming, painting, sleeping, surfing, dancing, skiing, snowboarding.
- Feel the joy, the love, the excitement of whatever you are doing, and breathe that emotion into your heart space.
- Now visualize a balloon, tennis ball, surfboard, cupcakes, presents, ocean, parrot, kangaroo, Sun, Moon, flower, rainbow.

- Bring yourself back to the breath and think of one thing that you love about yourself.

- Now think of one thing that you are grateful for.

- Now send one person in your life a wish, a prayer, or a big hug.

- Now send that love to the whole planet, every living being, and creature.

Yoga Nidra Script for Kids Ages 7—10

- Bring your awareness of breath into the heart. Feel that breath expand your heart with love.

- Bring your breath now to your third eye and feel a peaceful light relax between your two eyes.

- Send light out from your third eye and expand it around your body like a bubble of light.

- Now in that circle of light, I want you to think of a time that made you so incredibly happy. It could be a kiss from your puppy, a friend's laughter, playing outside, a gift that was given to you, a delicious cake, winning in a game, or scoring great on a test. Now fill your bubble of light with that positive emotion. Really feel that energy surrounding your whole body and senses.

- Now bring your awareness back to your heart and create an intention or an open heart invitation that you would like to bring into your life. State whatever you want into your life with assertiveness. For example, *I read incredibly well, I love to do math, I am so good at soccer, I am strong, I am flexible, I am amazing. I am smart. I am healthy. I am beautiful.*

- Now bring your attention to your head, hair, scalp, face, eyes, ears, mouth, nose.

- Bring attention to both hands, elbows, shoulders, heart, ribcage, belly, back, hips, buttocks.

- Bring your awareness to both legs, knees, ankles, and feet.

- Now breathe into your entire body from head to toe, heart to hands.

- You are going to count backward from ten all the way to one. Inhale into the heart ten, exhale ten, inhale nine, exhale nine . . .

- Now wherever you are with your counting, stop, and we will do this again, but this time we will count back from fifteen. Inhale into belly fifteen, exhale fifteen, inhale fourteen, exhale fourteen to one. If you lose count, start all over again.

- Now, remember a time when you felt extremely hot.

- Now, remember a time you felt very cold.

- Now feel weightless as if a big fluffy cloud was beneath you and floating you up toward the stars.

- Now feel as if a ten-pound weight was put on you, and you were sinking all the way down, down, down to the ocean floor.

- Now feel a time when you were so happy and carefree and breathe in that elation and joy.

- Bring your awareness to the third eye center.

- Picture yourself walking through dense rainforest. With every step, the leaves crackle underneath your feet. You smell the thick, musky rain, and the dew is dripping off every tree. Open the ears to the sounds in the rainforest: the birds, the animals, the insects. Start to notice a break in the canopy and take your gaze upwards to the light in the sky between the dense vegetation. See the light mixed with the blue hue of the sky. Feel the warmth of that sunlight streaming down onto your face. Keep walking until you see a clearing, and you lay down on the soft earth with a small log that fits perfectly under your head. You close your eyes and start to drift away into a deep sleep.

- Now bring your awareness back to the breath and to your body and bring the awareness to that third eye center again.

- Visualize green grass, tan sand, blue ocean, red starfish, purple flower, blue skateboard, yellow banana, pink rabbit, brown book, silver moon, black ball, turquoise star.

- Now bring awareness back to the breath and the body, and as you stare with the third eye, see if you can extend that gaze with the eyes closed to about a few inches in front of your eyes. Notice how it looks like a fuzzy TV screen and picture the colors morphing into each other from black to red to blue to purple. Just stare into that empty space and relax the brain more and more. See if you can just focus on the colors and release any thoughts in the mind. If thoughts come in, just recognize them, and then place them on a floating lotus flower and see that flower drift down that stream further and further away from your body and mind. See if you can just be in that space without having any thoughts.

- Now bring your awareness back to your breath and think of a new and vibrant energy you would like to invite into your life. Think of something that you would like to manifest into your life, like a goal, a dream, a vision.

- Now think of it as if it has happened already and fill your body with tremendous gratitude.

- Now think of something that you really love about yourself.

- Think of a wish or prayer for someone else.

- Make a wish for planet Earth.

- Thank yourself for taking this time on your mat today.

Lesson Four – Equanimity

Equanimity is the ability to stay calm, composed, and peaceful at all times, even when faced with the most challenging situations. This is a difficult skill that can take a lifetime to master. Every day of our life and every situation is something we can we can learn from. Each experience provides us with wisdom for the next. Every experience, every situation is an opportunity to practices equanimity.

Practicing Equanimity

In these practices, we will learn to dispel unwanted feelings when they arise. These practices are important to do with the kids when they know they are experiencing stress.

Kriya Deep Breathing for Change

We learned about two body *kriya* practices in the Third Limb— *Asana* chapter in September. This *kriya* below deals with only the breath, the body is relaxed. It is an effective breathing practice to set up for meditation. I learned this breathwork through the Art of Living Foundation.

Kriya means to eliminate or burn off. This breathing increases the *tapas* (heat in the body) that burns away impurities, not only physically but mentally and emotionally. Whatever doesn't serve you in the highest is released through this breathing technique. This breath practice is a powerful oxygenator, so slow down or stop, if you start to feel dizzy or light headed. This feeling is a natural result of increasing the breath. In the end, it creates an incredible euphoria that is wonderful to bask in for meditation.

Notice you might feel a little dizzy or lightheaded. This is a natural sign of oxygenation. If you do, just minimize the breaths. This breathing detoxes the body and helps dislodge blockages. Start with just one round. Work up to two to three. Lying down after breathing has a very good grounding effect. Enjoy the clearing sensations this breathing brings on after you are done.

One full round of this breathing entails three different speeds of a breathing technique called bhastrika. We learned about the bhastrika breathing technique in October.

1. Breathe nice, slow, deep breaths into the belly. When you inhale, the belly expands, and when you exhale, the belly draws in, navel to spine. Slow down the breathing and take five to ten breaths just like this.

2. Inhale and exhale now, just a little bit faster. Inhale, push the belly out with a little more force and exhale, drawing the belly in. Repeat for twenty to fifty breaths.

3. Begin to inhale and exhale now as fast as you can, with the belly still expanding on inhale and drawing in on exhale. Breathe as fast as you can for twenty to fifty or so breaths.

4. Repetition- Now slow down and repeat steps one to three for two more rounds. You can also just do one round of this and lie down and relax—great breath for prepping to sit for meditation.

Bedtime Reprogramming the Brain *Meditation*

Right before bedtime is a good time for positive reflection. Sometimes, instead of reflecting on the good, we reflect on the not-so-good, things we regret, or the things we can't change. Then, we go to bed with these draining, negative thoughts stored in our subconscious. We may have nightmares or anxious dreams.

Choosing only positive thoughts before drifting to sleep is most beneficial for creating positive synapsis in the brain and creating positive outcomes in the days ahead. Affirmations can create a more positive self-view and build resilience. Priming the brain for positivity, especially right before bed as your brainwaves go into Alpha state, can help decrease anxiety and help with deeper sleep.

Before bedtime, think of all the things that are wonderful and beautiful in your life. Honor all the qualities about yourself that you love. Think of positive things, listen to calming music, find gratitude, listen to a *yoga nidra*, or do some deep breathing to fall asleep peacefully.

Being Aware — Which wolf are you feeding?

Sometimes we are not aware of the wolf we are feeding. When we get into bad habits, we become mindless to our thoughts and go right into automatic. Over time, this creates a series of negative thinking and behavior. The only way to change is to awaken and become aware of what we are telling ourselves or the negative patterning we are experiencing.

An old Cherokee teaches his grandchild about life.

"I feel a terrible fight inside me," he says to the child. *"Two wolves battle within."* The grandchild asks, *"Which wolf will win?"* The old Cherokee simply replies, *"The one you feed."*[4]

Being Aware *Practice*

Have the kids write down or talk about any negative feelings they are having. Practice letting it go with big inhales into those emotions, and big exhales of release. Now find the opposite emotion to what they are feeling and inhale those positive sensations throughout the whole body and exhale, feeling more relaxed and at ease, peaceful, and happy.

Discharging Energy — Shaking it Off

We are the only animals that do not shake off or dispel negative energy right after a stressor. All other animals in the animal kingdom have ways to discharge and release energy right after a triggering event. Whether we are running from a lion or engaged in a heated argument, if we do not consciously release that tension, we often carry it with us. As time goes on, those emotions can feel very heavy and debilitating. We often start living in that hyper state of awareness (SNS), and our bodies and minds break down. This practice is a resource for shaking off stress.

Discharging Energy *Practices*

Whole Body Shake:
Begin with your feet hipdistance apart or wider. Shake your hands vigorously, as if you were shaking water off. Let that movement move up into the arms and shoulders. Keep your knees slightly bent as you start to shake now through the whole body, still really focusing on the hands to release any pent-up emotion or cleansing any unwanted feelings. This will also stimulate the *chi* in the body and get the blood circulating and breath moving, having an overall relaxing effect on the whole body.

Shaking Off Tension in the Jaw:
Take your hands together in front of the chest, palm to palm. Relax your jaw and inhale, and on the exhale, let the breath out with a deep *AHHH* sound, shaking the palms together to start to rattle and shake the jaw. Shake and repeat three times. As the sound exhales out, feel loose, easy, comfortable, and relaxed in that jaw as if you were cleansing the throat *chakra* energy as well as any tension in the ears, cheeks, face, and head. This deep sigh with the shaking movement in the jaw is great for clearing the energy in the throat for clear communication.

Channeling Our Inner Poet

Inspire the kids with your favorite poetry. Read a poem while the kids are in *savasana*. For example, I love this poem by Rumi called *The Guest House*. I have read it over and over in all my teen and adult classes. Every feeling, emotion, and experience has a hidden meaning that can ultimately help us become more present, grateful, and loving. Our feelings teach us something about ourselves. We can learn a lot through stress and hardship. We also have a choice in either taking those emotions on or choosing to release them. All in all, recognize that there is a teaching in everything.

Allow the kids to bring in their favorite poems. Talk about the meaning and the feelings those words bring up for you. Have the kids get in touch with their feelings and/or something meaningful in their lives and have them make up their own poems to share. Writing poems are incredible resources to resolve and release emotions and experiences.

Dance Therapy — Ecstatic Dance Yoga Freeze Game

The song *Who Let the Dogs Out* by Baha Men is always fun and a terrific way to discharge negativity. When the song plays, the kids dance freely and spontaneously. When the music stops, the kids freeze. Now add a yoga pose to freeze in, the next time the music stops. It could be a tree pose, a butterfly pose, or any posture you can think of. You might have to demonstrate it. When the music plays, you can get goofy and have a great time. The song never gets old!

Lesson Five – Spring Equinox

The equinox in the spring and the fall are great ways to invoke balance back into our lives. It provides a chance to reconnect to the Earth, our life, and our daily practice. Embodied practice like Sun salutations and Moon salutations gives us a chance to use our bodies and minds as a vehicle for prayer and devotion. It is another auspicious time of reflection and renewal.

When the Sun positions itself directly over the equator, and the hours of daylight and darkness are almost equal, that is the equinox. In autumn, the equinox indicates the beginning of shorter days and longer nights. In the spring, the nights become shorter and the days longer. Honoring these *sandhyas* (sacred junctures) in time and space is a fun and inspiring way to reconnect with the Earth and the calendar like our ancestors did.

Surya namaskar and the origin of prostrations came about as an offering and devotion to the Sun. Every morning at dawn, the yogis would move in devotional and loving ways to honor and hold gratitude for the nourishment they received. However, each morning as they moved their bodies in prayer, they did not know that the Sun would rise. These bowing movements and observances gave way to an appreciation of the miracles and cycles of life that arose each day. In yoga, they are a traditional form of movement and flow.

- *Nama* is to bow.

- *Namaskar*—Bow to the energy in which you are cultivating.

- *Surya Namaskar*—Bow to the energy of the Sun (melting, heating, destroying)—Heating Sun Flow.

- *Chandra Namaskar*—bow to the qualities of the Moon (receptive, cooling, nourishing)—Cooling Moon Flow.

- *Sahaja Flow* is practice within the *asanas* connecting to the underlying creative intelligence. It's an instinctual flow that helps connect to the internal rhythms.

Sacred Movements for Peace

Yoga Mala

Yoga Mala was inspired by my teacher Shiva Rea. This movement meditation is most potent when practiced on a high energy day or around a seasonal shift. On the spring equinox, guide a practice of *pranams* or Sun salutations with intention and purpose. You can also use the auspicious number 108. With the kids, I like to do a derivative of 108 like 72, 36, 27, 9, etc. Add gratitude, appreciation, and love into every part of the flow. These are great questions to ask yourself or the class you are leading your *yoga mala*:

What am I balancing in my life? What am I grounding in? What is alive, present, and peaceful in my life?

With these practices below, honor the Earth, the balances of light, the beginning of the spring season, and the beauty and bounty that will flourish with new seeds of intention.

Turn to the June chapter for a more detailed explanation on how you can guide your own *yoga mala*.

Sun and Wind Blessing

Sun: Standing with feet wider than hip-distance apart, inhale while raising your arms up toward the Sun. Draw the rays down over the body as your arms cascade down to your sides. Inhale again, and with arms sweeping forward and up, pour that immense, healing light over your body. Feel this light cleanse and purify the body.

Wind: Sway the arms from side to side. With your knees bent, move and groove your body back and forth from one foot to the other like wind blowing through the trees. Feel the energy of the wind move your breath. Breathe as you find gentle movements that feel free and open. Move in whichever way wish, feeling the air support your every step, every sway, every breath. Feel the healing, spontaneous movement bring you back into your body and mind.

Prayer Wheel

Take one foot forward and one foot back into a basic *Tai Chi* stance. Place your fingers at heart level and, as you inhale, take the hands forward and out from the heart. Circle them down in front of you on the exhale and shift the weight into the back foot. Inhale as the arms scoop from the base *chakra* or tailbone area and have the fingers move up the spine toward the heart as you move the weight into the front foot. You are essentially creating an energetic circle, drawing the *chi* from the Earth, up your spine toward the heart, and expanding it out and back down.

Spring Equinox Projects

Prayer Stick Art and Meditation Project

Go on a nature hike and have the kids choose a stick. Bring it back to the classroom and have the kids notice that stick: the perfections and imperfections, the roughness and smoothness. Honor everyone's unique piece. Decorate them with ribbon, feathers, flowers, vines, or crystals until the stick is covered. Use the meditation stick as an anchor for meditation.

Hold it in your hands and feel deeply connected to the Earth. Feel the breath move along the limbs, breathing into all parts of your being. Sit with your breath and feel as if you were a tree, rooted yet free-flowing in the winds of the breath. Use the stick to anchor your energy.

Crystal Meditation

Sit or lie down, placing a crystal on your body or around your body. Focus on the energy of the crystal, drawing light within and around the body, protecting it like a force field. Crystal healing will be elaborated on in the month of July.

Sage Bundles or Earth Bundles

Gather some dried sage or any dried herbs from the Earth. Also, gather twine or embroidery thread and any small, flat, and skinny rock or crystal. You can also dry flower petals to use on top of the sage but under the rock/crystal. Wrap the rock/crystal with twine or thread. With an adult, carefully burn in a fire-safe dish.

Flower or Nature Crowns

Gather flowers and things on the ground from the Earth. Get a piece of twine to wrap and tie the flowers and earth items into the twine to make a crown.

PART **5**

Loving the Earth, Loving our Bodies

"Remember to love. Everything, everyone, yourself, the world around you. That is the work. Because if you can be with that love, embrace it, own it, and let it influence all the ways you are in the world, then you will know God, you will be home, and peace in every way possible will be your contribution to this life."

-Seane Corn[1]

April: Loving the Earth, Loving our Bodies

April is a month of self-discovery, self-awareness, and of honoring our contribution to making this world a better, more peaceful place. It's a time for learning about different ways to fall in love with oneself, over and over again. It's an opportunity to reconnect to the magic of nature and know that we can make an impact. When we learn ways to take better care of ourselves, we feel more inspired to take care of our planet. Self-care is the only way we can sustain and maintain this busy, fast-paced life.

Earth Day is on April 22nd. This is a time to honor the Earth and commit to keeping our planet healthy and vibrant. By being aware of our role in and impact on the world, we can inspire and educate others to take action. Knowledge is power. Nature is one of our greatest teachers. We can look upon her for guidance, energy, support, and bounty. Yet, when she suffers, so do we. We are so intertwined.

"You have to create love and affection for your body, for what it can do for you. Love must be incarnated in the smallest pore of the skin, the smallest cell in the body, to make them intelligent, so they can collaborate with all the other ones in the big republic of the body. This love must radiate from you to others."
-B.K.S. Iyengar[2]

This month, we will be learning more about ourselves and our unique environments. We will be exploring topics that generate healthy and sustainable habits. *Lessons on Nature, The Power of the Mind, Sacred Water, Ayurveda, Anatomy, Vital Organs, and Knowledge of the Energetic Systems (koshas, bandhas, and chakras)* will give your students an increased self-awareness and tools for them to design their unique self-care routines. The more we know how to take care of ourselves, the more we have to give to the world. This chapter is full of ideas for reconnecting ourselves to the Earth through embodied practices, breathing, meditation, *seva*, and art. Yoga philosophy has so much rich knowledge to offer us. Learning to listen to our bodies and becoming aware of our thoughts is the first step to healing.

Lesson One – Yoga and Nature

"Love the Earth and Sun and animals . . . dismiss whatever insults your own soul, and your very flesh shall be a great poem and have the richest fluency not only in its words but in the silent lines of its lips and face and between the lashes of your eyes and in every motion of your body."
-Walt Whitman[3]

Nature is supremely powerful. As beings of nature, our union with that power is real. The production of hormones and chemicals in our brains and bodies are dictated by the cycles of the Sun and Moon. Similarly, our health and wellness depend on our nutrition, sleep, and how grounded and connected we feel to nature, to that power around us. We now can measure electrons moving up into the body when we walk bare foot in the grass. The Earth's energy becomes and natural antioxidant. The healing power of the Earth is real and an easy way to boost our vitality.

As such magnificent beings, our impact on the world is significant. When we take the time to experience deep connections with nature, honor our resources, and take care of our land, it is a beautiful give-and-take cycle. This connection and commitment to the Earth can benefit us both.

Taking Care of Mother Earth

Sustainability is an important discussion to introduce to the kids. Sustainability is how we as humans interact with the environment to allow resources to remain for future generations. Every day we make big choices that can lead to huge impacts. We must be responsible in our decisions about the products we use and how we rely on natural resources such as food, water, plants, and minerals. We hope to live sustainably and allow the planet to continue to support people for many generations to come.

Our planet depends on us. We are all interconnected. There are small ways that we can start to create tremendous change. By creating habits and routines for our children, we are one step closer to educating the masses about sustainable living.

We can celebrate the Earth by being aware of our roles in keeping the planet alive and healthy. Everyday can be Earth Day!

Teaching Children How to Love the Earth

- Recycle paper to help save trees. Trees make our air breathable, provide resources for homes for animals and humans, and provide beauty around us.

- Limit the use of single use plastic. Use your own nonplastic or multiuse shopping bags. If you're eating out, bring reusable utensils. Plastics tend to end up in the oceans, making birds and marine life very sick.

- Recycle glass bottles to reduce greenhouse gases and save resources.

- Try to fix things instead of tossing them away. Be conscious and conservative.

- Turn out lights to save energy.

- Conserve water. Put a bucket in your shower and use the water you collect outside on a plant.

- Compost your kitchen waste for your garden.

- When shopping, choose environmentally friendly products first.

- Prevent water waste by turning off taps while not using the water.

- Think about what you need rather than what you want.

- Carpool with friends or ride the bike to school and sports.

- Organize beach, park, or school cleanups with all the kids in the neighborhood.

Nature and Yoga

There are so many teaching opportunities within the yoga *asanas*. Most yoga postures mimic nature and create a platform to educate kids on the importance of the Earth and habitat while exploring ideas of becoming one with the animals and their unique ecosystems. We can embody healing movements and learn about our environment at the same time. As we learn more about taking care of ourselves, we will become more empowered advocates for keeping nature alive and healthy. In these resources below, allow your students to dictate the things that matter most for them. Make these earth-friendly discussions, art, and meditations a way to share that love and peace inwardly and outwardly.

*"Every morning we are born again.
It's what we do today that matters most."*
-Gautama Buddha[4]

Seva *Practice*

Host an Earth Day-inspired clean-up. Clean up trash in your local park or beach. Rake the leaves in your neighbor's yard. Water your garden. Plant a tree or flowers.

Earth Day Tree *Art Project*

Draw your own tree. Talk about how trees are beautiful and unique just the way they are. Trees give off oxygen that feeds us. We breathe in oxygen and breathe out carbon dioxide to feed all of the trees. We are interconnected. Notice your surroundings, the Earth beneath you, and where you are on the planet. Certain trees grow specific to their environments and ecosystems. Talk about ways to keep trees healthy. Talk about the ways in which trees are endangered. What natural resources can we use instead of chopping down trees? In each leaf, draw ways you will dedicate to making this planet cleaner, brighter, and more sustainable. For example, recycle/reuse/reduce.

Earth Day Pots

Get little pots for the kids to paint. Bring seeds and starting mix. Have the kids plant a seed in their pots and make a wish for planet Earth

Animal *Yoga*

This is a fun practice to do with kids ages 3—10. Have them bring stuffed animals and create a yoga flow where they can incorporate the animals on their bodies during practice. For example, in tree pose, have the kids balance the stuffed animal on their head or knee, or in downward dog, have the kids place the animal on their backs for balance.

Allow the kids to have fun, make up an individual or partner yoga routine with their animals.

Allow the kids to share a story about their animals or fun facts about their animals as you practice yoga together.

Stuffed Animal *Meditation*

Talk about how animals meditate. Do they find peace in a cave, by a lake, under the grass, or in a hole? Talk about how animals sleep. What do they look like? Are they curled up, snuggled up, or stretched out? Now place a stuffed animal on your body or near your body and concentrate on feeling at peace and at ease. What animal are you, and how do you relax? Mimic that feeling and sensation in the body and do a short relaxation with your animal, giving prayers out that every animal gets good, safe, and restful sleep.

Animal Spirit Cards

Have the children pick a card from a deck of animal cards. I like to use the ones from Medicine Cards by Jamie Sams and David Carson. Talk about what superpower each spirit animal is giving you. You can also have the kids meditate on what their spirit animal would be and discuss what that animal is empowering in their life. Allow the kids to make up a yoga routine dedicated to their animal spirit. Kids also love to draw their spirit animal.

Nature Visualizations

Take your kids or students through outer space, an underwater ocean, jungle, forest, desert, mountains, or rainforest meditation. Guide them through a visualization of doing things that they love, like fishing, hiking, swimming, dancing, surfing, etc.

Nature Walk

Take a nature walk and spend five minutes either mindfully walking barefoot, sitting watching the clouds, laying down listening to the sounds, breathing in the universe, or dancing joyously with your surroundings. Soak in this infinite love. Feel the Earth's energy filling your body and soul.

Bhramari Breath - The Bee Breath

Bhramari, the Sanskrit word for bee. *Bhramari Pranayama* (also known as Bumblebee Breath) soothes the nervous system and has an overall calming effect. This *pranayama* gets its name because of the humming sound emanating from the back of the throat and the resemblance to a buzzing bee. Breathing this way relieves stress, anger, and frustration. It also helps calm the mind and body before going to sleep or in a stressful situation.

This breathing exercise also allows for deeper conversation to unfold about the importance of bees and our ecosystem. Bees are our biggest pollinators and provide high quality food and medicinal products like honey, royal jelly, beeswax, propolis and bee venom. We depend on bees for our survival. This is a great topic to explore with your students.

When you're finished with this cycle, consider how your body has changed. How has your mind changed? Do you feel more spiritually charged, or have the sensations in your body shifted? When you're ready, open your eyes and continue to absorb that awareness you've gained.

Bhramari *Breath Practice*

Begin in a comfortable position, perhaps cross-legged on the floor, and elevate your hips just slightly. You can also sit toward the front of a chair, feet flat on the floor. Elongate your spine. Close your lips, keeping your teeth slightly apart, and put the tip of your tongue in the space just behind your upper front teeth. Keep your jaw relaxed.

- Take a deep breath in through your nostrils, pulling your breath all the way into your belly. Lower your chin to your chest and slowly exhale. Make a steady, low-pitched hum, buzzing sound or '*ngg*' sound at the back of your throat, like a bee. As you exhale, bring your awareness toward the third eye.

- Now, slowly raise your head and straighten your neck and breathe normally. Keep the eyes still closed and feel this peaceful feeling permeate throughout your entire being. Begin the process again up to seven times.

Honoring the Four Directions *Meditation*

Sit and place four items like a rock, crystal, flower, or stuffed animal in all directions around your body like a square. Sit in the middle of that square and take your awareness to the four directions around your body. Honor these powerful navigational tools of the north, south, east, and west. This is fun to do outside where you can gather objects from the Earth like a leaf, flower, rock, or piece of bark and place them around you in the four directions. Feel the sacred circle holding your prayers for peace..

Honoring the Four Directions *Meditation*

Sit and place four items like a rock, crystal, flower, or stuffed animal in all directions around your body like a square. Sit in the middle of that square and take your awareness to the four directions around your body. Honor these powerful navigational tools of the north, south, east, and west. This is fun to do outside where you can gather objects from the Earth like a leaf, flower, rock, or piece of bark and place them around you in the four directions. Feel the sacred circle holding your prayers for peace..

Oneness with Nature *Meditation*

Relax in either a restorative posture with props supporting your body or a seated meditation. Inhale and exhale, feeling each breath as a continuation of one other. The inhale flows into the exhale and vice versa as if the breath was one long-sung note.

Feel the body rise on the inhale and, as you exhale, relax deeper into the Earth. Feel your body merging into Mother Earth. As you become more aware of the exhalations, feel your whole body energetically expanding into the ground.

You can imagine a green *bindi*, or spark of light, at the heart starting to shine and spread out into the room, then out into nature and beyond. Feel your presence and awareness as that green spark or bindi of heart space merges out of the area, city, county, state into the vast ethers of the entire planet.

Feel your awareness move through rivers, streams, oceans, mountains, hills, dams, deserts, jungle, rainforests, and through the planet. Feel a deep peace as you bless each being with light, each part of nature with your inherent goodness, your love for all of humanity, gentle kindness, and unconditional love. Feel it penetrate throughout every image that comes to mind.

When you finish exploring consciousness in the most peaceful way, allow the breath to bring you back into your body. Inhale that awareness of the green light of peace and love back toward your heart. Bring that oneness and compassion back toward your whole self. Bask in this state of being present, feeling unity and peace, seeing the entire world as perfect just the way it is. Honor yourself for taking this exploration and sending light to every being, every creature on the planet. Feel that love come back to yourself.

Lesson Two – Mind Power

The Power of Thought

"And I said to my body softly, 'I want to be your friend.' It took a long breath and replied, 'I have been waiting my whole life for this.'"
-Nayyirah Waheed[5]

Our thoughts are powerful, as is the mind, body, and spirit connection. What is important for all of us to understand, especially the youth, is that our thoughts directly affect our wellness. Being positive and gracious is just as important as eating well and exercising. Our mindset and treatment of ourselves both mentally and emotionally carries profound physical effects. Mindfulness gives us an awareness of our thoughts and the attention to choose the energies we invite into our lives.

Japanese scientist, Dr. Masaru Emoto, studied how thoughts and intentions impact our physical lives. He conducted experiments on water's molecular structure and how human words, thoughts, sounds, and intentions affected the composition of the water.[6] He found that when water was exposed to loving, compassionate, positive intentions, the water formed beautiful molecular formations. When subjected to fear, anger, or negative human intention, the water appeared disfigured or unpleasant.

Dr. Emoto wrote about this phenomenon in his book *Messages in Water*.[6] He also showed how positive emotions and feelings can repair damaged water from pollution and toxins. With evidence from magnetic resonance imaging (MRI) technology, Dr. Emoto demonstrated the power of thought by taking polluted water and restoring it to a beautiful composition using only prayer, beautiful words and positive intention.[6]

I love using Dr. Emoto's research to inspire my classes. The power of human thought, sound, and intention have an enormous impact on the water element everywhere. Ultimately, we can transform our own chemistry and internal vibration with the power of thought and willpower. Not only can we become conscious of the thoughts we are feeding ourselves, but we have the power to help heal globally with prayer.

Bringing this awareness to kids at an early age can help stop negative thinking and self-talk, comparing, judging, and criticizing, or at least help them to become aware of those negative emotions. When we can catch ourselves with mindless thoughts that don't serve and add thoughts of gratitude and kindness, it can not only change how we feel about ourselves, but it can shift how we see the world. We can then start to filter the overload of excess outside information so our minds can relax, and our bodies can heal.

Movement and Flow

Water is energy capable of more than we have ever imagined. It's an essential substance of living that has been worshiped formally and spontaneously by beings throughout time and culture. The water element within yoga is considered to be the sacred element that both purifies and nourishes at the same time. Water is a great carrier of energy, nutrients, vibration, and subtle information. Like our planet, we are composed of over 70 percent water. The water element is a commodity cherished for its purity and abundance. Water is sacred and an important topic to introduce to the younger generations, so nothing is taken for granted.

The teachings of Dr. Emoto[6] remind us that we are what we think. The thoughts we have about ourselves absolutely affect our health and wellness. Guiding the children through meditations of things they love and adore about themselves and their life will instill a positive vibration within. You can even take it a step further and show them how you can create intention with everyday activities like blessing your water or food before you consume it. You can have great talks on environmental conservation and stewardship, like how to cherish and preserve our water sources and not waste natural resources.

When we are more conscious of ourselves and our self-talk, we become masters of our own minds. We are happier people who make more conscious choices. By accessing the healing qualities within, we become stronger-willed, and more aware human beings. I feel that this is one of the most important aspects of this curriculum. For healthy self-esteem, we have to learn to be conscious of our thoughts. We have to be aware of what we are saying to ourselves. The power of positive intention and thought are beneficial practices we all can learn and grow from.

Here are some positive and mindful practices to share with the kids:

· Bless your food or drink with positive intentions

· Say prayers to a garden you have planted

· Sing with the birds or animals

· Hum in nature

· When you are in nature, breathe in the abundance that surrounds you into every cell of your body

· Every time you look in the mirror, smile and appreciate your beauty and unique part in the world

· Find gratitude in the small things

· Honor those moments where you feel full, balanced, and happy

· Pray for every living being and creature on the planet to be happy, safe, and nourished

· When you are doubtful or worried about a situation, think positively and tell yourself that "it is going to be great!"

Jala - Sacred Water *Meditation*

Guide the kids through a water-inspired meditation. Sit or lie down and imagine that you are underneath a waterfall or lying on a bed of water (ocean, lake, pond, or river). Feel the water quenching, releasing, relaxing, and nourishing. Feel every molecule of water soak into the skin and nourish and cleanse every muscle, tissue, and organ in the body.

Breath Wave *Meditation*

Lie on your back comfortably. Find your natural breath. Try not to control the breath, just allow it to move through you. Honor this magic passing through you every moment of the day. This is the breath. Honor this greater energy that is connected to something way more powerful than we can comprehend. Honor that you are a walking miracle—unique and beautiful.

Now take the breath into the lower belly as you inhale and allow that swell, like a wave, to move upward into the ribs, chest, heart, throat, and head. As your breath moves up toward the head, the wave of energy crests and crashes. As you exhale, feel the wave move back down from head to hips as you allow the body to relax deeper into your mat. Inhale again into that lower belly, allow the breath to rise up to the crown of the head and exhale, releasing that breath and moving awareness back down your spine to the tailbone. Inhale into the low belly, and feel the breath rising like the hugest swell, all the way to your head before the wave crashes and moves back down the spine from head to tail.

Inhale into the front body, pause. Exhale down the back body and pause at the bottom of the breath. Feel the ebb and flow of life, the rise and fall of the tide. Feel infinite consciousness. Feel the feminine healing energy of the ocean. Feel this magnificent love you have for yourself. Think about all the ways you can cradle yourself with self-love. Think about a daily practice that you can give back to yourself. Repeat this breath with affirmations seven more times.

Fountain of Youth Love *Meditation*

In a kneeling or sitting position, close your eyes. Imagine the fountain of youth in front of you. Take your hands and bring that water up toward the crown of the head. Feel that water cascade down over your body as the hands come back down and then grab more water. Inhale and sweep the arms forward and up as the water goes to the crown and exhale as the arms float down and the water flows over the entire front and back part of the body. *Amrita* is a Sanskrit word that means immortality. It is said to be the regenerative elixir of the Gods. It's the nectar that has all the wisdom, intelligence, and rejuvenation of the universe. Feel *amrita* bless and invigorate every cell in the body with health, youth, freedom, lightness, and love.

Lesson Three – The Fluid Body

*"You only have to let the soft animal
of your body love what it loves".*
-Mary Oliver[7]

Wave motion is the underlying movement of all creation. Being fluid is our very nature. As we honor the fluid body in our yoga practice, we are adding extra awareness into our being. When we open ourselves to the sensation of flow within the *asanas*, we are more in tune with our current state. As water is ever-changing and ever-flowing, we have a chance to honor whatever we are feeling in the present moment and attend to that. When we are aware to breathe into that space, we can purposefully begin to let it go. The buoyancy of breath can push open anything that feels stuck, like blocked emotion. We can hydrate and lubricate our inner body just through breath and intentional movement. Our practice becomes a meditation between the ever-expanding and contracting breath pulsation. This fluidity is called *spanda*. It's the magic of the inhale and exhale, our heart rhythm, and our brain waves. It's a subtle vibration that is the source and foundation of conscious movement and thought.

When we tap into the magnificent power of the water element through rejuvenated movement, we can experience the potency of healing and, therefore, an increase of the mind-body connection. With intention and affirmation added to these embodied practices, we can experience a heightened sense of self-love and an increased sense of well-being. Each new day is an opportunity to tap into the flow and to evolve in harmony by listening and attuning to what our body is saying, rest when we need to rest, modify when we need to modify. This is the ultimate yoga to be shared with kids. It's not all about the push but rather the steady flow. It's about remembering the water element in the body and in nature is potent, powerful and sacred.

Yoga Flows Honoring the Fluid Body

Prana flow yoga is the most liberating type of yoga I have ever experienced. It is the way I prefer to move my own body and teach from that experience. Some of these movements I learned from my training with Shiva Rea, and some I have created myself. In essence, we are honoring the water element within each *asana*.

Use this yoga flow sequence to feel the wave motion of breath pulsating through the body. Moving this way keeps the kids active and engaged. It can improve coordination and keep the mind steady, alert and present.

Moving Chair: Sit in a chair pose with your feet and legs together. Inhale and sweep the arms forward and up, feel the body pulse upward a little. Exhale, and allow the arms to sweep back gently and gracefully as you sit down a little deeper, keeping the abdominals engaged. Feel this breath supporting your movements.

Pulsating Plank: Fold forward and step back into plank pose either on your hands with shoulders over wrists or come down onto your elbows and forearms. You can also modify it with the knees down in both positions. Inhale and coil the spine like a C curve, gazing toward the navel and keeping the hips relatively low. Breathe deep into your back body, dissolving tension and stress. Exhale, engage the quads, and come back into your supportive and dynamic plank pose without allowing the hips to sink and the lower back to compensate. Feel the energy shooting outward through your heels and out through the neck and head as you exhale.

Spontaneous Cobra: Drop the knees and chest and bring your body flat down to the Earth. Take the fingertips outward on each side of your body and in front of the shoulders. Firm the legs and stretch into the toes, keeping the tailbone rooted down. Inhale and press into the fingertips. At the same time, lift the upper body off the ground with engaged legs. Feel a wave of breath movement lifting the chest. Exhale, and lower the chest to the floor. Inhale again and slither the body from side to side like a cobra snake. Feel the breath move the upper body into the neck and shoulders with spontaneous and intentional fluid movements. Exhale, lower down carefully.

Circular Downward Dog: In downward dog, press firmly into the hands and feet to feel grounded. Now move the wave motion through the body. Inhale and lift the heels up off the floor and feel this wave of motion move the hips toward the sky, rounding the back body. As that wave moves into the upper back, shoulders, neck, and head, bring the weight more into your shoulders and hands. Exhale, coiling back into the feet with very bent knees and the hips drawing way back. Inhale and bring that wave again through the heels, legs, back, and forward into the shoulders. Coil back again as you exhale into the steadiness of the legs. Feel the breath move freedom and lightness into the spine.

Crescent Flow: Step one foot forward and come into a crescent lunge pose. Take the hands in *hasta mudra* with the palms face up by your hips. Inhale and feel the legs draw inward like you were scissoring your legs in place. Feel this Earth energy move upward into the legs and draw up into the pelvis. As you inhale and pulse up, with this energy moving upward through your spine, gently lift the hands up toward the sky. As you exhale, move the hands with palms facing down and elbows slightly bent back toward the hips, feel the legs extending outwardly, bringing that front knee right over the ankle again back into a crescent lunge pose. As you exhale all the way out, keep that back quad engaged and extend into the heel.

Warrior One Flow: Inhale, sweep up into warrior one pose. Exhale, and sweep the arms back into airplane arms, and the chest comes forward, engaging the abdominals. Inhale, sweeping the arms up. Exhale, sweeping the arms back. Interlace the hands behind the back and fold forward into a humble warrior pose. Inhale to rise back up.

Pulsating Warrior Two Pose: Come into warrior two pose. Inhale and sweep the arms upward to touch as you stretch up toward the sky. Exhale and bring the arms down toward the Earth as you lunge back into a deep warrior two pose.

Moving Reverse Warrior into Side Angle: Come into warrior two pose. Inhale and sweep the front arm up to the sky as you take the back hand to the hip or thigh. Exhale and windmill the front elbow to the thigh and sweep the back arm over your head toward the front of your mat. Inhale and reverse the warrior pose and exhale into a side-angle pose.

Pulsating Eagle in Horse Stance: Come into horse stance (mini squat) with toes out, heels in, and knees bent, making sure the knees are over the ankle alignment. Take the arms into eagle arms. Inhale and pulse upward from a deep squat while lifting the elbows high and exhale; the elbows will press down into the chest as you squat as deep as it feels good and supported.

Separate Leg Stretch Flow: Step one foot out about three to four feet. Have the toes forward and the heels in one line. In this wide stance, extend the arms out and inhale. Feel the lift move through the heart and flow the upper body down toward the ground with the hands touching the Earth. Inhale, bringing your fingertips under the shoulders, and lengthen the wave motion through the spine with the neck long. Exhale, melting into a forward fold, keeping legs engaged. Inhale, pressing into the fingertips and extending the spine. Feel the breath move into the lower lobes of the lungs and exhale release the head and the neck.

Lesson Four – Self-care

Ayurveda

Ayurveda, the mother of all healing, is considered by many scholars to be the oldest healing science, originating in India over 5,000 years ago. In Sanskrit, *ayurveda* means the science of life. Accomplished masters taught this practice of ancient Vedic culture for many thousands of years using oral tradition. *Ayurveda* practices encourage the maintenance of health and wellness through close attention in balancing one's life through awareness of the seasons, ritual, right thinking, diet, lifestyle, self-care, personal constitution and the use of foods and herbs. The body is a temple, so whatever we put into our experience and bodies must be sacred.

Ayurveda is based on the concept that we each have our own individual constitution or *dosha* (combinations of *pitta*, *kapha*, and *vata*). Knowing our specific *dosha* enables us to tune into the seasons, and make appropriate lifestyle changes to create a balance of body, mind, and consciousness. A central tenet of *ayurveda* is that balanced energy supports all life. When we minimize our stress level and stabilize our energy flow, our natural defense systems kick into gear. We build a strong body that can defend against disease by addressing the mind, body, and spirit together.

Ayurveda recognizes that each of us is unique. We each respond differently to life events, hold different strengths and weaknesses, and each one of us contains the power to heal. *Ayurveda* encourages us to use our experiences, understanding, and deep insight to find information about ourselves.

Yoga and *Ayurveda* go hand in hand. They are sister sciences. You can introduce the healing benefits of *ayurveda* to youth through the explanations of *dinacharya*, or daily routines.

If we want to bring radical change to our mind, body, and consciousness, we must have a daily routine to establish balance. This daily routine also helps regulate our biological clocks, supports digestion, elimination and nutrient absorption. It is an act of self-care and a discipline that will set us up for success.

I like to introduce children and teens to these life-changing and life-giving practices:

Ayurvedic Daily Rountine

Dry brushing: *Gharshana*, or 'skin brushing,' helps to stimulate the lymphatic system, helping the body get rid of toxins. It leads to smoother, brighter skin by removing dead skin cells and supporting blood circulation. Ideally, you'll want to dry brush in the morning, moving from the outer extremities toward the heart

Oil pulling: Known as *kavala* or *gundusha*, this is an ancient *ayurvedic* dental technique that involves swishing a tablespoon of oil in your mouth on an empty stomach for up to twenty minutes. This action draws out toxins in your body, primarily to improve oral health but also to improve your overall health.[8]

Self-massage with oils: *Abhyanga* is the anointing of the body with oil such as sesame oil or coconut oil. It can be beneficial for maintaining healthy circulation and used as a medicine for some disorders such as pain and inflammation in the joints and tissues of the body. The actual act of self-massage is both soothing and healing. Use long strokes on the long bones and circular massage over the joints. Leave all the oils on for at least twenty minutes, rinse off in the shower without using soap.

Face-massage with a *gua sha* stone. A *gua sha* is a specially shaped stone traditionally carved from jade and other gemstones. This stone can help lift, tone, and stimulate the lymphatic system and drain fluid buildup. It can also relieve facial and jaw tension. Apply oil on the face and move the stone from the center gently outward towards the hairline and jaw. Massage from underneath the chin towards the collar bone. Face massage is beneficial to do before or after *abhyanga*.

Attuning to natural rhythms: Practices such as waking at sunrise and resting our bodies at sundown are beneficial for our internal clock. By doing so, our bodies balance hormones, blood sugar and our mood. Moreover, getting enough sleep at night and activity in the day will also help strengthen our immune systems, help with digestion and allow our bodies to rest easier. Meditating in the mornings with *pranayama* and yoga are great practices to reset and renew our natural rhythms and to allow energy to flow. Limiting screen time at night will help with a goodnight sleep.

Cleansing practices: Eating with the seasons and choosing whole foods specific to your *dosha*, is helpful for cleansing the body and improving digestion. Proper food combinations help with the assimilation and absorption of nutrients. Drinking warm lemon water first thing in the morning and doing *kitchari* cleanses with seasonal changes are ways to cleanse and reset the digestive system. Daily, we can practice eating less, having lunch as our biggest meal of the day, eating light and early each night. Teach kids that 'less is more' when it comes to healthy eating and digestion. Eat slowly and mindfully.

Sipping warm spiced water: Sipping hot spiced water or teas is helpful for eliminating toxins in the body. Steep hot water with various spices (nutmeg, ginger, turmeric, cardamom, cinnamon, fennel, coriander seeds) according to your *dosha* and sip it throughout the day for cleansing, hydrating, nourishing, and balancing.

Tongue scraping: *Jiwah prakshalan* is one of the best ways to keep the tongue healthy and to help the body release toxins by scraping it gently daily. Tongue scraping uses a tool or scraper to remove debris, bacteria, and other things stuck to the surface of the tongue. Sometimes toxins accumulate due to poor digestion and or lack of a strong metabolism. This can cause disharmony, blocked energy, and or a weakened immunity. Tongue scraping is best in the morning before eating and before you go to bed.

Oiling nose and inner ears: With oils such as coconut, ghee or sesame oils, use a cotton swab or your fingers to lubricate the inner nose and ears. The inner oiling can catch bacteria and viruses trying to enter through the nose. The oils create a protective barrier.

Finding your dosha: Support your individual and unique *dosha* through food, herbs, and practices. To find your *dosha*, try an online quiz at **Banyan Botanicals**.[9]

Two ayurvedic practitioners that I recommend for more information are **Cate Stillman** and **Cory Tixier**.[10]

Food as Medicine

Ayurveda can help balance certain *doshas* through taste. Food is very healing and the basis for balancing your constitution and learning how to eat throughout the seasons. Taste is also known as *rasa* in Sanskrit; it can be defined in several ways. Experience, enthusiasm, essence, and juice all form an integral part of taste. The six tastes are sweet, sour, salty, pungent, bitter, and astringent.

A fun discussion in the classroom is to talk about food as medicine and proper nutrition. It's so important that children know that food is fuel for the body. I like to share the metaphor of a car taking gasoline for energy. If you feed the car high-quality fuel, it will go the distance. What we put into our bodies makes the biggest difference in how our bodies and minds function as well as our energy. If we eat vibrant and fresh foods, we will have sustained energy, but our results can be very different if we feed ourselves excess sugar and hydrogenated fats.

Food *Meditation*

Talk about food as medicine. Have a theme for the month (like superfoods) and bring foods in like (goji berries, chia seeds, blueberries, avocado, coconut, cacao nibs) to the classroom and talk about their healing powers while you experience the taste sensations.

At the end of the practice, food meditation is a great way to introduce different foods and their benefits. It's also important to talk about their life-giving essence, how and where those foods were grown, and how they got onto your plate. Hopefully, by guiding the children through a taste meditation, they will become more involved and conscious of what they are putting into their bodies.

You can share a fun learning experience with the kids by bringing in foods that correlate with the six different tastes: sweet, salty, sour, pungent, bitter, and astringent. In *ayurveda*, we can use these tastes to help bring balance back to our bodies and minds.

Yogic Cleanse

Sacred junctures that happen throughout the year are powerful times to cleanse and renew. For instance, Spring and Fall are great times to reset the digestive system. There are many ways to cleanse: fasting, juicing, eating clean, mono diet, healing soups and or eliminating certain foods like meat, dairy, sugar, or processed foods. It could also mean eliminating negative thoughts or habits and may be as simple as drinking more water. For children, it's best to encourage healthy eating practices with life giving foods such as fruits and vegetables.

Self-Massage

Start by using your hands and massaging the different tissues on the body like the shoulders, hands, chest, legs, knees, and feet. Create friction in your hands as you massage the skin and muscles and get the circulation moving. Tapping, kneading, gentle percussion techniques are great ways to move stagnant energy and to improve blood flow.

Kitchari Jars

Kitchari is an Indian home staple recipe and one of the foundational foods in *ayurveda*. It's nutritious and easy to digest. It also has cleansing, balancing and grounding properties.

What you need:

- ¾ cup white basmati rice
- 1 cup mung dal
- Jar
- A bag for the spices

Spice packet:

- 1 bay leaf
- 1 teaspoon cumin seeds
- 1 teaspoon fennel seeds
- ½ teaspoon ground turmeric
- ¼ teaspoon ground coriander
- ¼ teaspoon granulated garlic or ginger
- ½ teaspoon Himalayan Sea salt

Jar assembly instructions:

1. Place rice and mung dal in a Mason jar.
2. Fill a small bag with spice mixture.
3. Roll or fold the spice bag to fit in the top of the jar and then secure the lid.

To cook:

1. Soak the rice and the dal for 30 minutes.
2. In a medium saucepan, sauté the seeds in the ghee or butter on medium heat until they pop.
3. Add the other spices and stir for one minute.
4. Add the rice and dal and stir for two minutes.
5. Add 6 cups of water to the saucepan and bring to a boil.
6. Reduce heat to low and cook covered for 30 minutes.
7. Add any vegetables to the cooked rice and dal mixture and cook for 10 more minutes. If you are adding vegetables that take longer to cook like carrots, add them in when you add the water.
8. Add mineral salt and chopped fresh cilantro or mint and serve.

Lesson Five – The Vital Organs

When kids know about their vital organs, they can build greater body awareness. Teaching kids the basics of how the body works and operates is profound. Kids can become advocates of their health and life choices.

Nervous system: This system carries messages from the brain throughout the body and includes the brain, nerves, and spinal cord.

Yoga practices that support the nervous system are calming, restorative, and gentle. Any posture that aligns the spine and creates movement and flow through the central channel is beneficial. *Yoga nidra*, *Yin* and Restorative yoga are balancing practices to the nervous system.

Respiratory system: This system uses the lungs, larynx, and airways to transfer oxygen to the bloodstream and remove carbon dioxide from the body.

Yoga practices that support the respiratory system are any breathing techniques and yoga postures that open up the lungs and chest like twists, backbends and side opening poses.

Circulatory system: Blood is carried through the body via the circulatory system to bring nutrients to the rest of the body. Organs in this system include the heart, blood, veins, arteries and blood vessels.

Yoga practices that support the cardiovascular system are inversions and heart openers like backbends.

Digestive system: The stomach, gallbladder, liver, intestines, and pancreas work together to process food into usable energy and nutrients for the rest of the body.

Yoga practices that support the digestive system are twists and forward folds.

Endocrine system: This complex system of hormones regulates most of the body's functions, including growth, hunger, thirst, mood, metabolism, and reproduction. The prominent endocrine organs are the pituitary gland, adrenal glands, and thyroid.

Yoga practices that support the endocrine system are calming *pranayama* and postures that create compression and release in the neck, back, and belly. Inversions are great for hormonal balance and the glands in the neck and head.

Excretory system: This system removes waste, food, and toxins the body doesn't need. This process occurs via the kidneys, bladder, and large intestine.

Yoga practices that support the excretory system are stretching in the hips, legs, and feet for grounding, balance postures, and twists. Squats and belly massage are beneficial. Longer exhalations (*apana vayu*) are also helpful in releasing stuck energy in the abdomen.

Integumentary system: This system protects the inside of the body from the world outside and includes the hair, skin, and nails.

Yoga practices that support the integumentary system are inversions and head, hand, and face massage.

Muscular system: All of the muscles in our bodies work together for supported posture, movement, and strength and are controlled by the nervous system.

Yoga practices that support the muscular system are heat-building and strengthening postures as well as long, slow, and deep holds like *Yin yoga*.

Reproductive system: This is the only body system that differs in male and female bodies. It includes all of the organs necessary for reproduction.

Yoga practices that support the reproductive system are postures on the belly to stimulate compression and circulation and back bending postures and twists.

Skeletal system: The bones, ligaments, tendons, and cartilage work together to support and protect other organ systems.

Yoga practices that support the skeletal system are postures that require great detail and alignment, power flow, and *Yin* or restorative yoga.

Interactive Anatomy Art Lesson with Food

When discussing the internal organs, you can pair them with their *Yin/Yang* counterparts and discuss the energetics of organ relationships. You can use healthy snacks like coconut, raw nuts, seeds, dried fruit, and healthy chocolate when identifying the organs and placing that food as a marker on the paper (instead of using a pen)—for example, placing two raisins or two sunflower seeds where the lungs are in the body. Another example is placing a cashew or piece of healthy chocolate where the heart is and discuss everything the heart does for us. It doesn't matter which foods go where. This project keeps kids interested and alert because, in the end, they can eat their art.

Organs of the Body

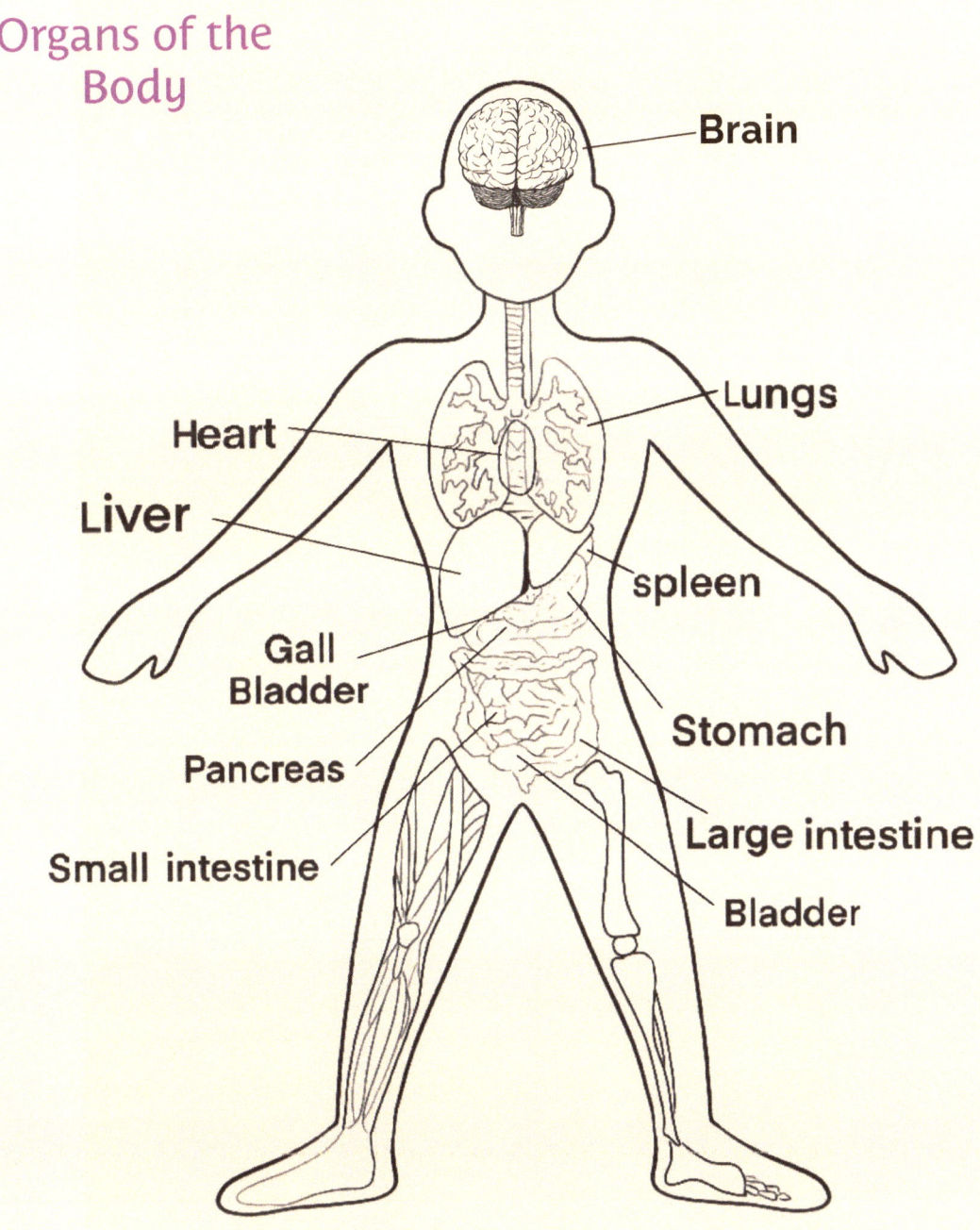

- Brain
- Lungs
- Heart
- Liver
- spleen
- Gall Bladder
- Stomach
- Pancreas
- Large intestine
- Small intestine
- Bladder

Lesson Six – Yoga Anatomy

Understanding basic anatomy and having awareness of one's body can help to enhance the yoga experience. This knowledge can be especially important in yoga *asana* because every posture targets a specific body part.

Body Awareness

Body awareness can be described as conscious embodiment, is an empowering way for all of us to understand our body mechanics and learn about the different muscles that help us move throughout the day. Our yoga becomes an exploration of dissecting certain areas of our bodies and learning how our bodies are powerful instruments of expression. Body awareness also allows us to realize where our bodies are compared to the space around us. Activities focused on body awareness help us with our own coordination and also help us understand how to interact with and relate to people around us and objects we encounter at home, school, and outdoors. Below are fun yoga postures that aid in learning about our anatomy.

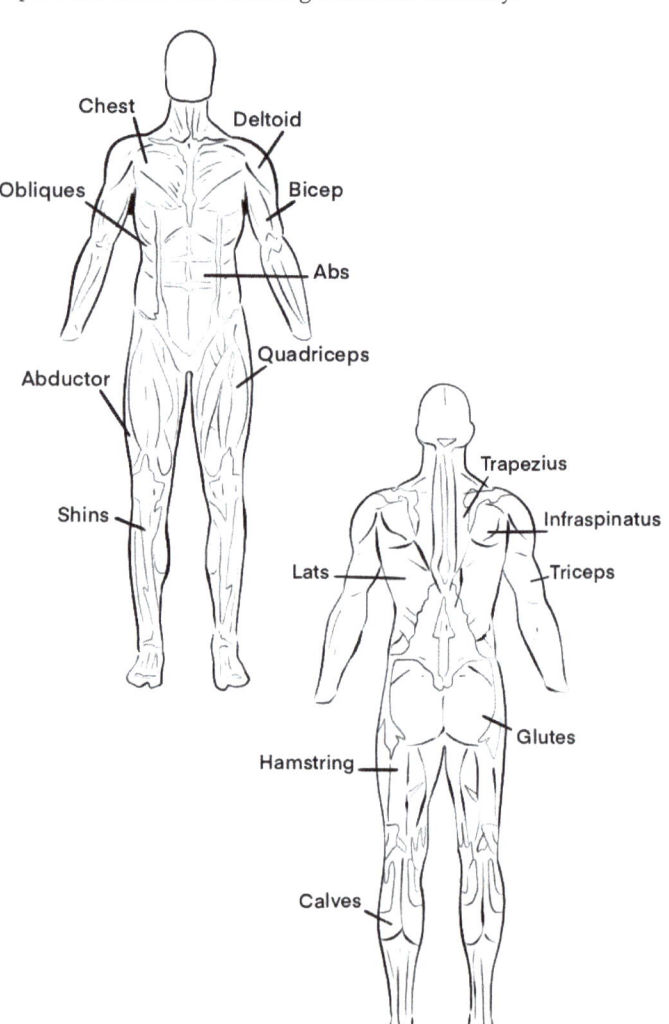

Yoga Anatomy Flow

Have the kids identify their muscles in these postures:

- **Biceps** – planks, *chaturanga*, handstands, backbends, arm balances
- **Triceps** – handstands, *chaturanga*, tabletop, lotus lift
- **Chest/Pectorals** – pushups, handstands, dolphin stands, arm balance, standing postures
- **Abs** – boat, core, pendulum, lifts, handstands, backbends, standing postures, arm balances
- **Quads** – standing postures, planks, handstands, backbends, warriors, bow, yoga headstands
- **Hamstrings** – splits, running, jumping, forward bends, sitting postures
- **Glutes** – lunges, handstands, chair pose, warriors, hip openers
- **Lats** – cobra, bow, backbends, forward bends, yoga headstand
- **Trapezius** – handstands, dolphin handstands, yoga headstands

Full Moon Healing *Meditation*

Relax on your back with your knees bent, feet hip-width apart, heels out, and toes slightly inward. If it feels better to do so, allow your knees to draw in toward each other.

Place your hands on your belly. Your elbows should be on the floor for support—if not, place a blanket or a pillow beneath them. Close your eyes and notice the breath moving in and out of the belly. Feel the rise and fall. Notice that your body relaxes deeper and deeper with every exhale, releasing any tension in the lower back, hips, and spine.

As the eyes stay closed, imagine a great big full Moon out in the night sky. Notice the brilliance in color, shape, and magnificence. Now imagine your whole center is a beautiful, serene, and still lake. As the Moon shines bright, visualize sparkles of light dancing on the surface of the lake. As those diamonds flicker and twinkle, notice how the light penetrates deep on the superficial layer of the skin, expanding now from the belly throughout the top surface of your skin.

Now, see the light move downward through the layers of tissue. First, the outer dermal layer, then into the connective tissue and muscle, joints, ligaments, tendons into the vital organs, until that light has sifted through the entire torso and down into the mat underneath the back body. Feel that light healing, transforming, energizing, relaxing, and opening all parts of your being from physical to energetic body. When you honor the light, think about what you are honoring in your life. Now bring yourself back to the breath and feel the belly rise and fall underneath your palms. Honor the miraculous healings of that great big Moon and all of her lunar cycles.

Lesson Seven – The Koshas

The Energetic Body

Practicing yoga profoundly affects all parts of our being—our body, breath, mind, heart, and soul. As a body-based meditation, yoga invites us to focus and experience ourselves with a deeper awareness. When we do this, we are moving through the layers of our being or otherwise called *koshas*.

The *koshas* are our energetic layers, from the outermost layer of skin to the deep spiritual core. Each layer, like the *chakra* system, has its own function on a physiological level. Practicing yoga allows us to track those subtle, deep *kosha* layers and access them more readily. We use an *asana* to prepare our outer body and then turn our attention inward to the *pranic* body via yogic breathing. The philosophy of yoga gives us awareness of our emotions so we can focus on becoming calm and healthy.

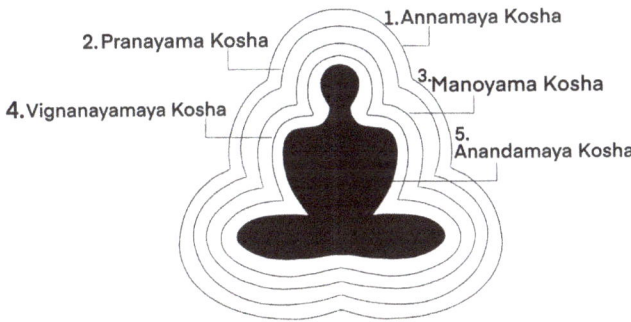

1. Annamaya Kosha
2. Pranayama Kosha
3. Manoyama Kosha
4. Vignanayamaya Kosha
5. Anandamaya Kosha

Koshas *Meditation*

Guide your students through a meditation of the *koshas*. As you begin this meditation, bring everyone's focus to the support for your body from the surface below—the floor, the ground, the Earth, whatever it is. Allow everyone to feel heavy and relaxed.

Anamaya Kosha

Anamaya kosha is the journey through the physical body, including the skin, muscles, connective tissue, fat, vital organs and bones. It is made of solid material and nourished by food and water. A physical yoga practice affects this *kosha*. Here you can elaborate on different body parts that you would like your students to meditate on—the eyes, ears, neck, and legs. Pay attention to the sensations that are present in the physical body.

Pranamaya Kosha

Pranamaya kosha is the journey of the natural breath. The subtle body includes the circulatory system for *prana* or 'life-force energy,' and our energetic body. We use *kosha* to regulate the flow of *prana* using the *nadis* and *chakras* we will learn about

below. In *yoga*, both *asanas* and *pranayama* affect this *kosha* by bringing vitality to every body's cell, energetic channel, muscle, tissue, and organ. Now bring attention to the sensation of this magnificent breath. This could be through the nostrils or the feeling of it rising and falling through the belly. If the mind wanders, just bring it back to the breath. Notice how your breath comes and goes, naturally.

Manomaya Kosha

Manomaya kosha is the journey of our attention, our thoughts, and our emotions. This is our mental body and a mindful way we become aware of the world perceived by the five sensory organs. The *manomaya kosha* sends messages through the brain and central nervous system, controlling our emotional and physical bodies. Here is where we transfer from physical feelings to emotions. Notice right now the state of your being. What are you feeling and thinking? Do you feel certain emotions inside the body? Just notice those sensations without being attached. Can you breathe into them and feel them move or shift?

Vijnanamaya Kosha

Vijnanamaya kosha is the journey through our intuitive selves. It's about paying attention to signals, responses, and gut feelings. This *kosha* is associated with a profound level of intuition and inner wisdom. It is our intelligence and our ability to process information with our entire being. In yoga, meditation and meditative *asanas* affect the *vijnanamaya kosha*. Quiet reflection and journaling can also help engage the wisdom mind and help promote greater intuitive understanding and increased willpower. Now start to notice thoughts or images that may be present. What thoughts or beliefs want to be seen right now? Does it feel good? Look upon choices you have made and discover if those feelings feel right and truthful. How does a good choice feel in the body?

Anandamaya Kosha

Anandamaya kosha is the journey through your whole being to find ultimate peace and freedom. You might experience connection with all things, freedom from sorrow, and a more relaxed state of being. For example, one can experience this within postures that feel so amazing that you get lost in that sensation. Another example is having a deep, spiritual connection with someone, and time just flies by or simply feeling at ease and at peace. Another way to experience this kosha is through devotion to a higher power or selfless service or feeling divine energy within and without. Now notice if there are any sensations of contentment, happiness, or presence in your life. Notice times where you felt completely at one with the universe; those times in which you feel that time and space have stopped, and you have melted entirely into nothingness. Your awareness is inside but also everywhere. You have merged with the one.

Lesson Eight –
The Chakras

Chakra means wheel or vortex and refers to energy points in the body. *Chakras* are disks of energy that spin as they remain open, balanced and aligned. They relate to nerves, major organs, and other parts of our bodies that regulate emotional, mental and physical well-being. There are seven main *chakras*, each with corresponding numbers, names, colors, and a specific location along the spine from the sacrum to the crown.

ROOT CHAKRA - *Muladhara*

The root *chakra* represents our foundation. On the human body, it sits at the base of the spine. When the root *chakra* is open, we feel confident, grounded, balanced, and secure. When it's blocked, we can feel unstable, fearful, scattered, and confused. It's the seat of our primal energy. It holds the basic needs of health, family, core relationships, security, survival, and safety. It opens to the nose and affects the adrenal glands and our immune systems. The *muladhara chakra* wants us to rest more. Some issues that deal with the first *chakra* are family and group safety, ability to provide for life's necessities (food, clothing and shelter), ability to stand up for oneself, and feeling at home. Some symptoms could include chronic lower back, hip, feet, knee, and ankle problems, sciatica, varicose veins, depression, and immune-related disorders when out of balance.

Location:	Base of spine, in tailbone area, hips, legs, feet, bones, teeth, immune system
What it controls:	Survival issues such as money, shelter, clothing, and food. The emotional imbalance is fear.
Mantra:	LAM *"I am balanced and connected."*
Color:	Red
Element:	Earth
Stone:	Hematite, bloodstone, tiger's eye, fire agate, black tourmaline
Practice:	All stretching and grounding flows dealing with the hips, low back, legs, knees, ankles, and feet, working with *mula bandha*.
Affirmation:	Reclaim your essence. Reaffirm your power and beauty. Know yourself. Honor transformation and wisdom. Connect to the beautiful Mother Earth.
Meditation:	We are all one. Breathe in the Universe. We are all made up of earth elements. The breath is a gift and an exchange. Honor existence and all that surrounds you. You are a part of the whole.

SACRAL CHAKRA - *Svadhisthana*

The sacral *chakra* helps to guide how we relate to ourselves and our emotions, and how we respond to the emotions of others. It also governs creativity and spontaneity. When this *chakra* is open, we feel connected, have healthy relationships, and feel confident and powerful. Those with a blocked sacral *chakra* could feel a lack of control in their lives, trouble in relationships, feel unworthy, and experience trust issues. It's about honoring our sensitivity, vulnerability, creativity, and the flow of life. Nothing is ever consistent; it's ever-changing, moving, and transforming. Some symptoms could include lower back pain, sciatica, urinary problems, and endocrine challenges when out of balance.

Location:	Lower abdomen, about two inches below the navel, hips, bladder, pelvic area, intestines, and reproductive organs
What it controls:	Your sense of abundance, well-being, pleasure, and sensuality; the emotional imbalance is guilt.
Mantra:	VAM "I am in the state of flow."
Color:	Orange
Element:	Water
Stone:	Carnelian, citrine, moonstone, coral
Practice:	*Uddiyana bandha*—belly lock, all movement that is free and flowy. Squats, pulsations, cat-cow movements, dance-like flow.
Affirmation:	I am powerful. I am in control. I flow in a state of grace. I am financially independent. I take full account of all my actions. I can adapt and change and move with the transitions in life.
Meditation:	Notice how it feels to have no agenda, no need to achieve. Notice how it feels to be just present with the flow and grace of the breath. Notice timelessness. Notice the sense of freedom. Feel carefree.

SOLAR PLEXUS CHAKRA - *Manipura*

The third *chakra*, the solar plexus *chakra*, speaks to your ability to be confident, outgoing, brave, and in control of your life. When open, there is self-assurance, independence, and a sense of purpose. If your solar plexus *chakra* is blocked, you might feel shame and self-doubt. Those with open *manipura chakras* feel inspired, empowered and motivated to accomplish and create. It's about self-empowerment, purpose, vitality, and energy. It's the *hara*, the seat of self, self-esteem, willpower, motivation, and inspiration. When out of balance, there is nervous tension, fear, doubt, and lack of trust or personal honor. One might experience arthritis, ulcers, intestinal problems, diabetes, indigestion, and liver dysfunction.

Location:	Upper abdomen in the stomach area, muscular system, and digestive system
What it controls:	Self-worth, self-confidence, and self-esteem. The emotional imbalance is shame.
Mantra:	RAM "Self-love starts when I accept all parts of myself."
Color:	Yellow
Element:	Fire
Stone:	Citrine, malachite, calcite, topaz
Practice:	Core work, planks, twists
Affirmation:	I care for myself because I love myself. I am confident and courageous. I am powerful.
Meditation:	I am beautiful, bountiful, and blissful. I am love. I am creative and magnificent.

HEART CHAKRA - Anahata

The heart *chakra* is the bridge between the lower *chakras* (physical) and the upper *chakras* (spiritual). This *chakra* influences how we can give and receive love, both from ourselves and others around us. An open heart *chakra* is full of understanding, compassion, empathy, and peace. Someone with a blocked heart *chakra* will have difficulty opening up and trusting people in their life. With an open heart, we can experience compassion and empathy on a deep level. Heart *chakra* essentially is about love and divine manifestation. When out of balance, one can experience heart problems, asthma, allergies, breathing problems, and upper back and shoulder tension.

Location:	Center of chest, just above the heart, lungs, breasts, shoulder blades, and arms
What it controls:	Love, joy, and inner peace. The emotional imbalance is grief.
Mantra:	YAM *"When I love myself, loving others comes easily."*
Color:	Green
Element:	Air
Stone:	Rose quartz, jade, green calcite, green tourmaline
Practice:	Rubbing heart in circles, *chi* ball to heart space, backbends and heart opening *asanas*, side body opening
Affirmation:	I am love myself unconditionally.
Meditation:	Listen to the whispers of the heart. Heart opening meditation. Be curious about the physical, mental, and emotional heart.

THROAT CHAKRA - Vishuddha

The throat *chakra*, gives power to the voice to speak from our hearts and communicate personal power. It allows us to express and articulate our authentic self with clarity and compassion when it's open. Someone with a blocked throat *chakra* could lack trust in themselves, their voice, or their passion. They could be fearful of speaking up or have an inability to listen deeply. When out of balance, one can experience throat issues, mouth ulcers, gum and joint problems, swollen glands, and thyroid problems.

Location:	Throat, mouth, lips, teeth, tongue, neck, shoulders
What it controls:	Communication, self-expression, getting your voice heard in the universe, and truth. The emotional imbalance is dishonesty.
Mantra:	HAM *"I speak my truth, always."*
Color:	Light blue/turquoise
Element:	Sound/music
Stone:	Aquamarine, turquoise, kyanite
Practice:	Using *OM mantra* in practice, inversions, restorative yoga, yoga poses or breathing that stimulate a throat lock or compression
Affirmation:	I speak my truth clearly. I am honest and trustworthy. I release all judgments.
Meditation:	Being vocal, singing, chanting, saying out loud what you really want from the universe.

THIRD EYE CHAKRA - Ajna

The third eye *chakra* is where we access intuition. It's about self-reflection, intuition, imagination, psychic perception, clear seeing, listening to the body, and tuning into a higher self. I like to tell the kids it's the eye that looks out for you. It's the eye that tells you right from wrong. It's your ability to see clearly. When out of balance, one can experience headaches, neurological disturbances, learning disabilities, and seizures.

Location:	Forehead between the eyes, face, eyes, ears, nervous system.
What it controls:	Intuition, imagination, wisdom, and dreams. The emotional imbalance is depression.
Mantra:	SHAM *"I am open to exploring what cannot be seen."*
Color:	Dark blue
Element:	Light
Stone:	Lapis, amethyst, purple fluorite, black obsidian
Practice:	Inversions, meditation, buzzing or humming in the brain, *yoga nidra*
Affirmation:	I have faith and knowledge. I have will. I am wise and intelligent. I trust the universe.
Meditation:	Shift the gaze up to the third eye center and ask what do you need to know right now.

CROWN CHAKRA - Sahasrara

The crown *chakra* represents our ability to be fully connected spiritually. One with an open *chakra* is full of wisdom, an open mind, and a strong sense of self. When your crown *chakra* is fully opened, you gain access to higher dimensions of consciousness. When out of balance, one might feel energetic disorder, mystical depression, lack of faith, chronic exhaustion, judgmental thinking, extreme sensitivity to light or sound, and environmental factors.

Location:	The very top of the head and all systems of the body.
What it controls:	Inner and outer beauty, spiritual connection. The emotional imbalance is attachment.
Mantra:	OM *"I am a vessel for love and light."*
Color:	Violet/white
Element:	Divine consciousness
Stone:	Selenite, clear quartz, amethyst, diamond
Practice:	Devoted practice to something greater, *yoga nidra*, meditation, *reiki*
Affirmation:	I am connected to something greater. I am a part of the divine. I am whole.
Meditation:	Becoming one with the universe, *metta* meditation, connection to higher power

Chakra *Meditations* to Balance and Energize

Chant for Intuition: HUUUU

The sound of *HUUUU* stimulates the third eye center and, as a result, can increase awareness and intuition. This sound can also help the functioning of the pituitary and pineal glands.

Sit up tall and close your eyes. Bring your awareness to the third eye center. Inhale through the nose and exhale the sound of *HUUUU* and feel the vibration buzz the brain.

Golden Ball Chakra Meditation

Sit comfortably. Imagine the golden light of the Sun flowing down through the *chakras*. The golden Sun light draws down into the crown and mixes with the purple light, then the dark blue of the third eye, then the light blue of the throat, the green of the heart, merges with the yellow of the solar plexus, then orange at the sacral area, and then all the way toward the red color at the base of the spine. Feel the golden ball melt into the Earth.

Circle of Light Chakra Activation

Take the hands toward the base of the spine and inhale, with the fingertips slightly up. Envision red at the root and then float the fingers to the lower belly and see orange. Move to above the navel (yellow), toward the heart (green), up the throat (light blue), to the third eye (dark blue), and all the way to the sky (purple). Take that purple light and wrap it around your body like a protective cloak as the arms cascade outward and downward towards the floor.

Chakra Color Visualizations

Find a comfortable seat or lying down position. Feel the breath move in and out. Bring your awareness to the physical body. Without any judgment, honor your physical body. Now bring the breath into the mind and notice all the thoughts moving through the brain today. Again, without criticism of what you have been thinking or not thinking, notice your thoughts while being detached from meaning or significance. Just notice them as they are. Now bring your breath inside that heart space and notice the fluctuations of emotions and memories that have flooded the heart lately. Without having any remorse or regret about what you have been feeling, observe those feelings and sensations. Know that everything is good—perfect—just the way it is. Feel the body, mind, and heart all connect with the ebb and flow of the breath.

We are going to move our awareness through the energetic system of the body. These energy systems are called *chakras*, and they have color, sound, vibration, and balanced and unbalanced personality traits associated with them. We are going to move our awareness through each *chakra*.

Start with *Muladhara Chakra*, the root *chakra*, which is located at the base of the spine. Visualize the color red. It can be a red flower opening, blooming, flowering, and flourishing, or it can be just a red light extending or a circle of light spiraling like a wheel of bright, brilliant red. The sound is *LAM*. Just picture a red color with an internal *mantra* of *LAM*.

Now bring your awareness to the area on the belly two inches below the navel, which is *Svadhisthana Chakra*, the sacral *chakra*. Visualize the color orange, either expanding, flowering, or swirling, and add the sound *VAM*. Picture the vibrant orange color with the internal mantra of *VAM*.

Bring your awareness to the area two inches above the navel, the *Manipura Chakra*, the solar plexus. Visualize the vibrant color of yellow just as bright as the Sun and the *mantra* sound of *RAM*.

Now bring your awareness to the heart, which is the *Anahata Chakra*. Visualize the color green radiating outward from the heart with the internal mantra of *YAM*. Picture the brilliance of green humming to the sound of *YAM*.

Now bring your awareness to the throat area, *Vishuddha Chakra*. The color is light blue. Feel that light blue color, just like the day sky, surround the throat and add the *mantra HAM*.

Bring your awareness to the third eye center, *Ajna Chakra*. Feel the color dark blue expanding from the third eye center and add the *mantra* sound: *SHAM*.

Bring your awareness to the *Sahasrara*, the crown *chakra* at the very top of the head. Picture the color purple shining out the crown of the head and radiating out like an umbrella of light. As you picture this bright purple color, add the *mantra OM*.

PART **5**

CHAPTER **10** (May)

Artistic Expression

"All of me is on fire. My voice, my body, my hands. I tremble with the need to express. Out of the Earth I celebrate, Out of the skies comes my answer. Out of the Earth I create his body. Out of space his abode. This bounty and his beauty is my source. My body is the instrument of my expression."

-Shiva Rea[1]

May: Artistic Expression

Express Yourself

May is a month of creativity and expression. It's the end of the school year in some areas, and kids are preparing for summer break. Art and movement are the perfect solutions to keep them focused and calm when their minds are less focused on the classroom. As we embark on the path of yoga, we will realize that there is a meditational component in all that we do; our art, our work, our physical and mental practices, and the way we live. We all need these creative outlets and resources to achieve the right headspace. We all need ways to express ourselves.

Art therapy is a wonderful way to channel our thoughts and feelings and also release stress. There are also other modalities that we can use as resources for times that we need them the most. As we flow and change with life, it's important to have many different tools to pull from for support. As a dancer and lover of music, I have always been drawn to spontaneous, therapeutic movement. Movement is life-giving and reconnects us to the natural flow, where we are liberated, uninhibited, and alive with the creative flow. Breath-induced movement meditation is our first form of meditation. As early as our womb, we are soothed by the rocking motion that puts us to sleep as babies. Dancing is a way to celebrate and express as well as renew and rejuvenate. This month we will learn to be an instrument of that expression.

In Lesson One, we will be tapping into our creative force by designing our very own *mandalas* and *yantras* using sacred geometry. Sacred geometry refers to the naturally occurring patterns found everywhere we look. You can find these universal designs throughout time and space. Introduce the kids to a practice of meditation that naturally occurs through creating such art. Such symbols within *mandalas* and *yantras* have tremendous meaning and balance the left and right brain. When both sides of the brain start working together, the mind and the emotions become balanced. In the end, gazing at our masterpieces can help enhance the feeling of being centered, grounded, and relaxed. Inner peace comes from being in harmony with the universe that we are an integral part of.

In Lesson Two, I will teach you how to plan a freeform, trance dance, or ecstatic dance session with your students. Trance dance is another way to merge the breath and body into an intentional, intuitive flow that dissolves negativity and creates a new vibration of hope. The body essentially becomes a vehicle of divine expression. This spontaneous dance experience lays the platform for intentional transformation and healing and is a powerful outlet. Children naturally love to dance and move, so this is a fun way to explore movement and music.

In Lesson Three, we will learn to harness life-force energy as a source of creative expression through *qigong*. *Qigong* is a way to connect the flow of energy in nature and the body through slow, intentional, healing movements. Both trance dance and *qigong* practices support our yoga evolution because they give us a chance to trust our inner and outer flow, and allow the greater force to move through us, in essence giving us support and energy from the universe. We learn what is best for ourselves in present moment awareness. As we learn more about ourselves, we start to understand that our bodies are different every day, and we have to adjust our practice accordingly. These alternative yogic practices can help us with just that. The wisdom of tuning into our natural state and rhythm is one of the most important practices we can learn from.

In Lesson Four and *Five* will dive into other practices such as partner yoga and hands-on intentional healing. These modalities use the body as a vehicle of expressive and healing energy and are powerful practices to add to the classroom. These are practices that create trust, communication, and connection with others. The healing power of touch is an art form. As we learn to trust our instincts and use our hands to heal, we can make a big difference in coping and extending care. Using our hands for art, movement, and healing are just some of the ways we can extend love out into the universe.

Lesson One – Yogic Art

Mandala

A *mandala* is a spiritual ritual symbol originating from Buddhist traditions. *Mandalas* are mostly notably associated with Tibet, China, and Japan. *Mandalas* are an instrument of meditation and generally represent a spiritual journey. As the eyes shift from the outside to the inside, a process of letting go, releasing, and healing can take place. As the eyes relax, so does the mind. Ultimately, using a *mandala* for meditation can help the practitioner move from a state of suffering into one of joy and happiness.

Spiritual and artistic *mandala*s exist in many different cultures. In my research, I have found three main types of *mandalas*: a sand *mandala*, a healing *mandala*, and a teaching *mandala*.

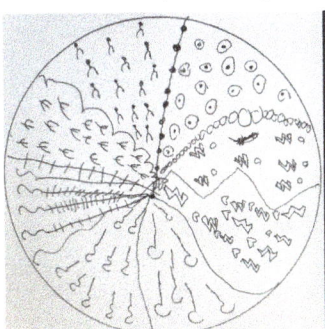

Mandalas usually consist of patterns of circles contained within a square and organized around a single central point. Despite their intricate patterns, common symbols are easily recognized. Traditionally, they include a wheel, tree, flower, or jewel. The center dot is the starting point, where we begin to contemplate and focus. From there, lines and geometric patterns symbolizing universal symbols of life (peace, love, joy) flow outward. An outer circle representing the cyclical nature of life surrounds the entire image.

When teaching kids, I like to simplify the *mandala* project to creative 'doodling.' Here, you can still encourage symmetry with alignment but kids can create their own geometric patterns. With the older kids, you can use rulers and compasses. Every *mandala* is unique and meaningful. At the beginning of each class, I like to guide the kids into a meditation on what feeling is represented in their artwork. Maybe it's compassion or unity, and maybe it's contentment or joy. Allow the kids to craft their own. Some added images can be used within the *mandala*, such as bells, wheels, lotuses, hearts, triangles, upside-down triangles, stars, suns, and moons.

Yantra

Where the Buddhists have a *mandala*, yogis have a *yantra*. A *yantra* is used as a visual point in meditation. The ancient yogis thought of *yantras* essentially as means of liberation from birth and rebirth or *moksha*.

A *yantra* consists of very specific patterns that aid in relaxing the mind. It has a square shape on the outer perimeter with circles and symbols moving inward. Like a *mandala*, its geometric patterns are made of several concentric figures like squares, spirals, crosses, hearts, dots, diamonds, circles, lotuses, triangles, stars, and points. Again, the eyes can meditate on a *yantra* moving from the center outward or vice versa.

When guiding a *yantra* class, I encourage the process to be relaxing and grounding. I like to have the kids invite specific energy in and to allow that creative force to move through them during the process. If the outer shape is too difficult for children to draw, I have them use a simple square shape. Every piece of art is beautiful—at the end of class, have the students share their masterpieces.

Lesson Two –
The Healing Power of Dance

Dance is a form of non-verbal expression. It's a release of rules and obligations, a way to feel the lightness of being. It is meditation in movement and a way to experience a shift from feeling the rigidity of life to the soft, soothing sensation of allowing the body to feel free.

"Dance when you're broken open. Dance if you've torn the bandage off. Dance in the middle of the fighting. Dance in your blood. Dance when you're perfectly free."
-Rumi[2]

Trance *Dance*

Trance dance is a very specific movement meditation that I have been trained in by Shiva Rea. Here is a template on how to design your very own dance experience with your students.

Select a music playlist of about five songs.

• The first song should be mellow and tranquil.

• The second song is a little more robust and upbeat.

• The third song is the energetic peak with the highest tempo.

• The fourth song is gentler and slows the pace.

• The fifth song is calm and relaxing.

Think of your intention for the dance. What will your prayers and blessings be? What are you dancing for? What is the meaning behind leading this gathering? How will you guide your audience? What dance and yoga flow will you be leading? What would you like everyone to get from this experience?

In the **first song**, begin with everyone on the floor in *savasana* or seated meditation. This is a great space for guiding students through breathing, gentle stretching, and embodying the wave-like motion through the body. It is also an important time to set intentions and prayer.

The **second song** enables you to lead transitions with gentle movements that slowly lead you to stand. Positions that take shape on all fours or tabletop pose, cat cows, hip circles, flowing downward dogs, and up dogs are good transitions. Creative movements that bring the belly to the Earth into various positions to open the body and breath with ease and lightness like cobra, airplane, and bow pose also make excellent transitions. Lunges, squats, and rag doll roll ups are mindful ways to get the body to a standing position.

The **third song** moves toward the peak, where you are fully expressing high energy movement. This can be guided by intentional movements or free-form, spontaneous dance. As the tempo lifts, you can choreograph certain hops, jumps, and moves to guide your fellow dancers into some delightful and fun expressions.

The **fourth song** helps guide the mood, the energy, and the body back toward the floor. This could look like slow-motion dance or gentle *chandra namaskars*, or any flow that gets you back to the Earth.

The **fifth song** moves the body toward *savasana* or seated meditation. It could be through leg stretching, pigeon poses, spinal twists, bridge, plow, or just free-form, soothing stretching. Guided relaxation, meditation, sound healing, or sharing a song seals this prayer in movement practice. Remember intentions, prayers, or anything you want to get out into the universe now while the soil is rich and fertile to plant those seeds of love and devotion.

Lesson Three –
Qigong

The Benefits of Qigong

Qigong is a healing movement practice that harnesses the energy of the universe inside of you. Found in traditional Chinese medicine, *qigong* combines movement, visualization, meditation, and breathing regulation to increase the flow of *qi* (vital energy) in the body. These centuries-old systems were used for the purposes of health, spirituality, and martial arts training.

Qigong is about gathering the *qi* or energy from the Earth and the cosmos and channeling it into the body and through the body. It's wonderful for enhancing the flow of energy in the meridians, the *chakras*, and the *nadis*. These exercises below are a mix of *qigong* and the stimulation of energy centers.

Qigong For Kids

Heart Rub: With feet wider than hip-distance apart and a slight bend in the knees, take the hands to the heart. Cross one over the other and hook the thumbs. Close your eyes and envision your hands resembling a butterfly. Move your hand around the heart *chakra*. Feel the movement start to sway from right to left, and you circle the hands over the heart's energy. Now switch and go in the other direction. Feel the unconditional love move through your whole body.

Belly Rub: With feet wider than hip-distance apart and hands to the belly, take three deep lower belly breaths. Feel the belly swell into the hands. Now take the hands around the belly in a clockwise circle. Feel the heat, the warmth, and the relaxation to all the vital organs. Feel empowered, centered, and strong.

Ear Massage: Massage all around the upper and lower lobes of the ears. This stimulates all the internal organs through acupressure points.

Shaking Tree: Stand, bend the knees, and shake the whole body. Feel the bouncing action shake off any unwanted tension or stress.

Chair Tap: Squat as though sitting in an imaginary chair and tap the inner thighs. Stand up and tap the lower abdomen right above the two hips. Repeat both taps five times.

Flossing the Shoulders: Just like cat-cow movements in standing position. Inhale, open elbows and shoulders backward, and arch the spine and lift the heart. Exhale, draw your elbows toward each other, bend your knees, and curl back. Repeat five times.

Figure Eight: Move the hands and arms into figure eights, shift weight from side to side. Now move the hips in a figure eight and feel the fluidity in the body.

Heart Belly Breath Meditation: Standing comfortably, place one hand to the heart and one to the belly. Inhale into the belly first, then all the way up to the heart. Feel the breath move through the body.

Lesson Four – Partner Yoga

Kids love partner yoga. Partner yoga consists of connecting yoga postures or creating shapes with one another. It's about learning how to work with other classmates, share, and be creative.

Find partner yoga cards online for good ideas. Or, kids can also come up with their own poses. They can choose poses they know or make ones up. You can get creative and ask them to make up a routine and or make up names for their creations. In partner yoga positions, the children are encouraged to connect their postures in some way or another. Invite the children after practicing to showcase their works of art.

Partner Poses	*Partner Stretching*
· Double Tree	· V Leg Stretch
· Double Butterfly	· Partner *dandasana*
· Double Chair	
· Double Downward Dog	
· Lizard on a Rock	

Giving Your Partner Love - *Adjusting in Savasana*

Adjusting a student in *savasana* can be both liberating and calming for the recipient. Little adjustments go a long way in the relaxation experience for kids.

Have the student lie on their back. Gently take one arm and stretch outward from the shoulder. Lay the whole arm out just below the shoulder. Repeat on the other side. Now, take a leg and gently lift it up and stretch it out and open. Carefully release it to the floor. Repeat on the other leg. Now come toward the head, gently lift it up, and stretch it ever so slightly back and down. A little head massage feels good here. Lastly, take both your palms and gently press each shoulder down, like a cat kneading a pillow, for about four gentle presses on each shoulder. The power of touch is effective, and kids love this attention and added relaxation.

Lesson Five – Magic Hands

Reiki: Hands-on Intuitive Healing

Reiki or hands-on intuitive healing uses the hands as instruments of healing. I call them magic hands for children because they are using their own hands as a resource to heal and calm themselves. They can use this technique when they are feeling hurt, sad, stressed, or on others to facilitate the natural flow of life-force energy.

Reiki originated in Japan and is built from two words: *rei*, meaning God's wisdom, and *ki*, which means life-force energy.[3] *Reiki* reduces stress and promotes healing and relaxation by using hands as conduits of universal life energy. When our energy is low or stuck, we are likely to get sick or feel more stress. Sometimes, we need to just relax and allow someone to facilitate the energy to move through us. Ultimately, *reiki* guides the life-force energy through us with intention and care.

Reiki offers a simple, natural, and safe practice for self-improvement and healing that is accessible to everyone. When used with the right intention, it can energize and improve the well-being of everyone involved. It combines nicely with other medical practices as a support for recovery and reducing side-effects. As you feel *reiki* move through your body, it resembles a heat building through and radiating around you, removing the malady and replacing it with light, health, and wellness. *Reiki* treats the whole person: body, emotions, mind, and spirit.

Reiki is an amazingly simple, sacred technique to learn, and I highly recommend going through an official training. *Reiki* is only passed on from *reiki* master to students during an attunement. Students learn how to tap into an unlimited supply of life-force energy to improve areas in the body that need attention. However, anyone can practice the simple basics of harnessing universal light into their hands to help themselves or someone else in their life. Animals love *reiki*. Children are really receptive to *reiki*. You can even use it on technology that is malfunctioning or use it on a situation or challenge with clear intention.

In the practices below, students who are learning to tap into universal life energy can simply imagine that they are harnessing the energy of the Sun, the Moon, or the universe and bring that light down through the body and into the hands for intentional healing. This is how I teach magic hands to kids.

Magic Hands

In this simplified technique, I am not teaching the students the *mantras* and symbols for *reiki* but the overall experience of using their hands for moving universal life energy. Our hands are powerful and magical, and they can access this sacred energy with their unique visualizations. The more we can learn to understand the healing capabilities of our own hands, the more love and care we can give to ourselves as well as our friends and families.

First, have the kids sit straight up with hands in prayer or on the lap. Have them breathe energy from their hearts upward toward the Sun. Imagine light from the heart touching the Sun. Capture that radiance and vibration as white, golden light and harness that energy back down through the crown, into the heart and down through the arms into the hands.

Feel the light and the heat within the hands. (You have the option to do the *qi* (*chi*) ball exercise below to increase energy vortexes in the hands). Have the kids place their two palms up and feel the energy in the palms. Now, think of a place on their bodies that needs that extra love and support. Place the hands with the powerful light onto their bodies. Now, partner up and practice on one another. For example, place your hands on your friend's back and imagine the light streaming from your hands into their back body. Tell them to take it home and do it on a pet, their parents, or even a tree.

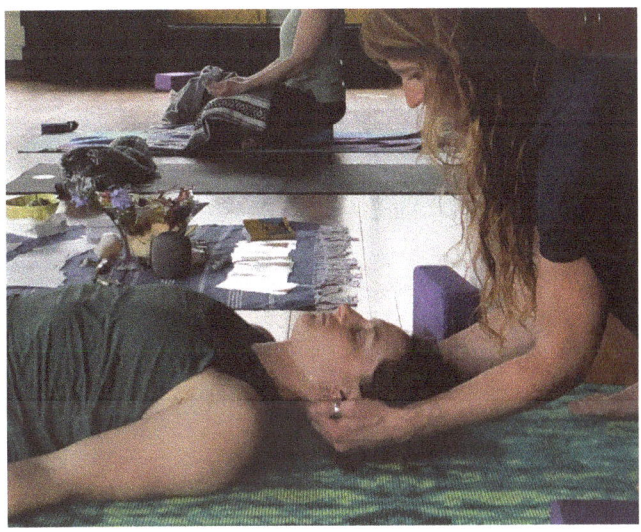

Intentional Healing

Qi (Chi) Ball Exercise

Have the kids rub their hands together and make friction. Now, pull the hands apart and feel like you are cupping your hands around an imaginary *qi* ball (also known as *chi* ball) or energy ball. Feel the energy between the hands. It feels like taking two magnets and turning them opposite to each other (that repelling sensation). Now, close your eyes and take that energy ball to wherever in the body that needs that extra love and attention.

Lightsaber Energizer

Close your eyes and imagine where in your body you need extra attention and healing. Imagine holding onto a lightsaber and taking that saber to parts of the body that need more energy. Feel the light and the heart soak into those areas. Use your imaginary lightsaber on others for increased energy and healing.

Body Scan

Lie down and bring awareness to all parts of the body. Every time your mind goes to a certain spot, imagine light penetrating in that area and feel the breath relax you deeper and deeper into a state of peace.

PART **5**

CHAPTER **11** (June)

The Yoga *of* Dreaming

*"Be kind to that sleepy heart. Let it out into the vast
fields of light and let it breathe."*
-Hafiz[1]

June:
The Yoga of Dreaming

The beginning of summer is a powerful time to dream big. School is out, and it's a perfect opportunity to dive back into the things in life that feed the mind and the heart. For kids, it's an opportunity to learn about things that spark play, interest, and hope. As a teacher, it's a great time to share more fun, exploratory resources on how to navigate through life with grace and ease. Together, we can learn how to focus our hearts and minds in order to achieve our dreams.

One way to create inspiration and joy is to offer summer programs with a continuous theme that reinforces goal setting. I call these offerings the "Yoga of Dreaming," in which the whole month is dedicated to fostering visions and dreams. This series of classes provides practices that create intentionality and consistency through yoga, art, and meditation. The themes will build upon each other. We will explore what we are inviting into our lives and create clear ways to support our endeavors. These everyday practices will give the students resources and tools to take a vision from start to finish. It takes focus, patience, and perseverance to see things to the very end. When we do, the overall feeling of accomplishment is so rewarding. It's through this growth that our self-esteem and self-appreciation can take leaps and bounds.

As we support our visions this month, we will be exploring other artistic and movement practices that connect ourselves to our higher purpose and passions. These practices can become a form of meditation and are great resources to invite goal-setting into our lives. The energy of summer is here to support kids and their extracurricular activities. Further, it is a time to inspire the dreamer, the believer, the innovator, and the entrepreneur. Kids will feel empowered by their ideas and curiosity.

My goal in this chapter is to introduce more creative practices that become resources for kids to use for manifestation. These resources will also help kids feel centered and confident as they navigate and carve out their own unique paths. We will also learn other modalities to heal and recharge. June's curriculum is chock full of creative outlets.

The lessons in this chapter include dream boards, dreamcatchers, malas and mala bracelets, mantras, mudras, summer solstice yoga mala, restorative yoga practice, and crystal healing. The focus in all of these activities is to inspire kids to feel passionate about their creations and innovations so that, when they go back to school at the end of summer, they feel full, happy, independent, and strong.

The Power of Vision

I like to share the story of Michael Phelps with the kids as an introduction to the power of vision. Michael Phelps is an American Olympic swimmer. In his training, his coach had

him visualize his races right before he went to bed and before starting his day. He did this over and over in his mind. He visualized the perfect race, every breath, every kick, and every stroke that got him to the end of the pool and back. He pictured himself calm, cool, and collected.

When it was time for his race, he got up on the stand, put his goggles and gear on, and, with the shot of the starting gun, he jumped in. However, as he dove in, his swimming goggles filled with water—he couldn't see at all! Without losing focus, he immediately went back into his visions and meditations of swimming every stroke and kick to finish the race with his eyes closed. In the end, he won the race, without even being able to see! The power of vision and dreaming big became a great support system to help him win the race and make his dreams a reality even when things didn't go as planned. This story inspires us to use the power of the mind, repetition, and meditation to support the very outcomes we so desire.

The Power of Positivity

One of the main themes in this curriculum is the importance and potency of intention setting (*sankalpa*). The more we can catch those thoughts that are holding us back, the more we have the ability to direct those thoughts toward positive intentions. Over time, these positive intentions, phrases, and thoughts chip away at old belief systems and, essentially, start to rewire the brain. Yoga becomes this relationship between our minds and our thoughts. The more we have mastery over our negative thinking, the more our willpower and self-esteem strengthen and renew.

Our willpower is the energy of choice. We can choose to be positive. When we create this vibration of opening to health and well-being, we attract it. Positive thoughts create positive returns. Over time, we can create positive change. When we start to feel good, we make better choices and feel more connected to our mission. This connectedness helps us to become more confident, more in touch with our intuition and increases our capacity to share the love of health and increased vibration with others. Our yoga practice can stoke that inner heart fire and create platforms that enrich, support, and allow our seeds of thoughts and vision to take shape and grow. Here are some incredible resources that help enable dreams to come to fruition.

Lesson one –
Activities for the Yoga of Dreaming

Dream Boards

Living out our dreams takes time and dedication. It doesn't just happen overnight. A vision always starts with a feeling. We have learned in our yoga practice that energy follows thought and our thoughts are, therefore, a gateway into manifestation. Dream boards are a wonderful way to put all sorts of those energies together to see everything clearly and get the momentum going. Dream boards are a powerful way to become clear about what we are welcoming into our life.

A dream board or a vision board physically identifies what we seek and are attracting in our lives. We can use it to manifest the things we desire by using visualization techniques. Olympic athletes and other powerful and successful people use imagery and visualization to keep focused on their goals. By keeping that intense focus, they actualize their goals into a reality. This phenomenon has been proven in neuroscientific studies. Repetition and visualization are everything when trying to attain one's goal.

To begin this process, lead the kids through a meditation on what dreams they invite into their life. Have them pick one to three things that they would like to achieve. On a sheet of paper, have them journal how they are committing themselves to their desired outcome. Include a plan to achieve their goals and a specific timeframe. For instance, to become a pro athlete, we need proper training, rest, and nutrition. This training might take months to years to achieve. After they have journaled a plan, they channel it into a dream board, cutting out pictures and/or inspiring words. Use markers or paint to draw your own pictures, too.

Another creative way to use dream boards is to have the kids meditate on what kind of energy, values, and morals they invite into their life. Have them choose images that inspire and align with their goals. Ask them questions like, "What do you wish to magnetize into your life?" Cut out phrases or letters from magazines to create your affirmations or mantras. Permit yourself to express your dreams into physical form. Dream boards can be created monthly, annually, or updated as time progresses. You have great flexibility in implementing this project with your students, so flex your creative muscles, ignite the inner artist, and have fun!

"Goals are just dreams with deadlines."
-Napoleon Hill[2]

Dream Board Supplies

·White paper

· Scissors

· Glue

· Magazines

· Markers, paints

· Journal and pen

Lunar Planning - Using Time on Your Side

Whether you are working on a positive affirmation, inviting energy, manifesting, or creating something amazing in your life, it's good to work with the Moon's energy or in a timeframe that feels good to you. Working with the Moon's cycle connects us back to nature and can empower us as we get more in touch with life cycles. We can identify with the subtleties of nature and the exquisite power she can support us with.

There are fifteen days between each new and full Moon; just over two weeks. If, for example, you were eliminating sugar from your diet, you might set the goal starting on the new Moon and lasting until the full Moon. Having a sensible timeframe that you can see on a calendar is a dependable way to stay accountable. The progression of nature within the Moon cycles can also inspire you to stick with your intentions.

Vision Planning and Preparation

Once you have a goal in mind, think about all the factors that contribute to achieving that goal.

Here are some strategies to incorporate:

· Training

· Nutrition

· Timeline

· Lifestyle

· Meditations

· Restoration

Dreamcatchers

Dreamcatchers are webbed and beaded circles with feathers hanging from the base. Good dreams flow down the feather into the dreamer's mind, while the web captures the bad dreams, and the morning Sun burns them away. Native American cultures also believe that a good and easy night's sleep will allow the dreamer to remember the messages and visions from the higher spirit that come during the night.

Traditionally, dreamcatchers are hung in sleeping areas and are believed to take away bad dreams and bring good dreams. They symbolize the removal of fear and general protection of our thoughts while we sleep. The process of creating and installing a dreamcatcher can bring about peaceful and purposeful resting energy. Dreamcatchers become an ally while sleeping and children can often rest easier with this sense of protection. Seeing a dreamcatcher can be a reminder that we have the power to control the thoughts in our mind by setting positive intentions before we sleep. It's important to think of your dreams and goals and everything you are grateful for before you close your eyes for bed, so those good thoughts resonate in your dreams.

How To Make a Dreamcatcher

I like to prepare the material ahead of time, so it is easy to do with the students. **First**, take the yarn or leather string and tie it to the wooden circle. This step is optional if you want to have the wooden hoops wrapped before making the web. **For the web**, take the yarn or hemp cord and cut it into individual balls of string for the students. Tie a double or triple knot at the top of the hoop to make it secure. I like to make the first weave of the web around the hoop for the younger kids. I use a demonstration loop for older kids to show them how to run the string clockwise, spaced approximately two inches apart around the hoop. Wrap the string around and back over itself, making a knot at each point. Pull it securely before moving on to the next loop. Once the first round of loops is made, the younger and older kids can go at their own rates and keep looping another round clockwise. Please note that younger kids really just like to wrap their own way, and it is all good and beautiful.

Kids are welcome to add beads into the web when they are weaving or at the end. The beads can symbolize these seed intentions of what they want to grow and evolve in their lives. They could also symbolize traits that they want to bring into their subconscious, such as *I am powerful. I am beautiful. I am creative. I am smart. I am courageous.*

After creating intentions within the dreamcatcher's web, help your students tie off the end knot. **Long**, wispy, and decorative ribbons can be tied at the bottom of the hoops. **Students** can add beads and feathers to string onto the bottom and allow them to hang down from the dreamcatcher. After creating each unique dreamcatcher, **guide** the students into a meditation where they are infusing peace, love, and wellbeing into their works of art. If it's a gift for someone else, have them send their prayers into the dreamcatcher for that particular person.

Dreamcatcher Supplies

· 5-inch (13 centimeters) wooden circles or hoops

· 2.5 yards (2.3 meters) leather string, buckskin lace, or yarn for wrapping around the wooden circles

· Individually cut yarn or hemp cord for the web, a piece for each child (approximately 2 yards or 1.8 meters)

· Beads

· Feathers

· Hot glue (optional) or tacky glue

Lesson Two – Malas

Traditional Indian *malas* are made with 108 beads plus the master bead or guru bead. These strands of beads can be used as a rosary for prayer or worn around the neck to energize and harmonize body systems and *chakras*. When using it like a rosary, take your thumb to each bead and recite a prayer or *mantra* 108 times. When you get to the guru bead, you know you have completed the meditation.

When wearing or using it as prayer, *malas* are great reminders of what you are opening your heart and mind to in your life. When making the *mala* with such intention, they become so charged that just seeing it, holding it, or wearing it can keep us grounded. The *mala* is a great resource for reconnecting to faith.

After you have strung your beads with intention, take the two loose ends and pull both of those through the master bead or guru bead. The tassel is optional. If you choose to leave the tassel off, just have the kids tie the *mala* off after the master bead. If you would like to make the tassel, make a knot at the end of the master bead, take six inches of your embroidery thread, place it into the center of your tied knot, and knot the middle of the threads. Then, fold both sides of the embroidery thread down to make a tassel. Pinch the top of the tassel and wrap it with another piece of thread to make the finishing touches. Comb the rest of the tassel string down and cut at the desired length.

The process of placing the beads onto the string is immensely powerful. Here we have a chance to invoke the dreams, visions, ideas, affirmations, and inspiration we wish to manifest in our life. The process is like a ceremony. Each bead has a prayer and intention, so it holds that specific vibration when you are using it for meditation.

If you want to modify the project and just make prayer beads for meditation, you can use a derivative of the significant number of 108. Making a *mala* with 54 or 27 beads is just as powerful.

Mala Bracelets

Mala bracelets are a great option if you are guiding a bunch of kids or have younger kids. Have the students pick out their beads and place them onto a paper plate or bowl. Guide the kids through a meditation of what energies they want to invite into their life. What positive thoughts or affirmations do they want to invoke? Encourage the kids to push this energy into the beads, using the power of their hands and that universal life force energy moving through them into their works of art. Take a piece of stretchy string about ten inches in length and tie it at one end. With every bead placed onto the string, have the kids internally recite their intention, dream, or prayer of devotion. *Mala* bracelets can also be dedicated to prayers for peace on Earth or blessings for mankind. Maybe you want to encourage them to dedicate the power of their *mala* beads to all animals on the planet or for saving the oceans. When you finish, tie off the bracelet and superglue the knot. Let it dry, and then cut the excess string. It is optional to have the kids bring in a shell, special bead or crystal with a hole in it to add to their *mala* bracelets.

Mala Bracelet Supplies:
· Beads
· Elastic String
· Scissors
· Special beads, shells, crystals, charms or guru beads (optional)
· Super Glue

Mala Supplies:

· 27, 54, or 108 *mala* beads
· Master bead or guru bead
· Silk beading cord with attached needle (size eight for smaller bead holes or size ten for larger bead holes)
· Embroidery thread for the tassel
· Scissors, beading tweezers (optional if you are making knots in between every bead)

Cleansing Ritual with the Mala

When you make your *mala* or *mala* bracelet, notice the beauty, the colors, the uniqueness, the sparkles, and know that you shine just as bright and beautiful. You can cleanse and energize your *mala* any time by burning sage or incense (with an adult) and wafting it over your *mala*. You can also lay it out under the Sun or the light of a full Moon. Another way to energize your *mala* or bracelet is to place it on your altar. Singing a song or playing music over your *mala* is also very powerful. When cleansing your *mala*, create the intention of what you release and what energies you add into it.

Mala *Meditation*

When you have made your *mala* or bracelet, take some personal time to reflect on things in your life that are no longer serving you. Have your *mala* or bracelet placed in your hands on your lap. When you know what that is, take three deep breaths with those thoughts and feelings in mind and exhale with a loud *HAAA* sound and cleanse your body from those feelings. Really feel like you are ready and willing to let that stuff GO!

Now, think of what you would like to replace those feelings with. When you are ready, hold your *mala* in your hands, place the *mala* to the heart *chakra*, and inhale three times the positive thoughts, affirmations, visions, and dreams that you have for yourself and your life. What are you ready to open your heart to? Be clear and know that you deserve it. Now, exhale and allow the breath to shower your whole body with peace and vitality.

Take a few moments in meditation and imagine the feeling that you have already achieved those dreams, and they have already come to fruition. Notice the sensations of being more relaxed and grounded and allow that pure peace to wash over you. Feel gratitude for opening your heart.

Your *mala* is a divine expression of your true self. It is an opportunity to take a deep breath and honor your unique journey in this world. It's a remembrance of who you truly are. It's a chance to be kind and loving to yourself, rejoice in your beauty and light, get back on that self-care track, and love yourself unconditionally.

Japa Meditation with the Mala

To use the *mala* or *mala* bracelet for prayer, sit comfortably and place a bead closest to the tassel between your thumb and forefinger. As you think of a prayer, *mantra*, or affirmation, recite it internally as you move your thumb and forefinger to the next bead. Keep reciting the prayer with every bead until you move around the entire *mala*, depending on how many beads you have on it, 27, 54, or 108 times. Alternatively, hold the *mala* in your hands, or lay down and place the *mala* on your *chakras* in a restorative position and meditate as you breathe in the prayer and affirmations.

Lesson Three –
Mantras

Mantras are a powerful tool to use along one's spiritual journey. It can reconnect one back to the source. Chanting or listening to *mantras* produces positive, life-affirming energy through vibrations. Chants are found in cultures all around the world because of their power to ground us. *Mantras* are a great resource for kids to anchor their intentions through sound resonance. Chanting *mantras* internally or externally is a way to enhance awareness and presence in daily life and move us into spaces of deep inner peace and silence. *Mantras* can open certain energy pathways, increase one's vibration, and enhance daily activities such as yoga, meditation, dance, and creative arts. Singing and/or chanting can be very healing and liberating. Traditional, ancient Indian *mantras* hold a tremendous amount of resonance and power from the ages. Try these *mantras* with the kids and enjoy the peace and calm that pervades.

Mantra *Practices*

Chant: *OM Mani Padme Hum*

The literal translation of this chant is '*I am the jewel within the lotus.*' There are many interpretations of this *mantra*. For me, it symbolizes how stress and the pressures of life help us rise to the occasion and sometimes help us on our path to becoming stronger and more resilient, even radiant, like the most precious jewel.

Jewels and diamonds form in their environments under tremendous pressure and stress from the geology surrounding them. This dense and powerful force pushes down upon these stones and creates the most precious jewel. Like the metaphor of this *mantra*, we can become that jewel within the lotus with hard work, patience, and determination. We can dust off the dirt and shine just as bright as the most beautiful stone. Setting the mind with patience and persistence is the key to achieving great things.

This *mantra* also can represent the purity of the Buddha in mind, body, and spirit. It also represents living a dutiful life full of compassion and love. I also like to think of it as a *mantra* for remembering that true, radiant, and resilient light inside.

Chant: *OM Namah Shivaya*

OM Namah Shivaya is a wonderful *mantra* to use when dealing with fear. This chant helps release worry and doubt so that our minds are clear. When we have a clear mind, we have more power to confront our fear. This chant is an ode to *Shiva*. Chanting this *mantra* builds the energy in our system to clear out negativity or to burn up the things that do not serve so they can be released.

Chant: *OM Gam Ganapataye Namaha*

This *mantra* invokes the elephant deity, *Ganesh*, who brings about new beginnings. Chanting this *mantra* helps remove the obstacles upon one's path to find freedom and renewal. It's a *mantra* for inspiring transformation and liberation.

Chant: *OM Aim Hreem Shreem*

A classic *mantra* meditation works with *bija mantra* or seed sound *mantras*. Chanting this *mantra* brings about creativity, wisdom, play, divine beauty, and harmony.

Chant: *Lam Vam Ram Yam Ham Sham OM*

This *mantra* energizes the seven *chakras* in the body. It's great for grounding, uplifting, and inspiring circulation and respiration. Chanting can help the movement of energy flow within the subtle, physical, mental, and emotional bodies.

Lesson Four –
Mudras

Yoga mudras are yoga positions for the hands and fingers. *Mudras* help to link the brain to the body, creating focus and coordination. *Mudras* also help encourage the energy to flow through our bodies by stimulating meridian and *marma* points. Through activating pressure points, we can influence our state of being. *Mudras* help us build balance between all of the elements within us. Grounding and centering *mudras* can be beneficial to practice when we feel stressed out. *Mudras* are also helpful in meditation.

Prayer Mudra: Hold your hands together at the heart. Feel the left hand press gently into the right hand and vice versa. Feel the elbows extend outward as the chest lifts upward.

Chin Mudra: Press the thumb and forefinger together and rest the backs of the hands on the knees. The other fingers are just resting peacefully. Place the hands the lap, palms down if you are turning inward for guidance, or palms up if you are looking for guidance from the universal energy. This *mudra* links us to our higher self by removing dull energy, calming our minds, and encouraging a more positive mood. It's often used in meditation, *pranayama*, and *asana*.

Lotus Mudra: Press your lower palms together and touch both pinky fingers together as well as both thumbs. The rest of the fingers splay out like lotus petals.

Butterfly Mudra: Press your thumbs together by crossing at the wrists, palms facing inward toward the body. As you extend all the other fingers out, place the hands over the heart center. Feel as if the fingers represent the wings of a butterfly.

Hasta Mudra: The palms face up to the sky as the elbows are pulled into the body, and the forearms are at a 90-degree angle. Feel the receptivity in your hands as yoau take a couple of breaths.

Lesson Five –
Summer Solstice Global Yoga Mala

A yoga *mala* is a collective practice of movement, breath, and intention. You can do this in a group setting or individually, harnessing peace on the planet. When moving together with the right intention, the practice of prayer can be powerful. My teacher, Shiva Rea, created the term 'Global *Mala*' to describe a type of energy-activism that unites people all over the world in a practice for peace. Your class can do this on a high powered day like the equinox, solstice, United Nations Peace Day, or any day that you create an intention to move as one. A *mala* is a sacred circle, within one's breath, one's community, all beings on this circular Earth, in our circular solar system, spinning through our spiral universe.[3]

Traditionally, a yoga *mala* or global *mala* is a practice of 108 Sun salutations. Of course, there are always variations and divisions of 108 that you can practice with potency: 9, 27, 54, 72. In this next section, I will be breaking down 108 into four rounds of 27.

In the first round, I like to start out with *pranams*, which are modified Sun salutations. You can also simply sit and move your arms in a meditational flow up and around the body, giving reverence to the sky and Earth as the arms come down to the floor.

The second and third rounds are traditional Sun salutations A and B. The fourth round can be, again, another modified variation. Anyone can sit in prayer with a *mala* necklace and participate or sit in a chair and absorb the increased frequency of everyone moving as a collective. At any time, you can take a child's pose or lay down in a *savasana* pose and take care of yourself. You still receive the prayer of peace.

The most important modifications:

1. Bend the knees in forward bends.
2. Bent knee *chaturanga* and lower the body safely to the floor to prepare for cobra pose.
3. Cobra pose on the belly, or cat's breath on all fours instead of upward dog.
4. Push safely back into downward dog or child's pose.

Yoga Mala Intentional Dedications

There are four rounds. At the top of each salutation, give a dedication. It may come slowly at first, but as your body moves and connects with your heart, you'll find more prayers moving though you. As you move, breathe, and meditate, allow devotion to lead the way.

First Round: This is dedicated to your individual revolution, transformation, and realization. This round is for personal activation, healing, and manifestation.

Questions to ask: *How are you living? What are you inviting into your life? How can you be a better person? How can you be the change you would like to see in the world? How can you love more, live more, and let go of the things that do not serve?*

Second Round: This is dedicated to the health and wellness of all your friends and family. It can also be for anyone you have unresolved conflict with. It can also be a dedication of gratitude to all your teachers and mentors who have impacted your life most positively. These people have influenced you, inspired you, and have helped you become the best version of yourself.

Third Round: Dedication for the world. This is dedicated to Mother Earth and the healing of every living creature and being on this planet, for everyone to live in harmony and to be kind, helpful, and loving to each other. This round tends to be the most powerful because it emphasizes our mission to take care of the Earth and each other. We pray for what we care about and are active in transforming and healing in this world.

Fourth Round: Dedication to Source. This is the conversation between you and your own unique understanding of the infinite divine universal consciousness. It could also be a round of peace offerings to your past and a chance to reconnect to your true self, path, and divine purpose.

Lesson Six –
Restorative Yoga

Restorative yoga is one of the most important practices to teach kids. While active postures are great for releasing pent-up energy, restorative yoga is equally important in replenishing the body and quieting the mind. Now more than ever, teaching stillness, ease, comfort, and relaxation is one of the most important skills to master. Kids' minds tend to be so busy with technology and screen time. It's not easy for anyone to be still, let alone to consciously let go. Our minds are programmed to assess things around us all the time.

Restorative yoga mirrors to us the fluctuations of our state of being. It brings up the discomfort of being still and being in these bodies. For kids, learning the skill of being aware of their thoughts and their breathing is powerful. Most of the time, we move through the day on automatic. Taking refuge in knowing we have the power over our thoughts and the ability to come into a state of ease is one of the benefits of a restorative yoga practice. We get to be a witness to ourselves without reaction. We learn how to be content with who we are.

Traditionally, restorative yoga uses props to support the body in postures of openness and ease to facilitate healing and relaxation. Restorative yoga is less about stretching and more about opening. Stretching and opening are not the same thing; they layer on one another. Restorative yoga restores the physical body and relaxes the stresses of our daily lives as we learn how to surrender to the moment. Restorative yoga is less doing and more being.

The use of props and blankets is intriguing for kids. I have found that they enjoy the comfort of setting themselves up for relaxation, especially when they can initiate the structure and form. Kids naturally love time to cuddle, creating spaces like forts and creative structures so they can feel safe. It's important that once they get into their positions, you encourage breath awareness and visualizations. Sometimes even music is appropriate for relaxation effects. Just like anything, it may take some practice to relax.

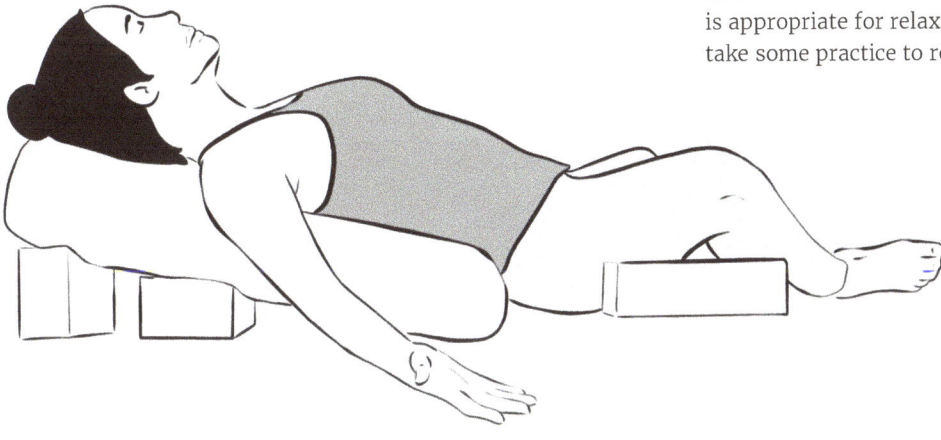

Restorative Yoga Tips

· **Create the environment:** Many aspects of our environment can distract us. I like to dim the lights—the darker the better—because the brain associates darkness with rest. I like to make sure the room is warm, so we feel more relaxed and comfortable. It's also nice to put something over the eyes for a deepening sense of relaxation. Cozy props, stuffed animals, and peaceful music or sound healing such as crystal sound bowls, chimes, bells, or drums are also remarkably effective. While meditation is the practice of learning to coexist and be unaffected by those things, our students will benefit from a supportive environment as they build these skills.

· **Support:** Demonstrating the pose can be helpful for kids, but sometimes they like to put their creativity into it. Support whatever way the kids can bring relaxation to their minds and bodies. For kids struggling with getting settled, guiding them through breathing relaxation or visualization is extremely helpful. Showing them how to use the props and sharing the experience with them is powerful as well.

· **Time for *savasana*:** Having an ample amount of time in *savasana* at the end of a restorative session is important. For adults, it can take about fifteen minutes to fully drop in and come to rest where we are able to release restlessness and curiosity. For kids, a three-to-five-minute *savasana* is sufficient. Celebrating any time toward rest is a job well done. Just be aware that kids might have a challenging time relaxing. You might have to have some tools in your toolbox to pull from, to engage their busy minds. For instance, music is calming, and so is telling a story. Sometimes, you will be guiding them through each pose with visualizations, and other days they might be so ready to let go on their own. Every class will be different.

Restorative Postures for Kids

· **Ultimate *Savasana*:** Place a bolster under knees, blocks under wrists, and rolled blanket under the neck.

· **Child's Pose:** Place bolsters lengthways under the belly and chest, turn head to one side, and then switch direction.

· **Reclined Butterfly:** Place bolster lengthways under the spine with the legs in the butterfly position and use either two blocks at each knee for support or tie strap around the knees.

· **Legs to Wall Pose:** Take a blanket, block, or bolster and mat to the wall and place hips as legs climb up the wall. *Optional:* Lift hips and place props underneath the sacrum.

· **Restorative Bridge Pose:** Take a block or bolster under the back of the hips, knees bent, and feet hip-width apart, and relax into the prop and breathe. Extending the legs might also feel good.

· **Heart Opener:** Place a bolster sideways underneath the heart for a chest opener or use two blocks, one along the upper spine and one under the head, for the same chest-opening effect.

· **Whole Body Opener:** Place the bolster lengthwise along the spine. Have the kids roll back on it and then scoot their shoulders and head off the bolster and onto the floor. Extend the arms and legs out and take deep, slow breaths.

· **Spine Twist One:** Lie on your back and have your bolster, pillow, rolled blanket, or block on the left side. Take the right knee up into the chest and fold it over onto the props for support. Extend the right arm out and rest and breathe. Then switch.

· **Spine Twist Two:** Place the bolster lengthways in front of you. Bring your left hip to the bolster with your knees bent towards the right. Extend the torso over the bolster and turn the right ear down. Place both hands on each side of the bolster with the elbows comfortably relaxed. Rest and breathe. Then switch.

Restorative Yoga Tips for Kids

Preparation for the Practice

Body Blessing - Movement Meditation

Sit comfortably. Inhale and float the arms up. As you exhale, take the hands to the top of your head slide your fingers down to the base of your skull. Bring your hands down the back of the neck to the shoulders and cascade the arms softly down each arm as if you were blessing your own body with love and reverence.

Take the hands to the chest, stomach, legs, and anywhere now that you intuitively need more love on and in your body. Bless your body with self-love. Give yourself permission to receive.

Swimmer's Breath

Inhale the breath and hold the breath from ten to twenty seconds. Exhale with a big *HAAA* sound. Kids love this one. It is great for relaxation and focus. It also strengthens lungs and respiration, and is great for athletic training.

Tension Relaxation

Lay on your back with arms and legs out wide. Inhale and squeeze the entire body. Exhale and relax with a nice *HAAA* sound. As you inhale, notice the breath moving into areas that feel tense and stressed. As you exhale, feel yourself let all of that go. Inhale and squeeze palms, arms, biceps, and triceps. Exhale and relax everything, every thought, muscle tissue organ in the body. Inhale and squeeze arms, legs, buttocks, point or flex the feet, then exhale and release to the whole body. Inhale, squeeze every muscle, exhale with a big SIGH, and let go of all the contractions. Inhale again, squeeze the muscles, exhale with more of an *AGGHHHH* sound deeply though the mouth, and feel the sound vibrate the inside of the head. Do it one more time with gusto. Exhale and release everything to the world. Pause in this space for at least five minutes.

You can do this breathing while sitting too. Inhale and make fists and squeeze the elbows into your sides as your shoulders go up towards the ears and exhale through the mouth with a great big SIGH, relaxing shoulders, arms and hands. Do this breathing exercise while sitting at the beginning of class or you can do it lying down at the end of class before *savasana*.

Guided Mindfulness Practices within Restorative Yoga

Viloma Breathwork

This technique can be practiced either seated or in a supine position. If you are sitting down, make sure you have a blanket, block, or bolster underneath the sitz bones so that your hips are higher than your knees. If this hurts the knees, place a rolled blanket under your ankles for support or place a block under each knee. Make sure the spine is nice and long, and you are comfortable and pain-free.

If you are lying down, place a bolster lengthwise under the spine and legs for support. If you don't have a bolster, place a blanket along the spine with another blanket crossways for a pillow. Extend the legs. Make sure you are comfortable. *Viloma* breath is good for focus, anxiety, fatigue, and depression.

In *viloma pranayama*, we will be inhaling in three stages or tiers. Take some normal and easy breaths to start. When you are ready, exhale the breath all the way out of the body.

· Inhale from pubic bone to navel and pause.

· Inhale from navel to heart center and pause.

· Lastly, inhale as deeply as you can without restrictions from the heart center to the head and pause. The pauses are just a two-second hold. Exhale a nice and slow fluid breath all the way out and then return to recovery breaths—breaths that are normal and natural.

Full Capacity Breathing

Sit comfortably with the hands on the lower belly and breathe deep into the belly six times. Now, take the hands to the heart, place them right over the chest heart area, and breathe into the heart six times. Take one hand to the belly and one hand to the heart. First, breathe slowly into the low belly and have the breath rise up into the heart and throat area. Feel the full capacity of breath. In our normal breathing, we only breathe at about ten percent. In this breathing, we are breathing using one hundred percent of lung capacity. This is great for maximum oxygen exchange and full use of lungs, cleansing the lower lobes of the lungs, strengthening the tissues, and the elasticity of the intercostal muscles. Great set up for relaxation.

Extended Exhale Breath

Sit or lie down comfortably. Place both palms on your chest or lap and close your eyes. Count three-to-five times and inhale deeply with each round. Slowly exhale to a count of six to ten. Your exhale should last twice as long as your inhale. I personally like the four to seven ratio. Repeat for a few rounds. This breathing technique is good for anxiety, depression, and grief.

Counting the Breath Backwards

Count the breath backward from any number you choose. I like to encourage the kids to count backward from twenty-seven (a derivative of 108). Inhale twenty-seven, exhale twenty-seven all the way to one. This is great breathing exercise for releasing thoughts and allowing the body to release and relax with every exhalation.

Breathing in Child's Pose

Come into child's pose, and the teacher can place their hands on the backs of the students (optional) to help them find and direct their breath into their back bodies. Have them breathe into your hands or just breathe into their back body. This breath is great for anxiousness and restlessness and teaches kids to breathe into anything tight or sore in the back. It is also useful for the kidneys and adrenal glands and for releasing fear in the body.

Breathing with a Prop

Get a stuffed animal, a crystal, or a yoga block and place that item on the student's back body in child's pose or on the belly in *savasana* pose. Have the child breathe ten breaths, allowing that item to rise and fall, to lift and release. This breathing teaches the kids to focus, to inhale and exhale fully, and to relax.

Being a Witness

Lie on your back and see if you can just observe. Observe the sounds, the breath, the temperature, the floor beneath you, the taste in your mouth, and the smells without letting the mind go down the storyline. Be a witness to your thoughts but not attached to them. Notice how our senses can pull you away from being present. Now see if you can let go and be present. Can you relax deeper and go within? Can you notice stillness and then thoughts? When thoughts come in, can you erase them and just concentrate on the emptiness of space or nothingness?

Moving Inward

Find a comfortable place to sit, lie down, or come into a child's pose. Bring your awareness to the sounds in the room. Now bring your awareness to the borders of your mat. Now bring your awareness to the edges of your skin. Now bring your awareness to the sounds of your breath. Notice the texture, temperature, and sound of your breath. Now feel the pulsation of your heartbeat. Rest in this space inside.

One Minute Meditation

Set the timer for one minute and see if the kids can focus on the sounds of nature. If thoughts come in, give them these strategies to deal with the distractions: have them picture those thoughts surrounded by a balloon and visualize releasing the balloon, letting those thoughts floating away. After one minute is up, talk about the distractions and allow the kids to share.

Third Eye Relaxation

Sit and lift the gaze to the third eye center. Focus on the colors behind the eyes, noticing how the colors morph into each other, maybe from black to red to purple. Whatever you experience is perfect. Relax the brain and all thoughts. Be with this visualization for one to three minutes. At the end of the meditation, honor whatever came up for you. Be aware of your thoughts but not attached to them.

Circle of Light Meditation

Lie on your back with support under your knees and your head. Feel the body rise and fall with the breath. Count back from ten and with every exhale and every number, see if you can peel away the layers of stress, agendas, thoughts, and distractions. Imagine you're peeling back the layers of life, like you are peeling an onion, layer after layer releasing as you return to the source and reconnect with that sacred center, the pearlized iridescent shiny center of the onion, which is your true self.

Once you get to number one, feel the body the most relaxed. Stay here for a few moments, being in a relaxed space without thoughts. If thoughts come, honor them but let them pass and bring your attention back to the breath. Now bring your awareness to your feet. As you increase the breath, notice a white light, a light that has all the healing of the universe, and has the information our body, mind, and heart needs, soaking in through the feet. Inhale this white light up through the ankles, into the calves, up through the knees, thighs, and hips, surrounding the flesh, the muscles, and all the bones. Allow the white light to be inhaled up through the hips into the torso, into the chest, up through the heart, and allow the white light to flow down through the arms and cascade out through the fingertips. Inhale the white light up through the throat, into the face, head, skull, and brain and shine out through the crown of the head.

Now visualize that white light turning to whatever color you like: purple, silver, gold, rainbow. Now take that color around the body in a big bright circle of light around and around and around. This circle of light is creating a bubble of protection, a barrier so that if anything negative comes at you, it will bounce right off. Now color your bubble in with a mother-of-pearl color—an iridescent rainbow sheen. Shade the front, back, sides, bottom, and top. Color the entire inside of the bubble. Now think of a positive affirmation inside that heart space and radiate that emotion from the heart to inside that circle of light.

Practice this meditation when you go out into a crowd, when you feel your energy is low, if you are sensitive to energy, if you're feeling emotional, sick, or if you are an empath. This circle of light will ground your energy and protect your health.

Lesson Seven – Yoga and Crystals

Crystal Healing

Crystal healing is another tool for kids to use to ground down, relax, and soak in the Earth's energy when feeling stressed or scattered. Crystals are powerful conductors of energy. Crystal energy can help us on our spiritual journey because crystals hold our intentions and prayers and remind us of our connection to the Earth. The beauty of crystal healing is that each crystal has a unique vibration. The vibrations of these energy crystals can help us reach a higher state of being. When your body contacts a crystal, you attune to the higher frequency of the crystal. Physical, mental, and spiritual blockages melt away with positive and uplifting energy.

We continuously have the ability and responsibility to choose our thoughts. Every day brings a new challenge or new beginning, and as we use healing crystals, we remember to take the time to slow ourselves down. We reconnect to the healing vibrations within the Earth. We learn to be patient; just as it took millennia for the crystal to form, it also takes years for us to evolve. Discovering the power of crystals and learning how to harness that energy takes time, as well. As you study, grow, and change, crystals remind you to be thankful for the abundance of Mother Nature and the great mysteries of the universe around us.

A great way to harness the healing power of crystals or stones is to perform yoga, meditate, or lay with the crystals on your body. Whichever you try, first create an intention of what you want to create in your life and what affirmations you want that crystal to hold. Crystals connect us to the Earth as physical forms with powerful vibrations. Their energy connects you to the universe as the crystals touch your skin or become part of your environment. As you put your intentions and thoughts into the universe, the crystals recognize your

individual vibrations and serve to amplify the energy you share. Crystals have the intelligence to hold your prayers and mantras. They are a reminder of our power and beauty and our unique imprint in this world. We shine just as bright as those precious jewels.

Meditation and Relaxation with Crystals

- **Meditation Pose**: Sit comfortably and place crystals in each hand. Create an intention that reflects what you call to you in your heart, mind, or for healing.

- **Relaxation Pose**: Lay on your back and place the crystals on your body. You can also surround your body with crystals, for example, putting one in each of the four directions. Laying the crystals on the *chakras* is also a powerful practice or simply place a crystal on the heart.

Crystal Guide[4]

Quartz: Protection, problem-solving, cleansing, charging other crystals, supports immune system & pineal gland, energizes all *chakras*

Smoky Quartz: Aural cleansing, grounding, detoxifying, absorbs negativity, encourages humor, base and earth star *chakra*

Rose Quartz: Love, forgiveness, heart opening and releasing, supports circulation, uplifts and protects heart *chakra*

Citrine: Attracts wealth and prosperity, calms stomach and digestion, energizes second and third *chakras*

Amethyst: Energy protection, stress reduction, mood regulation, crown *chakra*

Opal: Love, inner peace, communication, loyalty, faithfulness, balances throat *chakra*

Moonstone: Calms stomach, safe travels, karmic healing, communication, joy, enhances reflection and introspection

Labradorite: Energy protection, spiritual alignment, rational and intuitive wisdom, energizes throat and third eye *chakra*

Turquoise: Stress and pain reduction, letting go, freedom, strength, safe travels, helps with communication and intuition

Aquamarine: Good luck, ocean travel, cooling, calming, introspection, throat *chakra*

Black Tourmaline: Energetic protection, absorbs negativity, shields from electronic emanations

Obsidian: Grounding, confronting inner demons and dark truths, earth star *chakra*

Rhodonite: Self-love, heart activation, healing emotional wounds, stress relief, compassion, and earth star *chakra*

Malachite: Energetic clearing, reduces swelling and inflammation, detoxification, breaks past cycles

Amber: Space clearing, energy protection, stress reduction, physical alignment

Orange Carnelian: Energy boosting, stimulating, charging other crystals, supports reproductive organs

Tiger's Eye: Abundance, knowledge, vision, courage, integrity, power

Lapis Lazuli: Soothes migraines, calming, sedate energy, metaphysical attunement

Auralite: Stillness, serenity, simplicity, stress relief, quiets mind

Agate: Centering, calming, self-acceptance and harmony, crown *chakra*

Jasper: Aural cleansing, problem solving, organization, imagination

Hematite: Protection, grounding. This crystal closes your aura to keep out negative energy

Jade: Ambition, inspiration, motivation, longevity

Pyrite: Defense, protection, enhances strength of mind and will power

Garnet: Health, creativity, helps to prevent nightmares, heals broken bonds of love, helps depression, heart and blood stimulant

CHAPTER **12** (July)

The Yoga *of* FUN

"When I was five years old, my mother always told me that happiness was the key to life. When I went to school, they asked me what I wanted to be when I grew up and I wrote down 'happy.' They told me I didn't understand the assignment and I told them they didn't understand life."

-John Lennon[1]

July: The Yoga of FUN

July is a wonderful time to celebrate the divine self, marvel in nature, and feel gratitude for being alive. It's the height of the summer season, and it's about keeping the mind clear and the heart full. It's a wonderful time to let loose, feel the freedom of being carefree, and soak in all that incredible energy of the Sun. It's a great time to reconnect with your inner child and strengthen that intuition. It's a chance to rediscover how to be in the moment and get in touch with our feelings and emotions. It's about learning how to take responsibility for our happiness.

As we get older and feel more of life's duties, obligations, and stressors, we forget how to feel free and spontaneous like we were when we were children. We forget how thrilling it is to run, jump, hike, climb, be silly, laugh, and be totally carefree. We forget how it feels to be timeless and lost in the state of flow. One of the most healing things for all of us is to cherish that inner child and get to know them again and again. Flow arts such as learning how to hula hoop, jump rope, use poi balls, and get creative with scarves and belly skirts are fun ways to invoke that state of thrill and joy. Flow arts are another way to weave presence, breath, and coordination, and face the fear of doing something new. It's rexperiencing how to be lost in fun and be a kid again. For kids, it's about feeling gratitude for the opportunity to learn more about oneself through these different practices and to rejoice in the state of play.

The summer months are an exciting time to continue doing kids' yoga offerings and providing ways to manage their feelings and emotions through yoga, games, and art projects. Special nature retreats or doing yoga and art outside are great ways to teach the kids something new and have fun. July is a month of self-empowerment and learning about ways to take full responsibility for our life and our health. It's a month to celebrate our yoga practice and all the wisdom we have learned throughout the year. It's about finding further ways to nourish the heart space so that we feel rested, vibrant, connected, and ready to shine when we return to school.

In Lesson One, we dive back into arts and crafts to create *Ganesh* masks. This art project is a wonderful way to celebrate the elephant deity, who symbolizes this carefree and jovial attitude about life. *Ganesh* is a resource to remind us that we have the power to overcome any obstacles on our path. I love to add the mantra *'I am strong, beautiful, and free'* as we dive into making these cool and creative masks.

In Lesson Two, we will learn how to eat clean and healthy. Various modalities will be introduced that support a healthy body and mind, like learning how to cook fun foods and the importance of nutrition.

In Lesson Three, we will explore the benefits of pure essential oils and how to use these natural modalities as a safe and effective way to care for ourselves and others.

In Lesson Four will explore flow arts such as hula hoops, poi balls, jump ropes, and belly dancing. These incredibly fun activities spice up your class just enough to keep it lighthearted and interconnected.

In Lesson Five, we will learn about the importance of heart-centered practices.

Lesson One – Ganesh Masks

As we learned before, *Ganesh* is the lord of success and the destroyer of evils and obstacles. Throughout the world, he is honored as a symbol of education, wisdom, and wealth. Followers recognize his place as the destroyer of vanity, selfishness, and pride. He is the embodiment of hope and peace.

Ganesh's body and head represent the soul and our earthly existence. His elephant head represents wisdom, his trunk symbolizes *OM*. By making elephant masks out of plaster gauze, we are embodying and celebrating *Ganesh's* playful and childlike ways.

These *Ganesh* masks make an imprint of the child's facial bone structure. These masks are something to treasure as the child grows and evolves. The masks can be ornamental wall hangings that can symbolize their youth. The decorative nature of these masks is something to hold near and dear to the parent or caregiver's heart.

When tackling this project, it's helpful to have volunteers . If you do not have volunteers or extra help, the other kids can plaster gauze their elephant trunks while you plaster gauze each student's face.

Ganesh Masks: *How to Make them...*

step 1. Prepare your supplies and create the mold.

a. Place all the plaster gauze strips in large bowl and fill another flat dish or tray with water.

b. Have the child lay down and place a twelve-inch square piece plastic wrap over the forehead. Make sure it covers a little past the hairline, eyes, cheeks, and top of the nose. Make sure the child can still breathe easily, either through the mouth or nose. Have the plastic wrap extend on each side past the ears.

c. Take a strip of plaster gauze, dip it in the water and place it on the forehead on top of the plastic wrap. Continue with this process, covering the forehead.

d. Then, take a skinny piece of plaster gauze dipped in water over the third eye down to the tip of the nose and mold around the nose and eyes. If you wish to cover the eyes, you can paint over them later and make your own eyes on the dried plaster gauze. If you leave eye holes open, then the kids can use it as a mask to see through.

e. Continue by covering the cheeks and temples all the way to the hairline with plaster gauze. Smooth the gauze around the face, making sure it feels even, with no bumps or air bubbles. The plaster gauze doesn't have to be perfectly even on each side of the face and head. When it dries, there is an opportunity to cut it the way you like and or add ears and a crown to cover uneven edges. Once the plaster gauze has dried a bit (it usually takes about five to ten minutes), the mask should slide nicely off of the child's face.

f. Next comes drawing the ears, crown, and tusks onto paper plates and cutting them out. The students can even start to plaster gauze the ears, tusk, and crown.

g. Take a paper towel roll for the trunk and have the kids plaster gauze all around the roll. If they want a curved trunk, they can curl it or bend it at the end and gauze over.

h. Dry the plastered masks, trunks, tusks, ears, and crowns overnight.

Supplies:

· Plaster gauze cut into 1 x 3-inch pieces

· Washable paint and paintbrushes

· Feathers, beads, jewels, sequence

· Stapler · Paper plates ·Plastic wrap

· Paper towel rolls for the trunks

· Tacky glue and or glue gun

step 2. Assemble the masks.

a. After everything is dry, staple the ears on each side and the crown on top.

b. If necessary, trim off any jagged edges of dried plaster gauze under cheekbones.

c. Take the plaster gauze trunk and staple it under the nose part of the mask. Add the tusks. If the staples are really bumpy, plaster gauze over where the mask and ears, crown, and tusk meet for a smooth surface. Use a good amount of gauze for sturdiness.

d. Let it dry overnight again.

step 3. Paint the masks.

a. Place the paint onto paper plates and have the children paint their masks. They can add eyes or eyelashes, third eye, or do whatever they wish to decorate it.

b. Let it dry overnight again.

Step 4. Decorate the masks.

a. Adding the jewels, feathers, and accessories with glue. I like a hot glue gun for heavier accessories like bigger gems or tacky glue, which works great for sequins, feathers, and light beads.

b. Add elastic bands to the back if the masks will be worn, or string to use them as wall hangings.

c. Let them dry overnight and they are ready!

Lesson Two –
The Yoga of Food

Food As Medicine

Proper nutrition is important for growing children because it plays a significant role in their well-being. Food affects every aspect of our bodies: we are what we eat.

Food and nutrition are essential to health and feeling good. Making smart food choices helps support balance in our emotions, mental clarity, focus, concentration, and physical strength.

Clean and conscious eating is part of the yogic lifestyle for both adults and kids. The good news is that when we embark on the healing journey of yoga, our body naturally craves better, cleaner food. Clean, healthy food is food without fillers, preservatives, artificial flavors, and excess sugars. Nutrition is best when it comes from the basic elements of sunlight, soil, water, and air. The more we encourage our children to eat whole foods from the Earth and make healthy choices, the stronger their bodies and spirits become. They find a connection and a deeper respect for organic farming and all the workers who are in the food industry providing for all the people on Earth. The spiritual aspect comes from honoring where our food is produced and how it gets on our plate. The meditation is experiencing the food entering our body and being aware of all the nutrients, minerals, and vitamins our bodies integrate and soak in. The prayer is about blessing all of the food and drinks to nourish us in all the ways. The body is a temple, and what we put into it should be pure.

Knowing what is in our food is essential for health. As we teach our children the basics of healthy eating, it will serve them well throughout their lives. We can support them by offering healthy snacks and meals to balance every part of their being. Food is medicine, and teaching kids how to take their health and well-being into their own hands is very empowering.

Eating Seasonally

Bring in foods that are being grown within that particular season. There are so many fresh fruits and vegetables in the summer to bring for the kids to try. Allow the students to learn the healthy components and benefits of these foods. Talk about superfoods and the benefits of eating a plant-based diet. Revisit sustainability—how and what we eat affects not only ourselves but also our environments.

Yogi Cooking Class *Recipes*

Hummus

Homemade hummus is easy and delicious. With only a few ingredients, you can create traditional hummus. Traditional recipes include chickpeas (or garbanzo beans), lemon, tahini, garlic, and salt. A good food processor helps make smooth, creamy hummus.

Ingredients:

- A high-powered blender or food processor
- Canned garbanzo beans (chickpeas), lemon juice, sesame seeds or tahini, garlic, salt
- Spatula and serving dish
- Chopped fresh parsley for garnish
- Hummus dippers like pita bread wedges, crackers, or raw vegetables

Instructions:

1. Drain the beans, holding back some of the bean liquid for later.
2. Place beans, lemon juice, sesame seeds or tahini, garlic, and salt in the food processor.
3. Blend at high speed, stopping to scrape the sides if necessary.
4. Add reserved bean juice as needed until consistency is uniform.
5. Put dip in a serving dish and sprinkle with garnish.
6. Serve with pita bread, crackers, or raw vegetables.

Cacao Cashew Butter Energy Balls

Ingredients:

- ½ cup pure maple syrup
- 1 cup cashew butter
- 2 ¼ cup sprouted rolled oats
- ¼ cup cacao powder
- ½ cup coconut or ground flax
- ½ cup vegan chocolate chips

Instructions:

1. In a medium-size bowl, mix together the cashew butter and maple syrup until well blended.
2. Add the rest of the ingredients and stir; it should have a sticky, crumbly texture.
3. Roll into small balls and store them in an airtight container.

Healthy Granola[3]

Ingredients:

- ¼ cup unsweetened applesauce
- ¼ cup agave, honey or maple syrup
- 1 tbsp coconut oil, melted
- ½ tsp vanilla
- ½ tsp cinnamon
- ⅛ tsp salt
- 1 ½ cups rolled oats
- ¾ cup total of extra add ins, chopped nuts, seeds, coconut, dried fruit (optional)

Instructions:

1. Preheat the oven to 325 degrees Fahrenheit.
2. In a bowl, combine the applesauce, agave, coconut oil, and vanilla.
3. Stir in the cinnamon and salt until well-combined.
4. Stir in oats, nuts, seeds, or dried fruit.
5. Coat a large, rimmed baking sheet with coconut oil or non-stick spray.
6. Spread out the granola into a level layer.
7. Bake on the middle rack for 12-15 minutes until the bottom begins to brown.
8. Flip with a spatula, being careful not to let it crumble apart.
9. Bake for another 12—15 minutes until the granola gets crunchy.
10. Set aside to cool.
11. Transfer to an airtight container for storage.

Caramel Popcorn

Ingredients:

- 1 cup of white or yellow corn kernels
- ½ cup unrefined coconut oil
- ¼ cup maple syrup
- 5—6 drops of food-grade cinnamon bark oil (optional)
- Sprinkle with ground cinnamon and salt to taste

Instructions:

1. Pop the popcorn, either in an air popper, or on the stove with ¼ cup of the coconut oil.
2. In a separate pan, melt the remaining ¼ cup of coconut oil and stir in the maple syrup and optional cinnamon oil.
3. Pour the mixture over popcorn, pausing to toss and mix.
4. Sprinkle it with ground cinnamon and sea salt. Mix thoroughly and enjoy.

Pamela's Gluten Free Banana Bread[2]

Ingredients: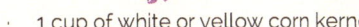

- 4 tbs melted butter
- 2 eggs beaten
- 1 cup bananas mashed
- ½ cup sugar or honey
- ½ tsp cinnamon
- ⅛ tsp salt
- 1¾ cup Pamela's Baking and Pancake Mix[2]
- ¾ cup total of extra add ins, vegan chocolate chips, carob, chopped nuts, oats, seeds, coconut, dried fruit (optional)

Instructions:

1. Preheat the oven to 350 degrees Fahrenheit.
2. In a bowl, beat together butter, sugar or honey, eggs and banana.
3. Add in the remaining ingredients and mix together.
4. Stir in optional add ins.
5. Pour into a greased loaf pan.
6. Bake for one hour, or until an inserted toothpick comes out clean.

Lesson Three – Aromatherapy

The Benefits of Aromatherapy

Aromatherapy is an alternative medicine practice that utilizes pure essential oils derived from many different healing plants. Essential oils have been studied to promote energy, help with relaxation, stimulate the immune system and have powerful effects on brain health. The oils are extracted from the whole plant and can have positive impacts on our entire system. Oils can be used topically, aromatically, and some oils internally. Each essential oil contains hundreds of different compounds. Each compound has different medicinal benefits. The oils can help boost mood and bring a sense of well-being. When you inhale an oil, the olfactory nerves bring the aroma to the limbic system in the brain. The smells stimulate the amygdala, where all of our emotions are stored but can be released. The important chemistry behind the aromatic compounds are the terpenes/terpenoids, and aliphatic molecules, all of which improve cognitive function.

Studies have shown that certain oils, like frankincense, can pass through the blood-brain barrier and have an incredible healing effect on the brain resulting in mood stabilization and improving brain health. These oils support learning, focus, and mood disorders like depression. They can also help with our concentration and ability to learn new things. Essential oils have neuroprotective, anti-aging potentials and may help with dementia, epilepsy, anxiety, and other neurological disorders. The oils get absorbed by the body, and they work their magic. Essential oils are antiviral, anti-bacterial, anti-microbial, anti-tumor, and anti-fungal. Having oils in the room can help kill airborne pathogens, boost the immune system, disinfect, and energetically clear the air.

Essential oils are a powerful addition to all yoga classes. They are naturally grounding and are fun to add to discussions about the healing power of plants, nature, and science. I have found that sharing oils at the beginning of each class helps create focus and intention for our session to come. It also brings the children into the present moment. Different oils aid in different things. However, when inhaled, all oils help us take a moment to stop, take a deep breath, and connect to the now. With added intentions, the brain can start to re-wire with positive behavioral patterns. Oils are an incredible and natural way to help children with first aid, relaxation, and for physical complaints like stomach aches, pain, bruising and bug bites.

For more information or to purchase pure essential oils:

Breathing Techniques with Pure Essential Oils

Balancing Emotions

Relaxation/Stress: Six belly breaths. Inhale deep into the lower belly, lower abdomen six times.	**Oil choices:** Lavender, bergamot ylang-ylang, Roman chamomile, patchouli, geranium
Anxiety/Depression: Longer exhalations. Inhale four counts, pause, exhale seven counts, pause (exhales are longer). Boxed Breathing. Inhale four counts in, hold for four, exhale for four, and pause for four.	**Oil Choices:** Wild orange, basil, frankincense, sandalwood, myrrh cedarwood, vanilla, tulsi
Energy: *Bhastrika* Breath. Inhale, belly out, exhale, belly in (rapid breaths) twenty times. *Kapalabhati* Breathing. Exhale through mouth or nose by drawing belly in. Exhale rapidly twenty to sixty times.	**Oil Choices:** Lemon, peppermint, wild orange, white fir, lemongrass, rosemary, ylang-ylang, cinnamon, thyme, spearmint, cypress, eucalyptus, wintergreen, grapefruit
Vision/Intuition/Balance: Alternate nostril breathing or *Nadi shodhana*. Close off one nostril and inhale through the open nostril and pause. Close of the other nostril and exhale through the open nostril and pause and repeat five to ten times.	**Oil Choices:** Sandalwood, myrrh, frankincense, blue tansy, tea tree, patchouli, jasmine, vetiver, lemon balm
Anger: Tension release breath. Inhale, elbows in and make fists, shoulders up to ears, shrug tight and exhale through the mouth with a *HAAA* sound and relax the whole body.	**Oil Choices:** Geranium, lemon-grass, vetiver, cypress, lavender, Roman chamomile, bergamot, ylang-ylang, rose, marjoram

Some Helpful Tips

· Always have parent or guardian's permission before applying essential oils to the skin or spraying essential oils in the air.

· Safe places for application for the roll-on bottles are inner wrists, neck, and feet.

· Safe places to spray are in an open room, your pillow before bed, or any place that smells stinky. Never spray directly at someone or at yourself. The spray can get into the eyes, nose, or mouth.

· Wash your hands after every application, so you don't rub the eyes. If you rub your eyes, don't use water to flush. Instead, get a cloth or napkin, put a carrier oil on it like coconut oil or olive oil, and gently swab the eye. The aromatic compounds will gently lift out of the eye and into the heavier, more dense oil.

· If the skin starts to feel hot or irritated, get a lotion or carrier oil and apply to skin. Don't wash with soap and water.

Potion-Making Project with Essential Oils

What you will need:

· 5 ml or 10 ml roll-on bottles

· 2 oz glass spray bottles

· A variety of pure essential oils

How to put together:

1. Fill the larger spray bottles with mostly water and have the kids add the drops of oils to the bottles. Five to ten drops per bottle.

2. Fill the smaller roll-on bottles with avocado oil or grapeseed oil and add five to ten drops of essential oils. Bless the bottles before use.

3. Make sure the kids know what oils they are using and their benefits. Discuss safety (especially allergies).

Lesson Four – Flow Arts

Flow arts such as hula hooping, the use of poi balls, jump ropes, and dance encourage us to be comfortable in our bodies through fun and spontaneous movement. This rhythmically induced state of natural flow is innate within all beings. The activation of free-form movement is a powerful way to generate flow and experience collective meditation. These dynamic practices can release tension, increase energy, connect new neural pathways, and train the breath. They teach joy, spontaneity, and confidence. These are supplemental activities that I have used for decades to either add to the curriculum or to generate comradery within the classroom.

Hula Hoops

Hula hoops are a useful resource to have in the classroom. I like to have them out when the kids come in for class so I can meet and greet the parents and know that the kids have something to do when they arrive. Hula hoops are an enjoyable way to warm up for a yoga class. You can even use them during class as a way to break up the energy. There are many fun tricks to teach with the hula hoops, and they are a great resource for coordination, balance, breath, and body awareness.

Poi Balls

Poi balls also teach patience and coordination. They are fun to play with and learn different moves and tricks. They are a terrific way to warm up for yoga class. I like those with a foam ball on the end, so they are easier and lighter to use and won't hurt if they collide with our bodies.

Jump Rope

I like to have the jump ropes available at the end of class. If you have the space where the kids can hang out after class, jump ropes are a great way to create new friendships. You can have a single long rope (I like the beaded ones) and teach the kids the basics of jumping rope. They can learn to run in when they get better, and older kids might like to learn double Dutch with two ropes.

Belly Dancing

Belly dancing is a supplemental activity that invokes bodily awareness through controlled movement. The kids love the spontaneity of the free-form movement. They also love to make up their routines.

Here are some moves I like to teach with belly skirts:

· Snake Arms

· Hip Bump in a circle

· Shimmy and Hop

· Figure 8

· Basic hip circles

· Skipping, Hopping, and Free Dance

Lesson Five – Heart-Centered

Our hearts have so much power and magnificence. The heart has both an intelligent energy and an electromagnetic radiance. It's a sensory organ that, like the brain, generates a powerful energetic field. The heart is our illuminating guide toward love, creativity, and deep knowing. It's that which connects us all.

The heart center is one of the most important and powerful places to rest awareness every day. When we can think, act, love, and respond from that place in the heart, our yoga forever connects us to our highest self and our highest will. Use these meditations below to foster a cohesive and unified heart.

Teaching heart-centered practices to kids is a way to enhance comfort, connection, self-love, and compassion.

Heart-Centered *Practices*

Heart Yoga

Warm up the shoulders, hips, back and legs. Heart yoga is any postures that open the heart like; camel, upward dog, cobra, swan, bow, bridge and full wheel pose.

Heart Opening Circles

Take one arm and move it in a big circle and feel the shoulder open. Repeat with the other arm. Now take one arm in the other direction and then repeat on the other side. Now, take both arms up and see if you can take one arm forward in a circle and the other arm backward in a circle. This is good for the right and left brain! Try it on the other side.

Heart Awareness Breathing

Place your hand to the heart and notice the breath moving through the chest and into your hand. Now, feel the heartbeat. Honor that life force moving through you that connects to something greater. Some bigger energy is regulating your heartbeat. Feel that power and know that you are magical. Know you are full of love.

Spiral Heart Movement Meditation

Sit comfortably and take the hands one in front of the other at the base chakra. Criss-cross them forward and back up toward the head, envisioning a DNA helix. As the hands extend up to the sky, take them outward and down as if you were creating a circle of light around the body. Now take the hands to the heart center and honor your life, your DNA, all that you have received from your parents. Feel grateful for being alive in this time and space. Honor that you are unique. Honor your mission. You are the only one on this planet who is just like you. This meditation can be a way to heal and pray for family. It can also be a way for connecting to ancestors and healing generational trauma. It can also be a prayer for yourself to stimulate internal health and the flow of energy in your body.

Connecting Heart to Third Eye Breathing Meditation

Sit comfortably and bring awareness into your heart space. As you inhale, bring awareness from the heart into the third eye. As you exhale, bring awareness back into the heart. Inhale heart to the third eye. Exhale the third eye back down to the heart. Repeat a few times and end with exhaling the energy back into the heart. This is a great breathing technique for bringing awareness and energy to both the heart and mind. As the energy passes through the throat *chakra*, this breathing helps bridge the gap between our hearts and minds and between our emotions and thoughts. Clearing the throat energy can help us think, act, and speak more from our hearts and intuition. It's about honoring that third eye energy of the inner teacher, higher self, and that self that knows best. It's about living in our highest truth.

Cooling the Heart Fire Breath - *Sitali*

Sometimes in the summer, there is a lot of heat. This could be externally from the Sun, but emotions like anger and frustration have a lot of heat, too. Certain foods also carry a lot of heat. Use this sitali breathing to cool yourself down and to calm the heart fire.

Coil the tongue or purse the lips, inhale deep into the lungs and feel the cool breath come in, and exhale the heat out through the mouth with one long exhale. This is great when feeling literally hot or overheated and is a great breath for releasing heat or *ama* (toxins) from the body. *Sitali* breathing is cooling and relaxing to the mind and emotions like anger, hate, frustration, and irritability.

Nourishing the Heart with Chocolate Meditation

Take your kids or students through a chocolate meditation, either while seated in circle time or lying down. Start by talking about where chocolate comes from and what the individual ingredients are. Talk about how all those ingredients got to you. Did they come by plane, boat, or train? Talk about the health benefits of chocolate. Raw cacao is an antioxidant, chock full of vitamins and minerals. Talk about slowing down when eating and having all the five senses come in for the tasting. Have them be in communion with the whole experience.

Heart Star Meditation

Lie on your back comfortably or sit with the spine nice and tall. Bring breath in and out of the heart with a sense of gratitude, feeding your soul's purpose and surrendering your whole life as is to the universe. Honor that everything is as perfect as it needs to be, that every experience is a lesson, and everyone you have met is a teacher. Honor all the wisdom and learnings you have discovered in this life. Feel gratitude for this opportunity to be here now. Amplify the breath within that heart space. Notice a flicker of light emerging in the center of the heart. Breathe deeper into that spark and allow the flame to get bigger and brighter. Fill the heart up with light, like the brightest star in the night sky. Allow the shards of light to emerge from the physical heart, move toward the flesh, and shine out every part of the body—the pores, the fingers, toes, eyes, ears, nose, mouth, and crown of the head. Imagine the whole body like a vibrant, shiny, and radiant star. Honor this light within you, this spark of divinity. Be the light, live the light, feel the light, travel with the light, spread the light. Know you are of that light.

Hand Massage for the Heart Energy

Massaging the hands stimulates the meridians of the lungs, heart, pericardium, small intestine, large intestine, and thyroid. Use one hand to massage the other with essential oils (optional) and give the middle finger (pericardium) and the pinky finger (heart meridian) lots of love.

Love Meditation

Lie down on your back and feel the Earth beneath your body. Now honor the natural breath that you are breathing that is connected to all things. This breath naturally rises and falls, and moves in and out. Bring your awareness into your heart space and think of three things that you love and adore about yourself.

Rainbow Hand Heart Meditation

Sit with both palms facing up in *hasta mudra*. Imagine a rainbow. Feel the rainbow starting and ending in each of your palms as the brilliance of colors bows over. The rainbow can feel like a toy slinky; you can hold this rainbow and play with the rainbow between your hands. Now, inhale the colors from the top of the bow into the heart. Inhale five times, taking all the vibrant colors into the heart *chakra*. Allow those colors to vibrate around the *mandala* of the body, drawing health and healing to every cell.

Notes:

PART **6**

CHAPTER **13**

Youth Yoga Resources

"If you feel lost, disappointed, hesitant, or weak, return to yourself, to who you are, here and now, and when you get there, you will discover yourself, like a lotus flower in full bloom, even in a muddy pond, beautiful and strong."
-Masaru Emoto[1]

End of the Year -
Reflection Journaling

These broad and open ended questions are always good for the kids to contemplate at the end of the school year, over summer break, or any time within this curriculum. These also can be teaching points. *Have the kids journal these questions or use them as discussion topics.* Revisit the questions and answers over time. It can be surprising how the answers change.

· Yoga is . . . ?

· Do's of a Yogi:

· Don'ts of a Yogi:

· The symbol *OM* means:

· My favorite pose:

· My least favorite pose:

· The pose I am working on:

· This summer, my *seva* Project is:

· This summer, my yoga *sadhana* will consist of:

· I am letting go of this:

· I am opening my heart, my mind, my body, and my awareness to:

· I love this about myself:

· This is whom I am sending love to right now:

· These are my prayers for Mother Earth:

Journaling All About ME:

These are great questions to ask your older yogis, who have been in your program for a while. You will get to know a lot about your students as they get to discover more about themselves! Revisit these questions and answers next year. Has anything changed?

· Name:

· Age:

· Birthdate:

· Allergies

· Astrological sign and element:

· What traits resonate with me?

· Chinese zodiac:

· Positive traits?

· Traits out of balance?

· What do I love about myself?

· What am I working on loving?

· What am I grateful for?

· What are my talents or "superhuman powers?"

· What energies am I inviting into my life?

· What energies am I ready to let go of?

· What in life depresses me?

· What in life scares me?

· What in life excites me?

· What is my intention for the week? The month? The rest of the year?

· What am I affirming in my life?

· What am I praying for? Can I pray for this wish to bless every living creature on this planet?

· What does 'world peace' mean to me?

· What is the change I would like to see in the world?

· How can my words, thoughts, and deeds affect all of humanity?

· What would I like to contribute to or what is my passion in this life?

· What would I like to be when I grow up?

· What is my dream? How can I reach that dream?

Yamas & Niyamas

Bonus Journaling and Classroom Discussions

Have the kids create homemade mini journals (see below) or have them journal their truths and appreciations on a piece of paper. You can also use the template below for a guided meditation or *savasana* at the end of class. I have found that kids also like to share their answers in circle time or at the end of class. Revisit these questions throughout the year or throughout the time you get to spend with them.

Questions to ask:

What can you work on with the yamas?
For example: Being kinder, thinking more positively, helping others, sharing, speaking from the heart, not wasting time, protecting energy, releasing attachments, connecting to universal energy, sitting quietly, non-harming practices, taking responsibility for all actions.

What can you work on with the niyamas?
For example: Using yoga and breathwork to purify, washing hands and keeping clean, helping with chores, appreciating what you have, paying attention and being more mindful and grateful, reading inspiring and spiritual books, reflecting on self, connecting to nature.

Further Discussion:

· How can you be of more service?

· How can you give back to the planet?

· Teach someone something worthwhile. What would that be?

· Tell someone you love them and appreciate them. Who would that be, and how would you express that?

Self-empowerment Art Projects

Homemade Journals

Take two pieces of paper, fold them in half or three ways, and cut them at the folds. Stack the papers together and then staple them together into a mini journal. Use the mini journal for the *yamas* and *niyamas* discussion.

The Lotus Flower

The lotus flower represents purity, beauty, and a fresh start. The metaphor of the lotus flower blooming has an incredibly special meaning. The lotus flower grows out of muddy and murky waters yet grows to be the most beautiful entity. It doesn't matter where you have come from in your life or what has happened to you in your past. What matters most is how you transform those lessons into something beautiful and great. It matters how you rise to the occasion. You can always become that beautiful flower if you choose. You can always change your thoughts. Willpower is about taking full responsibility for your life. It's about choice. You can always begin again by learning from those lessons and moving forward with grace. You can always grow into that most auspicious and beautiful flower, while letting go of the past and starting new one thought, one word, and one deed at a time.

Lotus Flower Reflective Journaling

- Reflect on the phases of your life. What can you improve upon? How can you be a better yogi? How can you take better care of yourself? Your family? Your friends? Of Mother Earth?

- What has been hard in your life? What can you let go of but don't want to? Where are you stuck? What is holding you back? What are your strengths? What are aspects of your personality that you can work on? What lessons have you learned in this life?

- How can you nurture that flower within to help it grow into an amazing lotus?

Lotus Chant

Om Mani Padme Om – *I am the jewel within the lotus*

A diamond is just a rock that transforms into the most lustrous of gems under extreme amounts of pressure and heat. Just like in life, sometimes it takes pressure, challenge, commitment, and even hard, demanding times to transform into the most beautiful diamond. What is overwhelming or hard to overcome in your life right now? Can you see the healing within that situation? Sometimes stepping out of our comfort zone helps us grow and become stronger.

Lotus Art

Make a five-petal lotus flower for each *yama* and *niyama*. Have the kids write out the Sanskrit letters in each petal and or write ways in which you can practice that discipline.

Paint a lotus flower. Think of aspects of the divine that you would like to dedicate to each petal. For example, grace, beauty, kindness, love, friendship, connection. Paint a symbol of those representations on each petal or simply bless each petal with beautiful color and artistic expression.

Lily Pads

Gather tissue paper, paper plates, glue, and markers. Color the back of a paper plate the color of water. Now draw in some lily pads. Scrunch the tissue paper to look like flowers and glue it onto the plate. Let it dry. Lilies symbolize new growth and new possibilities. What seeds of intention are you planting or nourishing?

The Lotus Flow

Sequence a yoga flow that will open the hips and knees for the lotus pose. Show the variations in lotus, especially because this posture is either really easy or really hard for kids. Give choices. Have everyone make up their own lotus poses and showcase them if they want to. Lotus pose 'warm up' includes postures to open the hips like pigeon posture, thread the needle, leg stretching, lying down on bent knees, ½ lotus, leg behind head, or over the shoulder and splits.

Celebrate lotus posture in spider pose, short man pose, broken leg pose, grasshopper pose, fish pose, lotus in headstand, lotus in handstand, lotus in plow, lifted lotus, humbled lotus pose, sleeping yogi, rooster pose, peacock in lotus pose, and mountain pose.

Lotus Flower Heart Opening Meditation

Lie on your back, supporting your knees with your arms out wide. Feel the breath and start to feel very relaxed and open. Bring your awareness to the lotus of your heart. Picture your heart as the most magnificent lotus flower. Notice the colors, the smell, the vibration, the shape, and the texture. As you breathe into the heart and your flower, allow petal after petal to unfold all the way naturally out to the edges of the skin—petal after petal unfolding, flourishing, opening, and expanding. Feel the beauty of that flower expanding and feel your unique beauty, your unique creative path. Realize that there is no other flower just like you: the shape, the size, the smell, the incredible beauty. Start to honor your unique path that will be different from that of your friend, your sister, your brother. Know that you have your own unique timing in the grand scheme of things and there is no need for comparison. Start to honor your journey on this planet and love all the things about you that make you, you. Appreciate your gifts, your strengths, the infinite wisdom from your past. Honor your unique footprint on this Earth and relish in that incredible magic and power. Now bring your mind back into the lotus of your heart and breathe in love, light, healing, and health. Feel the vibrancy. Know your potential. Feel the love for yourself radiate out from the heart like the most beautiful lotus flower.

Lotus Flower Pulsation Meditation

Bring your awareness to the lotus of the heart. When you inhale, envision the lotus flower opening. When you exhale, visualize the lotus flower closing. Feel the pulsation of life expand and retract. Feel this *spanda* sensation of the heart, this quality of the ever-expanding universe within the breath. Inhale and feel the opening of the heart's energy, and the petals expand. Exhale, and feel the petals fold in toward each other as the breath releases from the lungs. Honor this expansion and contraction. We are always moving and pulsating, flowing, and shining, and rising and falling. Change is the only constant. Honor these dimensions in your life. Release the expectation. Appreciate the good in the moment, be grateful for the experience. Do not hang on to it, nor grapple with it. Honor it and then let it go. Feel the Self accepting all that is.

Bring your awareness back to the opening of the lotus of the heart on the inhale, petal after petal unfolding. As you exhale, allow those petals to fold back into a bud, opening, and closing with every cycle of breath. Honor this unique pulsation that is your very own rhythm. Notice the beat of your heart, unique to you. Feel the magic in the life-giving inhalation and then let go. Release with the exhale. Connect with your heart's delight in the moment. Honor the experience and this beautiful moment to be one with your breath. Honor your precious heart.

Asana Practice

Yoga Practice for Little Yogis (ages 3—11)

- **Warm up**: Optional to use essential oils and cue breath work. Try *swimmer's breath, drum breath, lion's breath, fire breathing, dragon breath*, or any breathing that allows connection between mind, body, and the present moment. Tapping and *kriyas* are also a fun way to get the energy flowing. These practices can help the kids to connect their minds and their bodies to the group's energy. You can also pick from the *Prana* Flow Warm Up Arm Variations listed in Chapter One in the *Pranayama* section.

- **Butterfly pose**: (Ask the kids *Where are you flying to? Can be on Earth, imaginary, astral . . . anywhere!*)

- **Flying butterfly**: Grab big toes with the first two fingers and lift the heels off the floor. Fly your butterfly in the air. Try not to lean back or fall back, using the core.

- **Butterfly forward fold**: Fold your forehead toward your ankles and ask *who can touch their nose to their toes . . . then, laugh at how stinky their feet are!*

- **Extend legs** into *dandasana* (staff pose). Put imaginary markers on feet and hands and rotate them in circles (circles in the sky) to warm up wrists and ankles.

- **Make a 'sandwich pose.'** In *dandasana*, pretend that your extended legs in front of you are the bottom of a sandwich. Call on the children who are quiet and paying attention and ask them what their favorite sandwich is. Once the child answers, pretend you are spreading that filling (jelly, ice cream, cheese) on the bread, which is technically the legs. Once you get all kids to participate, inhale and reach your arms up (the top half of the sandwich), and fold forward and reach for the toes and pretend to take a big bite of the sandwich in a forward fold. This exercise is silly because there are so many fillings inside your imaginary sandwich that it's funny, and kids get a kick out of this. They don't realize that they are stretching out their hamstrings in a forward fold pose. Breathe while you stretch the fingers toward the toes.

- **Rock-the-baby pose with one leg**—Ask the kids to give their "baby" (the foot) a kiss and then have them take the baby up to the third eye, take the baby to the ear, take the baby over the shoulder and cross feet, press into the hands to lift the booty up or come into eight limb staff pose. Have the children lie on their backs and proceed to try and take the leg behind their head in sleeping yogi pose. Repeat the other side because the baby is a twin!

- **Try tabletop pose** and ask the kids about their favorite things to eat. Call on kids who are listening and paying attention to share with you their favorite food or what they like to eat for dinner.

- **Core**: Boat pose, low boat, high boat, or row, row, row your boat, with knees bent and hands grabbing an imaginary paddle and moving it from right to left and singing row, row, row your boat song.

- **Dog Pose**: Cross legs and jump back into down dog (take your dog for a walk), flip the dog, puppy pose, up-dog and howl like a wolf, down dog and bounce, down dog and karate kick legs, down dog and handstand kicks, donkey kicks, or simply walking the dog out.

- **Building heat and strength**: High plank, knees down or up, one foot up at a time, one hand lifts up at a time, mini *chaturanga* push-ups, and add side planks on each side.

- **Side plank**: Try tree pose or five-pointed star pose within side plank pose.

- **Fallen star pose**

- **Mini push-ups** (getting ready for *chaturanga*). Count in different languages or ask a student how old they are and do that many push-ups.

- **Back Warm up**: Moving into gentle backbends to warm up like moving cobra, swan, bow, up-dog poses.

- **Balancing dog pose**: Work on creating strength in the arms (no heads on the ground) and lift one arm and one leg up. Add the meditation of drawing Earth energy up the arms and through the body and flowing down and out through the feet and back into the Earth. Try a hip *mandala* in dog pose or ask the kids to take their dog for a walk!

- **Warrior one and warrior two poses** (add bow-and-arrow along with *khanda*/sword movements invoking what you are aiming for or cutting out from your life), shooting laser beams out the fingertips (go around and test your students' arm strength). Warrior three pose is a nice balancing pose. Take the arms into a flying airplane pose. Kids will have fun making up warrior four, five and six poses too! Switch sides.

- **Creative warrior two sequence**: Find reverse warrior, side angle, triangle, triangle bind, birds of paradise and switch sides.

- **Split pose sequence**: Dragon with the dragon breath, half splits, splits. Switch sides.

- **Fun inversions**: Donkey kicks and then jump back into downward dog pose (shake the booty here). Bounce the hips and legs in downward dog. You can work on mini handstand kicks here too.

- **Crescent lunge sequence**: Crescent twist with bind, warrior three, eagle, tree, toe stand, airplane pose and back to crescent and other side.

- **Chair pose sequence**: Moving chair, chair twist, side crow, back to chair and move through *vinyasa* and repeat on the other side.

- **Arm balances**: Crow pose, baby crow, dolphin handstand prep, tripod, turtle, *OM* pose, eight limb staff pose.

- **Arm balance challenge**: Crow, headstand, crow, jump back into a *vinyasa*.

- **Sun salutation A or B** (optional).

- **Backbend variations**: Heels up, one leg up, one arm up, walking back and forth.

- **Wall backbends**: Bridge pose for modification.

- **Inversions**: Handstands, headstands, forearm stands. Use the wall as a teaching tool.

- **Wall work**: Wall splits, king Arthur pose, lunges, king pigeon pose.

- **Cool down stretching**: Pigeon, mermaid, king pigeon, separate leg stretch or V stretch and forward fold pose, butterfly pose, cow face pose.

- **Healing inversions**: Plow, shoulder stand, supported bridge with block, both legs up on block, legs to wall pose.

- **Fish pose** and spinal twist pose

- **Relaxation**: Guided visualizations with imagery, breathwork, music and or sound healing.

- **Savasana**: Full-body relaxation. Try one minute of silence.

Yoga Practice for Older Yogis (ages 8—15)

- **Centering**: child's pose, reclined butterfly pose, forward fold, or restorative of choice or relaxing *savasana* pose

- **Cue Breath work**: Use boxed breathing or extended exhales. Throughout class, cue slow inhales and exhales moving in and out of postures with conscious breathing.

- **Creative Warm-up with Sun A and Sun B**: Feel the energy of the class and warm-up accordingly. Ask the kids what poses they would like to work on.

- **Intelligent flow to support the peak pose**: Peak poses need proper opening in the specific areas you are looking to stretch and strengthen.

- **Core work**: boat pose, plank, dolphin plank

- **Handstand fun**: donkey kicks, frog jumps, baby handstand kicks (hop switch the legs)

- **Wall work**: (break out and give options for wall work). Can be energizing like handstands, backbending and or downward dogs to the wall or cooling like leg stretching with a strap to the wall.

- **Inversions**: bridge pose, backbends, more handstands, headstands, forearm stands

- **Peak pose flow**: Finish sequence and flow into designated peak pose.

- **Cool-down**: twists, pigeon, double pigeon, leg behind the head (sleeping yogi), separate leg stretching, thread the needle, happy baby, bridge with a supported block

- **Inversions and counterpose**: shoulder stand and fish pose

- **Savasana** with sound healing or guided meditation.

- **Sit up for meditation** (optional) with cooling breath like *sitali* or alternate nostril breathing for preparation.

- **Closing practice**: prayer, gratitude, *OM*, dedications, intention setting, circle of light visualizations

Yoga Games and Fun

My Daddy is a Pretzel

Book and Yoga Cards by *Baron Baptiste*:
A great book to talk about yoga, life, careers, family, environment, and the cards have great games and partner yoga postures.

Peaceful Piggy Meditation

by *Kerry Lee MacLean*:
A great introduction to meditation for kids.

Yoga Altar:

Have the kids bring altar items to class to practice. Have them place their items at the front of their mats. Create intentions and prayer and even host a show and tell at the end.

Show & Tell:

Have the kids bring special items in and try to tie it into something yogic and meaningful.

Animal Bag with Yoga Postures:

Have a bag of small stuffed animals that the kids can grab at circle time. Just like animal spirits, that animal picks you. Create an altar of the animals and make up postures according to that animal in your yoga practice. Have the kids make up yoga routines devoted to their animal of choice.

Yoga Flow with Animals:

Take an animal on a 'yoga flow ride.' Try and balance the animal on the body and or creatively move through a yoga flow while being attached to your animal. Balance with it, flip it, catch it, move with it, and make up a fun and challenging flow with it.

"Who Let the Dogs Out?"

Ecstatic Dance Yoga Freeze Game:The song, *Who Let the Dogs Out* by *Baha Men* is always fun and a wonderful way to discharge negativity. When the song plays, the kids dance freely and spontaneously. When the music stops, the kids freeze. Now add a yoga pose to 'freeze in' the next time the music stops. It could be a tree pose or a butterfly pose, or any posture you can think of. You might have to demonstrate it. When the music plays, you can get goofy and have a great time with dance and fun intentional movements.

Animal Spirit Cards:

Art and Reflection Game: Kids love these animal spirit cards. I like the Medicine Cards by *Jamie Sams* and *David Carson*. Lay the cards out face down, and have the kids use their intuition to pick the animal they are most needing that day. Tell the kids to ask the cards 'what they need to know right now' before they pick out the card. When they pick out the card, they can draw it on paper or have the kids in circle time talk about what powers that spirit animal gave them. Kids can even make up yoga postures that correspond with their animal. There is a terrific book that explains the animal's powers that goes along with the deck of cards. Disclaimer: the kids will sometimes not like the animal that picked them! Just tell them that the animal picked them for a reason and then discuss why!

Yoga Jenga:

Play the game Jenga. When the kids pull out a block to balance on top, have them write their favorite yoga posture onto that block and demonstrate and teach their pose. Eventually, every block will have yoga postures, so when you play Yoga Jenga, every block that gets pulled out has a posture for each player and for everyone to practice.

Yoga Memory:

Get a yoga memory card game, and when someone gets a matching pair, everyone has to do that yoga pose.

Yoga Bingo:

Get a yoga bingo game, and when someone has BINGO, everyone has to do all the yoga postures on the winning card.

Yoga Contest:

Have the kids do a contest for these different poses. It is hard and challenging but the kids love it! Some examples are: boat pose, downward dog pose, tree pose, and handstand. Add fun movements to those postures if it takes a while, like eyes up in tree pose or three-legged dog pose

Yoga Red Light Green Light:

Have the kids in one line to start and you are at the finish line. Just like the red light green light game, explain the rules. What happens on a red light? What happens on a green light? Yellow light? Then make up how they get to the finish line. For example, moving tree pose on green light and downward dog on red light. Yellow light is more of a slow-motion moving tree. The child who gets to the finish line first gets to make up the next postures.

Alphabet Yoga: *Letters with our Bodies*

In groups of three to five kids, pick a letter for each group and have them place their bodies on the ground forming those letters.

Alphabet Yoga: *Turning words into poses*

In class, start with A and come up with a word beginning with the letter A that you can make into a yoga pose. **A** is for ape pose. **B** is for boat pose. **C** is for cat pose. If there is no known yoga pose for that animal, make it up!

High Intensity Movement:

Make up movements to get the wiggles out like skiing, surfing, cross country skiing, jump rope, running and or jumping jacks. Sometimes the kids come into the classroom with lots of energy. This is a fun way to shake it off and get ready for yoga.

Partner Yoga:

Partner Yoga is always a success. Partners of two to five have to make up poses or coordinate poses they already know and have them connect the postures creatively. Have the kids make up their posture names and at the end sit in a circle with a mat in the middle and let the kids showcase their masterpieces! If the kids do not want a partner, encourage them to make up their own posture or routine to share

Creative Yoga *with Yoga Props*:

Have the kids make up their routines with the props (straps, blocks, wedges, rollers, bolsters). Have them notice how they feel. Do they want a Sun flow or a Moon flow? Are the props there to support or empower? How can the props help open the body?

Obstacle Course *with Yoga Props*:

Take whatever you have; straps, blocks, bolsters, and make up an obstacle course. This tends to get a little messy, but if you have it all set up at the beginning of class, it is a fantastic way for kids to come in and start burning up some energy while you meet and greet everyone.

Yoga Stations:

Set up yoga stations around the room. For example, a wall space for headstands and handstands, a middle spot for restorative yoga, another section for splits and stretching. Separate the kids around the room, play some good music, and have the kids' yoga at the different stations for three to five minutes each and then change. Some other ideas for stations are wall yoga, partner yoga, jump rope, hula hoops, poi balls, juggling, instruments, hoop toss, scarf dance, and hopscotch.

Storytime Yoga:

In circle time, have the kids start a yoga story. For example, one person starts, "once upon a time, there was a monkey" (and then demonstrates the monkey pose). Then another kid goes next and makes up another part of the story, "and that monkey lived in a banana tree" (then do the tree pose) etc.

Yoga Routines:

Have the kids make up their own yoga routine, and at the end, they can showcase their unique flow. Start with three postures and work up to five. They can write them down if they know how to write.

Make Up Your Own Yoga Pose:

Have the kids make up their own yoga pose and share it if they want to.

Yogi Says:

This game is like "Simon Says," in which one person gets to lead the group through yoga postures or fun positions cueing their friends in a way that one has to listen very carefully. The kids only do what the Yogi says if they say, "Yogi Says, do tree pose," for example, all the kids do tree pose. If the Yogi doesn't "say" to do something and you still do it, you have to sit down until the last yogi is standing.

Old Macdonald Had a Farm... *for little ones:*

Sing the song and go around the circle, and each kid gets to pick out an animal that they can demonstrate the yoga posture for.

Jumping Jacks: *Counting in Different Languages*

Great tool to get the energy out and learn how to count in different languages. Take your jumping jacks into circles.

Notes

Preface and Introduction

1 Corn, Seane. Revolution of the Soul: Awaken to Love through Raw Truth, Radical Healing, and Conscious Action. Sounds Ture, 2022.

2 "A Quote by Mark Twain ." Goodreads, Goodreads, https://www.goodreads.com/quotes/505050-the-two-most-important-days-in-your-life-are-the.

3 Raumai, J. a., Moyne, J., Barks, C., J. a. R. (1999). The Essential Rumi. United King-dom: Penguin.

4 Baptiste, Baron. 40 Days to Personal Revolution: A Breakthrough Program to Radically Change Your Body and Awaken the Sacred within Your Soul. Simon & Schuster, 2004, 177.

5 Baptiste, Baron. 40 Days to Personal Revolution: A Breakthrough Program to Radically Change Your Body and Awaken the Sacred within Your Soul. Simon & Schuster, 2004, 64.

6 Watkins, Light. Bliss More: How to Succeed in Meditation without Really Trying. Bal-lantine Books, 2018.

7 "No One Is Quite Sure Who Wrote These Quintessential Yogic Texts." Gaia, https://www.gaia.com/article/patanjali-the-luminous-sage-divine-channel-of-the-yoga-sutras.

8 Dave Druz Yoga Philosophy Course, NS Oahu, www.yogaphilosophy.net

9 Spiritual Beings on a Human Journey.. https://www.psychologytoday.com/us/blog/inviting-monkey-tea/201507/spiritual-beings-human-journey-remembering-our-stardust.

10 "A Quote by Pablo Picasso." Goodreads, Goodreads, https://www.goodreads.com/quotes/607827-the-meaning-of-life-is-to-find-your-gift-the.

11 "A Quote by Haim G. Ginott." Goodreads, Goodreads, https://www.goodreads.com/quotes/81938-i-ve-come-to-a-frightening-conclusion-that-i-am-the.

12 "A Quote from Yoga the Science of Well-Being." Goodreads, Goodreads, https://www.goodreads.com/quotes/7730139-yoga-is-the-space-where-flower-blossoms.

13 Mindfulness Is a Way of Befriending Ourselves and Our ... https://www.do-bemindful.com/wp-content/uploads/2018/02/EP-lesson-10-P.pdf.

14 "'If Every 8 Year Old in the World Is Taught Meditation" Dalai Lama. The Responsive Universe, 29 Oct. 2014, https://responsiveuniverse.me.

15 Follow, et al. "'We're All Just Walking Each Other Home." Ram Dass Quotes to Guide the Way.: Elephant Journal." Elephant Journal., 7 July 2020. https://www.elephantjournal.com.

August: Limbs 1—4 of Patanjali's Eight Limbs of Yoga

1 "Light on Life Quotes by B.K.S. Iyengar." Goodreads, Goodreads, https://www.goodreads.com/work/quotes/697572-light-on-life.

2 "8 Limbs of Yoga." Eight Elements West, 6 Jan. 2018, https://www.eightelementswest.com/8-limbs-yoga/.

3 "The Power of Non-Violence." The Power of Non-Violence | The Voice of Truth | The Se-lected Works of Mahatma Gandhi, https://www.mkgandhi.org/voiceoftruth/powerofnonviolence.htm.

4 The power of non-violence. The power of non-violence | The Voice of Truth | The Select-ed Works of Mahatma Gandhi. (n.d.). Retrieved March 21, 2022, from https://www.mkgandhi.org/voiceoftruth/powerofnonviolence.htm.

5 PowerofPositivity. "10 Life Lessons We Can Learn from Buddhist Teachings." Power of Positivity: Positive Thinking & Attitude, Power of Positivity: Positive Thinking & Attitude, 25 July 2020, https://www.powerofpositivity.com/10-life-lessons-can-learn-buddhist-teachings/.

6 "A Quote from Light on Life." Goodreads, Goodreads, https://www.goodreads.com/quotes/976660-action-is-movement-with-intelligence-the-world-is-filled-with.

7 Igniting tapas (discipline). Awakening Self. (2020, January 13). Retrieved October 27, 2021, from https://www.awakeningself.com/writing/igniting-tapas-discipline/.

8 "My body is my temple, asanas are my prayers." (n.d.). Retrieved October 27, 2021, from https://iyengaryogacentre.ca/my-body-is-my-temple-asanas-are-my-prayers

9 "A quote from light on yoga." Goodreads. Retrieved October 27, 2021, from https://www.goodreads.com/quotes/943779-breath-is-the-king-of-mind.

10 Kundalini. citta vrtti nirodhah. (n.d.). Retrieved March 21, 2022, from https://cittavrttinirodhah.wordpress.com/tag/kundalini/.

11 Baron Baptiste quote from class.

September: Limbs 5–8 of Patanjali's Eight Limbs of Yoga

1 Goodreads. (n.d.). A quote from light on life. Goodreads. Retrieved October 27, 2021, from https://www.goodreads.com/quotes/976731-it-is-through-the-alignment-of-the-body-that-i.

2 Pranavee, W. by. (2021, September 28). The changing facet of yoga. Pranavee Talks. Retrieved October 27, 2021, from https://pstalks.wordpress.com/2021/09/28/the-changing-facet-of-yoga/.

3 Home. Aarogya Mandir. (n.d.). Retrieved October 27, 2021, from https://www.aarogyamandir.org/.

4 B.K.S. Iyengar. Center For Wellbeing. (n.d.). Retrieved October 27, 2021, from https://www.centerforwellbeing.net/b-k-s-iyengar.

October: Overcoming Fear and Inviting the Light

1 Goodreads. (n.d.). See what your friends are reading. Goodreads. Retrieved November 11, 2021, from https://www.goodreads.com/quotes/22783-i-wish-i-could-show-you-when-you-are-lonely.

2 Goodreads. (n.d.). A quote by Robert Heller. Goodreads. Retrieved November 11, 2021, from https://www.goodreads.com/quotes/46600-fear-is-excitement-without-breath.

3 Baron Baptiste Yoga Class quote

4 "courage is only an accumulation of small steps.." Inspirational Quotes - collated by Phil Stubbs. (2014, September 15). Retrieved November 11, 2021, from https://philstubbsquotes.wordpress.com/2014/10/28/courage-is-only-an-accumulation-of-small-steps/.

5 - Anonymous

6 Celebrating the festival of diwali. Astrology events, horoscope, palm reading, numerolo-gy, ayurveda. (2021, November 1). Retrieved March 26, 2022, from https://asttrolok.com/blog/celebrating-the-festival-of-diwali/

7 Goddess power. Sally Kempton. (2020, August 28). Retrieved March 26, 2022, from https://www.sallykempton.com/Goddess-power/

8 Hinduism. (2017, January 30). Meaning of ✕.... hinduism. Retrieved March 26, 2022, from https://ancientgk.wordpress.com/2017/01/30/meaning-of-%E0%A5%90/

9 Eleanor Roosevelt. FDR Presidential Library & Museum. (n.d.). Retrieved November 11, 2021, from https://www.fdrlibrary.org/eleanor-roosevelt.

10 www.yogahealer.com

November: Gratitude and The Buddha

1 Biddulph, D & Flynn D. (2009). The Teachings of the Buddha; the wisdom of the Dharma from the Pali Canon to the Sutras. New York: Sterling Publishing. p. 101.

2 O'Brien, Barbara. (2021, September 10). The Three Poisons. Retrieved from https://www.learnreligions.com/the-three-poisons-449603.

3 Goodreads. (n.d.). A quote by Gautama Buddha. Goodreads. Retrieved November 11, 2021, from https://www.goodreads.com/quotes/3181192-in-the-end-only-three-things-matter-how-much-you.

4 Corn, Seane. (2022). Revolution of the soul: Awaken to Love through raw truth, radical healing, and Conscious Action. SOUNDS TRUE.

5 Philosophy - Seva Foundation. (n.d.). Retrieved November 11, 2021, from https://www.seva.org/site/SPageServer/?pagename=about%2Fphilosophy.

6 Gannon, S., & Life, D. (2002). Jivamukti Yoga. Ballantine Books.

December: Celebrating Sacred Ritual

1 May the Long Time Sun Shine upon you ... (n.d.). Retrieved November 11, 2021, from https://www.worldprayers.org/archive/prayers/celebrations/may_the_long_time_sun.html.

2 Yin Yoga. Ekhart Yoga. (2021, August 11). Retrieved March 27, 2022, from https://www.ekhartyoga.com/resources/styles/yin-yoga

3 Duprée Ulrich E. (2017). Ho'oponopono and family constellations: A traditional Hawaiian healing method for relationships, forgiveness and Love. Earthdancer, a Findhorn Press imprint.

4 Kameko. (2018, June 22). DIY: Fizzing Bath bombs. Rainbeau Mars. Retrieved March 27, 2022, from https://www.rainbeaumars.com/post/diy-fizzing-bath-bombs

Notes

5 ThriftyFrugalMom.com, A. L. @, Author: ThriftyFrugalMom. com, L. @, Brittanie, Mom, L. @ T. F., kulakovska, I., Jan, Renée, & Robyn. (2022, February 10). Easy healthy 3 ingredient fudge. Thrifty Frugal Mom. Retrieved March 27, 2022, from http://thriftyfrugalmom.com/recipe-easy-3-ingredient-healthy-fudge/

6 From the kitchen of Brooke Doret, www.brookedoret.com, and used with permission.

7 Corn, Seane (2022). Revolution of the soul: Awaken to Love through raw truth, radical healing, and Conscious Action. SOUNDS TRUE.

January: New Year, New Beginnings

1 Goodreads. (n.d.). A quote by Harriet Tubman. Goodreads. Retrieved November 11, 2021, from https://www.goodreads. com/quotes/5935-every-great-dream-begins-with-a-dreamer-always-remember-you.

2 McGonigal, K. (2013, June 12). How to create a Sankalpa. Home. Retrieved March 27, 2022, from https://yogainternational. com/article/view/how-to-create-a-sankalpa

3 Xplore. (n.d.). Mahatma Gandhi quotes. BrainyQuote. Retrieved November 11, 2021, from https://www.brainyquote.com/ quotes/mahatma_gandhi_105686.

4 Goodreads. (n.d.). A quote by Martin Luther King Jr.. Goodreads. Retrieved November 11, 2021, from https://www.goodreads.com/ quotes/313566-if-i-cannot-do-great-things-i-can-do-small.

5 Xplore. (n.d.). Eleanor Roosevelt quotes. BrainyQuote. Retrieved November 11, 2021, from https://www.brainyquote. com/quotes/eleanor_roosevelt_100940.

6 Goodreads. (n.d.). A quote by Maya Angelou. Goodreads. Retrieved November 11, 2021, from https://www.goodreads. com/quotes/5934-i-ve-learned-that-people-will-forget-what-you-said-people.

7 The animal that hides in your heart: Your animal sign. (n.d.). Retrieved November 11, 2021, from https://www.jadedragon. com/animal091.html.

8 Moore-Hafter, B., Shaner, L., Zacharias-Miller, C., & Barbee, J. (2021, April). EFT Inter-national Free Tapping Manual. Retrieved March 28, 2022, from https://eftinternational. org/wp-content/uploads/EFT-International-Free-Tapping-Manual.pdf

February: Individuality & Conscious Leadership

1 Seane Corn. Off the Mat Into the World. (n.d.). Retrieved March 27, 2022, from https://www.offthematintotheworld. org/seane-corn

2 Wishes fulfilled. Hay House Publishing. (n.d.). Retrieved November 20, 2021, from https://www.hayhouse.com/ wishes-fulfilled-paperback.

3 Baptiste, Baron. 40 Days to Personal Revolution: A Breakthrough Program to Radically Change Your Body and Awaken the Sacred within Your Soul. Simon & Schuster, 2004.

4 Monkey pose. Yoga Journal. (2021, November 16). Retrieved November 20, 2021, from https://www.yogajournal.com/ poses/monkey-pose/.

March: Removing the Obstacles, Ode to Ganesh

1 Goodreads. (n.d.). A quote by Albert Einstein. Goodreads. https://www.goodreads.com/quotes/7275-in-the-middle-of-difficulty-lies-opportunity

2 8 tips on how to do yoga at home - practice and all is coming. Ekhart Yoga. (2020, Sep-tember 28). Retrieved November 20, 2021, from https://www.ekhartyoga.com/articles/practice/8-tips-on-how-to-do-yoga-at-home-practice-and-all-is-coming.

3 Iyengar, B. K. S. (2002), Light on the Yoga Sutras of Patanjali, HarperCollins, UK

4 Motivation, F. (2017, July 20). Which wolf are you feeding? story of the two wolves. Fearless Motivation - Motivational Videos & Music. Retrieved November 20, 2021, from https:// www.fearlessmotivation.com/2017/07/20/story-two-wolves/.

April: Loving the Earth, Loving our Bodies

1 Corn, Seane. (2022). Revolution of the soul: Awaken to Love through raw truth, radical healing, and Conscious Action. SOUNDS TRUE.

2 Quotes about love and affection. Quotes about Love and Affection (145 quotes). (n.d.). Retrieved November 20, 2021, from https://www.quotemaster.org/Love+And+Affection.

3 Dismiss whatever insults your soul. UPLIFT. (2021, April 26). Retrieved November 20, 2021, from https://uplift.love/ dismiss-whatever-insults-your-soul/.

4 Goodreads. (n.d.). A quote by Gautama Buddha. Goodreads. Retrieved November 20, 2021, from https://www.goodreads.com/quotes/81713-every-morning-we-are-born-again-what-we-do-today.

5 Goodreads. (n.d.). A quote by Nayyirah Waheed. Goodreads. Retrieved November 20, 2021, from https://www.goodreads.com/quotes/7685383-and-i-said-to-my-body-softly-i-want-to.

6 Emoto, M. (2005). The hidden messages in water. Pocket.

7 Oliver, M. (2020). Devotions: The selected poems of Mary Oliver. Penguin Books, an imprint of Penguin Random House LLC.

8 Nova. (2022, January 9). Oil pulling: What you should know. ME natural. Retrieved March 27, 2022, from https://www.menaturals.net/oil-pulling-what-you-should-know/

9 Banyan Botanicals. (n.d.). Dosha Quiz: Discover your ayurvedic body type. Banyan Bo-tanicals. Retrieved March 27, 2022, from https://www.banyanbotanicals.com/info/dosha-quiz/

10 www.yogahealer.com www.corytixier.com

May: Artistic Expression

1 Rea, Shiva. (2014). Tending the heart fire. Sounds True.

2 Goodreads. (n.d.). A quote by Rumi. Goodreads. Retrieved November 21, 2021, from https://www.goodreads.com/quotes/73137-dance-when-you-re-broken-open-dance-if-you-ve-torn-the.

3 What is reiki? Holistic Health & Living. (2022, March 18). Retrieved March 27, 2022, from https://holistichealthandliving.com/what-is-reiki/

June: The Yoga of Dreaming

1 Goodreads. (n.d.). See what your friends are reading. Goodreads. Retrieved November 21, 2021, from https://www.goodreads.com/quotes/579308-be-kind-to-your-sleeping-heart-take-it-out-in.

2 Xplore. (n.d.). Napoleon Hill quotes. BrainyQuote. Retrieved November 21, 2021, from https://www.brainyquote.com/quotes/napoleon_hill_152852.

3 Www.shivarea.com. (n.d.). Retrieved March 30, 2022, from https://www.shivarea.com/LiteratureRetrieve.aspx?ID=41690

4 A Quick Guide to Healing Crystals & Stones (Moon Magic 2022). Retrieved March 27, 2022, from https://moonmagic.com/blogs/news/healing-stones

July: The Yoga of FUN

1 Goodreads. (n.d.). A quote by John Lennon. Goodreads. Retrieved November 21, 2021, from https://www.goodreads.com/quotes/282517-when-i-was-5-years-old-my-mother-always-told.

2 "Banana Bread." Pamela's Products, https://www.pamelasproducts.com/products/gluten-free-banana-bread.

3 Thomson, A. L., & Thomson, L. (2021, May 8). Cinnamon Applesauce Granola. I Heart Vegetables. Retrieved March 27, 2022, from https://iheartvegetables.com/cinnamon-applesauce-granola/

Youth Yoga Resources

1 Masaru Emoto quotes (author of the hidden messages in water). Goodreads. Retrieved October 27, 2021, from https://www.goodreads.com/author/quotes/18732.Masaru_Emoto.

Bibliography

8 limbs of yoga. Eight Elements West. (2018, January 6). Retrieved Oc-tober 26, 2021, from https://www.eightelementswest.com/8-limbs-yoga/.

8 tips on how to do yoga at home - practice and all is coming. Ekhart Yoga

(2020). Retrieved November 20, 2021, from https://www.ekhartyoga.com/articles/practice/8-tips-on-how-to-do-yoga-at-home-practice-and-all-is-coming.

The animal that hides in your heart: Your animal sign. (n.d.). Retrieved November 11, 2021, from https://www.jadedragon.com/animal091.html.

Iyengar B.K.S.. Centerforwellbeing. (n.d.). Retrieved October 27, 2021,

from https://www.centerforwellbeing.net/b-k-s-iyengar.

Baptiste, B. (2004). 40 Days to personal revolution: A breakthrough program to radically change your body and awaken the sacred within Your soul. Simon & Schuster.

Biddulph, D & Flynn D. (2009). The Teachings of the Buddha; the wis-dom of the Dharma from the Pali Canon to the Sutras. New York: Sterling Publishing. p. 101.

Contributors, Trent T. Gilliss was the founding executive editor of On Being

Studios. He joined Speaking of Faith at American Public Media in 2003 as a web producer and later online editor, & Gilliss, T. T. (2020, April 2). Mary Oliver reads. The On Being Project. Re-trieved November 20, 2021, from https://onbeing.org/blog/mary-oliver-reads-wild-geese/.

Corn, Seane. (2022). Revolution of the soul: Awaken to Love through raw truth, radical healing, and Conscious Action. SOUNDS TRUE.

"Courage is only an accumulation of small steps." Inspirational Quotes - collated by Phil Stubbs. (2014, September 15). Retrieved November 11,2021,from https://philstubbsquotes.wordpress.com/2014/10/28/courage-is-only-an-accumulation-of-small-steps/.

Dismiss whatever insults your soul. UPLIFT. (2021, April 26). Retrieved

November 20, 2021, from https://uplift.love/dismiss-whatever-insults-your-soul/.

Eleanor Roosevelt. FDR Presidential Library & Museum. (n.d.). Re-trieved

November 11, 2021, from https://www.fdrlibrary.org/eleanor-roosevelt.

Follow, Engman, J., Ojala, T., DeNofa, S. A., Strada, D., Busse, M., Ferris, D. Y., Walker, J., Jackson, P., Garrett, S., & Ballard, G. N. (2020, Ju-ly 7). "we're all just walking each other home." Ram Dass quotes to guide the way.: Elephant Journal. Retrieved October 26, 2021, from https://www.elephantjournal.com/2019/12/were-all-just-walking-each-other-home-ram-dass-quotes-to-guide-the-way-julie-balsiger/.

Goodreads. (n.d.). A quote by Gautama Buddha. Goodreads. Retrieved November 11, 2021, from https://www.goodreads.com/quotes/3181192-in-the-end-only-three-things-matter-how-much-you.

Goodreads. (n.d.). A quote by Gautama Buddha. Goodreads. Retrieved November 20, 2021, from https://www.goodreads.com/quotes/81713-every-morning-we-are-born-again-what-we-do-today.

Goodreads. (n.d.). A quote by Haim G. Ginott. Goodreads. Retrieved Oc-tober 26, 2021, from https://www.goodreads.com/quotes/81938-i-ve-come-to-a-frightening-conclusion-that-i-am-the.

Goodreads. (n.d.). A quote by Harriet Tubman. Goodreads. Retrieved November 11, 2021, from https://www.goodreads.com/quotes/5935-every-great-dream-begins-with-a-dreamer-always-remember-you.

Goodreads. (n.d.). A quote by John Lennon. Goodreads. Retrieved November 21, 2021, from https://www.goodreads.com/quotes/282517-when-i-was-5-years-old-my-mother-always-told.

Goodreads. (n.d.). A quote by Mark Twain . Goodreads. Retrieved October 26, 2021, from https://www.goodreads.com/quotes/505050-the-two-most-important-days-in-your-life-are-the.

Goodreads. (n.d.). A quote by Martin Luther King Jr.. Goodreads. Retrieved November 11, 2021, from https://www.goodreads.com/quotes/313566-if-i-cannot-do-great-things-i-can-do-small.

Goodreads. (n.d.). A quote by Maya Angelou. Goodreads. Retrieved No-vember 11, 2021, from https://www.goodreads.com/quotes/5934-i-ve-learned-that-people-will-forget-what-you-said-people.

Goodreads. (n.d.). A quote by Nayyirah Waheed. Goodreads. Retrieved November 20, 2021, from https://www.goodreads.com/quotes/7685383-and-i-said-to-my-body-softly-i-want-to.

Goodreads. (n.d.). A quote by Robert Heller. Goodreads. Retrieved No-vember 11, 2021, from https://www.goodreads.com/quotes/46600-fear-is-excitement-without-breath.

Goodreads. (n.d.). A quote by Rumi. Goodreads. Retrieved November 21, 2021, from https://www.goodreads.com/quotes/73137-dance-when-you-re-broken-open-dance-if-you-ve-torn-the.

Goodreads. (n.d.). A quote from light on life. Goodreads. Retrieved October 27, 2021, from https://www.goodreads.com/quotes/976660-action-is-movement-with-intelligence-the-world-is-filled-with.

Goodreads. (n.d.). A quote from light on life. Goodreads. Retrieved October 27, 2021, from https://www.goodreads.com/quotes/976731-it-is-through-the-alignment-of-the-body-that-i.

Goodreads. (n.d.). A quote from light on yoga. Goodreads. Retrieved October 27, 2021, from https://www.goodreads.com/quotes/943779-breath-is-the-king-of-mind.

Goodreads. (n.d.). A quote from yoga the science of well-being. Good-reads.

Retrieved October 26, 2021, from https://www.goodreads.com/quotes/7730139-yoga-is-the-space-where-flower-blossoms.

Goodreads. (n.d.). Light on life quotes by B.K.S. Iyengar. Goodreads. Retrieved October 26, 2021, from https://www.goodreads.com/work/quotes/697572-light-on-life.

Goodreads. (n.d.). Masaru Emoto quotes (author of the hidden messages in water). Goodreads. Retrieved October 27, 2021, from https://www.goodreads.com/author/quotes/18732.Masaru_Emoto.

Goodreads. (n.d.). See what your friends are reading. Goodreads. Retrieved November 11, 2021, from https://www.goodreads.com/quotes/22783-i-wish-i-could-show-you-when-you-are-lonely.

Goodreads. (n.d.). See what your friends are reading. Goodreads. Retrieved November 21, 2021, from https://www.goodreads.com/quotes/579308-be-kind-to-your-sleeping-heart-take-it-out-in.

Home. Aarogya Mandir. (n.d.). Retrieved October 27, 2021, from https://www.aarogyamandir.org/.

"If every 8 year old in the world is taught meditation, we will eliminate violence from the world within one generation." Dalai lama. The Responsive Universe. (2014, October 29). Retrieved October 26, 2021, from https://responsiveuniverse.me/2012/1½ 0/if-every-8-year-old-in-the-world-is-taught-meditation-we-will-eliminate-violence-from-the-world-within-one-generation-dalai-lama/.

Igniting tapas (discipline). Awakening Self. (2020, January 13). Re-trieved October 27, 2021, from https://www.awakeningself.com/writing/igniting-tapas-discipline/.

May the Long Time Sun Shine upon you … (n.d.). Retrieved November 11, 2021, from https://www.worldprayers.org/archive/prayers/celebrations/may_the_long_time_sun.html.

Mindfulness is a way of befriending ourselves and our … (n.d.). Retrieved October 26, 2021, from https://www.do-bemindful.com/wp-content/uploads/2018/02/EP-lesson-10-P.pdf.

Monkey pose. Yoga Journal. (2021, November 16). Retrieved November 20, 2021, from https://www.yogajournal.com/poses/monkey-pose/.

Motivation, F. (2017, July 20). Which wolf are you feeding? story of the two

wolves. Fearless Motivation - Motivational Videos & Music. Retrieved November 20, 2021, from https://www.fearlessmotivation.com/2017/07/20/story-two-wolves/.

"My body is my temple, asanas are my prayers." (n.d.). Retrieved October 27, 2021, from https://iyengaryogacentre.ca/my-body-is-my-temple-asanas-are-my-prayers/.

Bibliography

No one is quite sure who wrote these quintessential yogic texts. Gaia. (n.d.).

Retrieved October 26, 2021, from https://www.gaia.com/article/patanjali-the-luminous-sage-divine-channel-of-the-yoga-sutras.

Philosophy - Seva Foundation. (n.d.). Retrieved November 11, 2021, from https://www.seva.org/site/SPageServer/?pagename=about%2Fphilosophy.

The power of non-violence. The power of non-violence | The Voice of Truth | The Selected Works of Mahatma Gandhi. (n.d.). Retrieved October 27, 2021, from https://www.mkgandhi.org/voiceoftruth/powerofnonviolence.htm.

Power of Positivity. (2020, July 25). 10 life lessons we can learn from Buddhist teachings. Power of Positivity: Positive Thinking & Atti-tude. Retrieved October 27, 2021, from https://www.powerofpositivity.com/10-life-lessons-can-learn-buddhist-teachings/.

Pranavee, W. by. (2021, September 28). The changing facet of yoga. Pra-navee Talks. Retrieved October 27, 2021, from https://pstalks.wordpress.com/2021/09/28/the-changing-facet-of-yoga/.

Quotes about love and affection. Quotes about Love And Affection (145 quotes). (n.d.). Retrieved November 20, 2021, from https://www.quotemaster.org/Love+And+Affection.

Rea, Shiva. (2014). Tending the heart fire. Sounds True.

Spiritual beings on a human journey—remembering our … (n.d.). Re-trieved October 26, 2021, from https://www.psychologytoday.com/us/blog/inviting-monkey-tea/201507/spiritual-beings-human-journey-remembering-our-stardust.

When you own your breath, nobody can steal your peace.-anonymous:

Anonymous quotes. Quotss. (n.d.). Retrieved November 11, 2021, from http://www.quotss.com/quote/When-you-own-your-breath-nobody-can-steal-your-peace.

Wise, J. (2021). Let us begin the journey home, episode 77. Turning Towards Life. Retrieved October 26, 2021, from https://www.turningtowards.life/home/2019/03/25/let-us-begin-the-journey-home-episode-77.

Wishes fulfilled. Hay House Publishing. (n.d.). Retrieved November 20, 2021, from https://www.hayhouse.com/wishes-fulfilled-paperback.

Xplore. (n.d.). Eleanor Roosevelt quotes. BrainyQuote. Retrieved November 11, 2021, from https://www.brainyquote.com/quotes/eleanor_roosevelt_100940.

Xplore. (n.d.). Mahatma Gandhi quotes. BrainyQuote. Retrieved November 11, 2021, from https://www.brainyquote.com/quotes/mahatma_gandhi_105686.

Xplore. (n.d.). Napoleon Hill quotes. BrainyQuote. Retrieved November 21, 2021, from https://www.brainyquote.com/quotes/napoleon_hill_152852.

Index

Index

Special Dedications

My Love, Dave Crowley
Mom and Dad
Yoga Inspiration: Shiva Rea, Seane Corn, Baron Baptiste, Rusty
Wells, Ana Forrest, Nicki Doane, Sally Kempton, Yogi Charu
May Rose Huntley, Serese Kudar,
Hailey Harber and Shelley Sailer
Pinedale Wyoming Yogis
North Shore Oahu Yogis
North Shore Meditation Gardens and Dave Druz
My Beautiful Illustrators: Elisa Reynard and Rachel Halbert

To all the children I have been so blessed to teach!